Stories for Every Classroom

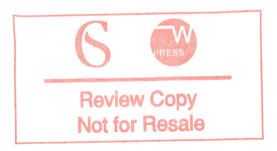

Stories for Every Classroom

Canadian Fiction Portraying Characters with Disabilities

BEVERLEY A. BRENNA

Canadian Scholars' Press
Toronto

Stories for Every Classroom: Canadian Fiction Portraying Characters with Disabilities
by Beverley A. Brenna

First published in 2015 by
Canadian Scholars' Press Inc.
425 Adelaide Street West, Suite 200
Toronto, Ontario
M5V 3C1

www.cspi.org

Copyright © 2015 Beverley A. Brenna and Canadian Scholars' Press Inc. All rights reserved. No part of this publication may be photocopied, reproduced, stored in a retrieval system, or transmitted, in any form or by any means, electronic, mechanical, or otherwise, without the written permission of Canadian Scholars' Press Inc., except for brief passages quoted for review purposes. In the case of photocopying, a licence may be obtained from Access Copyright: One Yonge Street, Suite 1900, Toronto, Ontario, M5E 1E5, (416) 868-1620, fax (416) 868-1621, toll-free 1-800-893-5777, www.accesscopyright.ca.

Every reasonable effort has been made to identify copyright holders. CSPI would be pleased to have any errors or omissions brought to its attention.

Canadian Scholars' Press Inc. gratefully acknowledges financial support for our publishing activities from the Government of Canada through the Canada Book Fund (CBF).

Library and Archives Canada Cataloguing in Publication

Brenna, Beverley A., author, compiler
    Stories for every classroom : Canadian fiction portraying characters with disabilities / Beverley A. Brenna.

Includes bibliographical references and index.
Issued in print and electronic formats.
ISBN 978-1-55130-729-9 (paperback).—ISBN 978-1-55130-730-5 (pdf).—
ISBN 978-1-55130-731-2 (epub)

    1. Picture books for children—Canada—Bibliography. 2. Young adult fiction, Canadian (English)—Bibliography. 3. People with disabilities in literature—Bibliography. 4. Children—Books and reading—Canada—Bibliography. 5. Youth—Books and reading—Canada—Bibliography. 6. Language arts (Elementary). I. Title.

Z1378.B74 2015   016.80883'99282   C2015-901332-1   C2015-901333-X

Cover design: Em Dash Design
Text design: Susan MacGregor/Digital Zone

15   16   17   18   19   5   4   3   2   1

Printed and bound in Canada by Webcom

Canadä

for Myra Smith Stilborn, 1916–2012
whose stories continue to inspire

TABLE OF CONTENTS

Acknowledgements • ix

INTRODUCTION: The Value of Stories • 1
    My Journey with Books Portraying Characters with Disabilities • 1
    Writing Books about Characters with Disabilities • 6
    The Value of Diverse Perspectives in Children's Literature • 7
    Changing the World through Critical Literacy • 9
    Three Essential Questions for This Chapter • 10

CHAPTER 1: The History of Characters with Disabilities in Children's Texts • 11
    The Evolution of Disability • 11
    The Definition of Disability in the Context of This Book • 14
    Historical Patterns and Trends • 15
    Contemporary Trends • 17
    Future Predictions • 21
    Three Essential Questions for This Chapter • 21

CHAPTER 2: Critical Literacy and the Value of Shared Reading as a Teaching Context • 23
    Rationale for Sharing Stories with Children • 23
    Evaluation of Children's Literature • 24
    Critical Literacy • 25
    Three Essential Questions for This Chapter • 38

CHAPTER 3: Contemporary Canadian Picture Books • 39
    Introduction to Picture Books in Canada • 39
    Summary of Picture Books Portraying Characters with Disabilities • 40
    Annotated Bibliography of Canadian Picture Books Portraying Characters with Disabilities • 44
    Three Essential Questions for This Chapter • 50

CHAPTER 4: Contemporary Canadian Junior Novels • 51
    Introduction to Junior Novels in Canada • 51
    Author Portrait: Rachna Gilmore • 52

Annotated Bibliography of Canadian Junior Novels Portraying Characters with Disabilities • 57
Read-on Bibliography • 62
Three Essential Questions for This Chapter • 63

CHAPTER 5: Contemporary Canadian Intermediate Novels • 65
Introduction to Intermediate Novels in Canada • 65
Author Portrait: Pamela Porter • 69
Annotated Bibliography of Canadian Intermediate Novels Portraying Characters with Disabilities • 75
Read-on Bibliography • 98
Three Essential Questions for This Chapter • 103

CHAPTER 6: Contemporary Canadian Young Adult Novels • 105
Introduction to Young Adult Novels in Canada • 105
Author Portrait: Beverley Brenna • 107
Annotated Bibliography of Canadian Young Adult Novels Portraying Characters with Disabilities • 118
Read-on Bibliography • 147
Three Essential Questions for This Chapter • 151

CHAPTER 7: Contemporary Canadian Books on an International Landscape • 153
Book Selection Ideas • 153
The Promise of Radical Change • 153
Concluding Thoughts • 157
Three Essential Questions for This Chapter • 158

References • 159
Copyright Acknowledgements • 171
Index • 177

ACKNOWLEDGEMENTS

Thanks to the Social Sciences and Humanities Research Council (SSHRC) for the funding that supported this project; gratitude also to the University of Saskatchewan, the University of Alberta, and the team at Canadian Scholars' Press for their encouragement. Particular thanks to my long-term research assistant for this project, Jean Emmerson, without whom this book would not have materialized, in addition to other student research assistants whose work has been greatly appreciated: Shelby Fitzgerald, Qiang Fu, Andrea Lendsay, and Summer Morin. As well, thanks to my inspirational doctoral supervisor, Dr. Joyce Bainbridge, for her immense help along the original path of a portion of this research. Hugs to my colleagues at Saskatoon Public Schools and my students, family, and friends for all their wisdom, especially Dr. Christtine Fondse, whose classes instilled in me a fond admiration for children's literature. A special thank you to my sons for all they have taught me about teaching and learning, and my husband Dwayne for his everlasting support and encouragement.

INTRODUCTION

The Value of Stories

My Journey with Books Portraying Characters with Disabilities

This book exists as the culmination of my work exploring the treatment of disability in Canadian literature for young people. A combination of PhD research and my own fiction writing, as well as my experiences as a classroom and special education teacher and school consultant, piqued an interest that has extended into my current research platform at the University of Saskatchewan. I am thankful for the many people who have supported this interest, as well as the granting organizations that have financed what has been a lengthy journey into fascinating Canadian literature. I am also thankful for the children who were my first inspiration regarding this project—and it is to them, and their families, that I extend my gratitude for exemplifying a range of possibilities in life stories.

Early Questions

In 2003, I was part of a governmental advisory committee on Saskatchewan curriculum. Foregrounding my special education background, I identified that part of my role on this committee would be to seek out books containing characters with disabilities, intending to support diversity in classrooms through recommendations of resources that portrayed diverse characters. It had occurred to me earlier, as a classroom and special education teacher, that books about characters with disabilities were limited on the school landscape. Where were these books? How might their presence offer, to students, affirmations of lived lives and extensions of notions about diversity?

Now, when I had the time to devote to a focused search, I was surprised at the small number of titles I was able to locate. Of these titles, I was taken aback at how few of them had characters with disabilities in leading roles. It seemed as though authors had employed characters with disabilities as supports for the main character, rather than as main characters themselves. But I kept searching.

And I started writing about a teen with her own list of exceptionalities—later to become Taylor Jane in *Wild Orchid*, the first novel in my young adult trilogy. How, I wondered, might my own work as a researcher and as an artist help fill in the gaps that I perceived related to diverse characterizations?

Early Discoveries

Two striking and inspirational texts that I located in my preliminary research exploration were written by the authors we meet through interviews later in this book: Rachna Gilmore and Pamela Porter. Both are previous winners of Governor General's Literary Awards for children's text—Gilmore for *A Screaming Kind of Day* (1999), a stunningly beautiful picture book illustrated by Gordon Sauve, about a little girl with a hearing impairment, and Porter for her poignant verse novel *The Crazy Man* (2005), about a friendship between a young girl with a physical disability and a farmhand from the local mental institution. Each of these texts particularly inspired me to strive for diverse qualities in my own fictional characterizations and to conduct further research.

My initial search for titles led me into a short literature review for a paper I presented at the 2006 International Conference on Education in Honolulu. Positive response to this paper directed me toward a larger commitment to research than I had originally envisioned. In 2008 I embarked on PhD studies in Education at the University of Alberta, where my doctoral dissertation focused on contemporary Canadian novels for children published since 1995, as well as influences on particular authors who write about characters with disabilities. This dissertation appears in the U of A library as *Characters with Disabilities in Contemporary Children's Novels: Portraits of Three Authors in a Frame of Canadian Texts* (Brenna, 2010b), with various related articles available in academic journals (Brenna, 2010a).

Current State of the Field

My research on books about characters with disabilities has been immensely rewarding. Although given far less attention than other minority groups, there does exist a small but powerful body of Canadian children's fiction portraying people with disabilities as viable protagonists who learn and grow throughout the course of a story. There is also work that spotlights characters with disabilities in secondary positions yet who are developed as full, worthy entities, capable of learning and growth. There are still titles that involve static, unidimensional characters with disabilities included as plot devices within their respective tales, but these, too, have a place within the critical literacy approaches today's classrooms can offer.

A number of other researchers are also examining the representation of disabilities in children's literature. These include Dr. Nicole Markoti (University of Windsor), as well as Tina Taylor Dyches and Mary Anne Prater (Brigham

Young University). Further work in this area can be examined in the *Canadian Journal of Disability Studies* and through children's literature journals such as *Bookbird*. Particular Canadian honours, such as the IBBY Outstanding Books for Young People with Disabilities, parallel American awards such as the Dolly Gray Award and the Schneider Family Book Award in spotlighting noteworthy titles.

IBBY Canada (the Canadian chapter of the International Board on Books for Young People) currently hosts the broadly defined IBBY Collection for Young People with Disabilities, which officially arrived at the North York Central Library in Toronto in 2014 from Norway (www.torontopubliclibrary.ca/ibby). This collection for all ages, in over 40 languages, has grown to 4,000 titles from around the world. Special formats include Blissymbolics (a writing system of basic symbols conceived by Charles K. Bliss), Braille, sign language, and tactile and textile books, and books that portray children and teens with disabilities are included, as well as subjects geared toward adults with developmental delays, language disabilities, or reading difficulties.

Goals of This Book

In this volume I focus on the *why*, the *what*, and the *how* of classroom practice, concentrating on particular Canadian contemporary picture books and novels for young people and the authors who created them, as well as educational frameworks to support their use with students. Marsha Rudman, in her comprehensive 1995 text *Children's Literature: An Issues Approach*, indicates that criticism of a book is not the same as censorship. I, too, make this distinction, believing that students can be encouraged to think critically about what they read, developing skills that will serve them well in a digital society where evaluation and discrimination are as important as decoding skills. In terms of the specific goals of this research-based product, I anticipate that readers will discover the following: supports for critical literacy; titles contextualized in a wide reading framework; supports for social justice; Radical Change theory as a lens for exploration; a consideration of societal values and definitions; and a focus on Canadian materials.

Supports for Critical Literacy

While difficult to assess in terms of its effectiveness, and certainly not measurable by objective standards, a critical literacy approach to education teaches young people to ask questions about what they read, nudging them toward independent thinking as an element of aesthetic as well as efferent reading, where the goals of reading include both enjoyment and information acquisition. From whose perspective is a story told? Whose story is missing? These two questions lead the way into further considerations of the messages embedded in reading material.

It is thus a primary goal of this text to assist educators and parents in finding and using books about characters with disabilities, enriching the body of resources we consciously share with youth for the purpose of developing imagination, empathy, self-acceptance, and critical literacy skills. Such pedagogy addresses the lack of attention we have previously given to disability as a topic for critical literary study. It also interrogates the manner in which disability is treated in contemporary fiction for young people. Do these texts offer fresh, new perspectives on uniquely lived lives, or do they further entrench traditional ableist (discriminatory) stereotypes about normalcy?

I anticipate that spotlighting literature about characters with disabilities in a volume such as the one at hand encourages books about characters with disabilities to be shared alongside other books in our classrooms, our libraries, and our homes. This literature will continue the very important function of helping readers explore commonalities and differences, promoting self-esteem as children identify with the protagonists in books, and facilitating understanding as young readers encounter characteristics they may recognize in themselves and others. Because my goal is that the literature in the annotated bibliographies in this text be shared, I have not included fiction published prior to 1995, seeking only contemporary titles currently in print.

Titles Contextualized in a Wide Reading Framework

In my survey of titles that have been published over the last two decades, worthy reading materials may have been missed, such as Sandra Richmond's (1983/2009) *Wheels for Walking* and Mary Blakeslee's (1991) *Hal*. Some of these titles, however, have been included as connecting reads, termed *read-ons*, in the annotations. Certainly Jean Little's (1972/2012) *From Anna*, while not included in the annotated bibliographies except as a read-on, is highly recommended for its incisive plotline and the warm characterization of a little girl with a vision impairment.

I am not suggesting that the books listed in this text be introduced in collections unto themselves. For this reason, I have provided read-ons for the novels in the annotated bibliographies in chapters 4, 5, and 6 to help situate particular titles in a wider frame of other books that are thematically related. Because the picture books mentioned in chapter 3 are easily connected to other materials due to their brevity, no read-ons have been included to accompany them.

Supports for Social Justice

I am conscious that many of the books introduced here open a space for the possibility of living with a disability, offering an opportunity for readers to acknowledge a part of life that is inevitable for many, and yet does not preclude happiness. Disability is a category of difference that occurs alongside all other differences and can occur at any time in one's life. Disability can be, among other things, "painful, comfortable, familiar, alienating, bonding, isolating, disturbing, endearing, challenging, infuriating, or ordinary" (Thomson, 1997, p. 14). Characterizations that present a wide range of responses to disability, through authentic descriptions, support individuals, but they also support society. Along with affecting individual identities, I believe that reading can change the world—offering new perspectives that shape landscapes both local and worldwide, and contributing to perspectives everywhere that forward social justice.

Radical Change as a Lens for Exploration

I anticipate that researchers will find in this text a seminal discussion of the current titles available in Canadian literature for young people, and negotiate their way into further research questions that arise from the studies I have conducted or summarized here. As we continue to promote children's literature as a worthy artifact through which to examine societal values and understandings, as well as a resource that provides what Lee Galda (1998) so eloquently calls "mirrors and windows" for readers, investigations are still needed into the existing content of children's literature. It is valuable to understand the current landscape of children's books, and consider the future in a field that is always in flux, an idea encapsulated by Dresang's (1999) theory of Radical Change—how books for young people continue to evolve. Radical Change recognizes that "temporal and spatial relationships in the digital world" have resulted in "interactivity, connectivity, and access in books for youth" (Dresang & Kotrla, 2009). A consideration of the impact of digital technologies helps us think about how changes to texts related to their forms and formats, content-related boundaries, and perspectives may have influenced the characterizations that contemporary children are encountering in literature (Dresang, 1999).

Consideration of Societal Values and Definitions

Explorations of a country's aesthetic products shine a particular kind of light on the societal expectations and norms embedded in artifacts that emerge from authors who are a product of that society. Wood (1979) discusses how depictions of gender and ethnic minority groups have been constructed as metaphors of evil in American horror films. The disappearance or death of the "monster" signifies, in Wood's view, "the restoration of repression" (p. 10).

Characters with disabilities can be similarly viewed as a social construction, somewhat reflective of how disability itself may be considered a social construction, and illustrated by changes over time toward representations more reflective of authentic experiences. Theories of social constructionism allow that "some part of the social world ... is better explained in social rather than biological or (individual) psychological terms" (Crossley, 2005, pp. 296–297). The use of the term *social construction* links to disability theories where a distinction is made between *disability*, a bodily configuration, and *handicap*, a set of social meanings assigned to a particular physical example (Klages, 1999). For instance, people with physical differences may be actually *disabled* in particular social contexts, depending on perceptions about their bodies and the structures around them.

Focus on Canadian Materials

Because of this book's potential to exemplify societal ideas related to disability, offering fuel for discussions on critical literacy, I have selected for the target books in the annotated bibliographies only titles by Canadian authors professionally published by Canadian publishing houses. Since one of the purposes of this book is to provide resources for educators, titles published prior to 1995 are not included, so as to maximize the potential for available and current resources. Foreign titles republished in Canada are also not included, although an attempt has been made to include these and other non-Canadian materials in the connected read-on sections of the annotated bibliographies in chapters 4, 5, and 6. While the read-ons are primarily Canadian, it is important to situate Canadian literature in the wider field, and I have attempted to do so whenever appropriate.

This extensive sample of children's and young adult books was derived with the help of my research team. We explored published book reviews, local bookstores, and online sources (such as Global Books in Print), and contacted 42 Canadian publishing houses known for producing children's and young adult books, requesting information about titles portraying characters with disabilities. In addition, we added other titles located by word of mouth, including materials discovered at conferences and through communication with other professionals in the field. While I have had excellent support in developing the lists of titles presented in this volume, I am aware that some books meeting the criteria of our search will most certainly have been missed. An up-to-date online compendium of further titles that come to my attention is intended, as new titles are suggested or produced. Monique Polak's (2014) book *Hate Mail*, for example, was in press at the time of writing, and thus its inclusion has been restricted to this brief mention.

While this book is intended for any reader, each chapter concludes with three essential questions to support preservice and inservice teachers interested in the combined study of children's literature and exceptional learners. These questions represent key topics from each chapter, and attempt to assist readers in connecting to the chapter through critical thinking and personal response.

Writing Books about Characters with Disabilities

As I considered the need for books to represent the diversity of all people, I began to work consciously to present characters with disabilities in the fiction I write for children. I have thus developed protagonists with identifiable disabilities whose challenges and accomplishments are shared by real-life students I have known in classrooms: kids with Fetal Alcohol Spectrum Disorder, with autism, with intellectual and physical disabilities—kids whose disabilities are merely one aspect of their lives and who demonstrate, as individuals, universal themes shared by many. A discussion of some of my books is included in this text in chapter 6 as part of my own author portrait, and although my characters are not based on any one person from real life, I wish to acknowledge here the terrific children and families who have been, and continue to be, part of my learning journey.

Eliza Dresang's 1999 title *Radical Change: Books for Youth in a Digital Age* reminds us that the landscape of children's and young adult literature is ever changing, and that what is unique now will someday recede to commonality in favour of other new emergent traits. As I read through the list of 2010 nominees for the Governor General's Literary Award for children's text, all intended for teens, I was struck by the diversity present among the titles—what Dresang would refer to as changing perspectives. *Me, Myself and Ike* (Denman, 2009) presents the story of a young man with schizophrenia. *Tyranny* (Fairfield, 2009) portrays a young woman with an eating disorder. *Free as a Bird* (McMurchy-Barber, 2010) offers the first-person narrative of a girl with Down syndrome. *Scars* (Rainfield, 2010) deals with cutting as a survivor's response to sexual abuse. *Fishtailing* (Phillips, 2010), the winner of the award that year, offers four different narrators who convey through free verse their stories related to school bullying. Dresang would describe another aspect of Radical Change at work here: evidence of changing forms and formats, with verse novels increasing as a commercially viable textual literary form for young readers.

Clearly, radical changes are continually occurring in the field of children's literature. A number of forces are currently nudging the field forward, including contemporary media and performance arts. The stage adaptation of Mark Haddon's (2003) mystery novel *The Curious Incident of the Dog in the Night-Time*, a book whose first-person protagonist is a 15-year-old boy with autism, premiered at the National Theatre on August 2, 2012, and since then has been broadcast live to cinemas worldwide. Culture is rich ground for propagating contagious innovation. At some point, my contributions to literature portraying characters with exceptionalities will no longer be radical. And that is a good thing.

The Value of Diverse Perspectives in Children's Literature

The evolution of diverse perspectives within children's books has compensated for literature's previous lack of attention to differences in gender, sexual orientation, and cultural background, a pattern accounted for by Dresang's (1999) Radical Change theory (a theory I further address in chapter 7). While disability can be considered as just another "culture-bound, physically justified difference to consider" (R. G. Thomson, 1997, p. 5), books for young people are beginning to include realistic characterizations of ability, and although not large in number, there exists a powerful body of Canadian children's literature that offers particular renderings of characters with disabilities in historical and contemporary settings. However, unlike curricular intent to include diverse renderings of differences such as ethnicity—and more recently lesbian, gay, bisexual, and transgender (LGBT) characterizations—in classroom resources, a consideration of books about characters with disabilities is often left to chance. We might ask ourselves what titles depict characters with disabilities fairly and accurately, where the character with the disability is allowed to grow and change throughout the story, and where the traditional miracle cure or tragic death is not employed as a plot device. For many readers, the list will be short.

As a child, I never questioned the portrayal of characters with disabilities in *Heidi* and *The Secret Garden*, books I read with interest and in which secondary characters with physical disabilities experience miracle cures. I also gluttonously devoured folktales, such as "Jack and the Beanstalk" and "Three Billy Goats Gruff," where characters with physical differences are presented as the embodiment of evil. In later experiences with children's literature, I did not encounter characters with disabilities at all. Yet as a child who enjoyed wide reading, it did not occur to me to wonder at the stereotypes and lack of presentation in literature. Critical thought about the distortions or absences of people with disabilities, in depictions as people, was my own personal "null curriculum," to use a phrase of Elliot Eisner's (2002). And I was not alone.

What prompts a person to move from the null to a consciousness of what's missing? What, in Canadian children's fiction, has informed particular authors who are now writing about realistic characters with disabilities, while other authors still rely on stereotypes? What informs teachers who have learned to embrace all students within their classrooms as equal members of the community, while other teachers philosophize about inclusion and exclusion according to traditional templates? In my case, the connections between unawareness, exclusion of difference, and the embracing of differences occur through stories read alongside deepening understandings of stories heard and lived. My mother's oral stories, in particular, have had a powerful effect on my conceptualization of ability and identity, and have affected both my writing and my teaching. Some of these oral stories are recorded in chapter 6, as part of my self-portrait as an author.

As we prepare our classroom landscapes to respect the stories of all children, it's clear we have work to do. The annotated bibliographies included in this book as part of chapters 3 through 6 are designed to assist teachers with this very important task, as well as offer ideas for further research regarding the resonance of these books in critical literacy discussions. Chapter 3's focus on picture books does not include age ranges for the titles annotated, as picture books can now be used across the grades. Chapter 4's focus on junior novels includes titles for ages six and up. Chapter 5's focus on intermediate novels includes titles for ages nine and up. Chapter 6 spotlights young adult novels for ages 12 and up. Upper age limits have been left open to support diverse reading abilities and interests.

Changing the World through Critical Literacy

Paulo Freire, a leading Brazilian educator, wrote poignantly about reading the word and the world, connecting literacy and social justice. In 1962, Freire applied his theories about liberation theology as he taught 300 sugar cane workers to read and write in just 45 days, offering them the chance to vote in parliamentary elections—a right they were previously denied on the basis of their illiteracy. In response to this venture, the Brazilian government approved the creation of thousands of cultural circles where literary learning was connected to the vocabulary of the people, although in 1964 a military coup put an end to Freire's efforts and he was imprisoned for 70 days as a traitor. Even now, with many published volumes to his name, work by the late Paulo Freire is not a welcome topic in some contexts where it is still contested: what some people viewed as supporting the lower class, others viewed as anti-government.

It is important that educators develop classroom climates within which to support the development of critical literacy—necessary in a society where goals for respecting diversity continue to be promoted. Kliewer (1998) discusses the representation of students with disabilities as "cultural burdens," a factor in their "long history of segregation from the wider school community," and outlines the "narrow and rigid interpretations of who and what constitutes community usefulness" (p. 9). Through segregation, people with disabilities have been made invisible, and, in Spufford's (2002) view, such invisibility through segregation is desirable. The lack of critique of Spufford's view of people with disabilities—in the context of *The Child That Books Built*, a compendium ostensibly heralding reading but with an underlying message about escape from the disability of a family member—is remarkable. His support of his childhood reading as a way to ignore a sister with disabilities, and his dislike of "vulnerable people," is left unexamined. Spufford's narrative is a striking example of an ongoing societal problem, offering support to Freire's (1998) indictment: "It is the irresistible preference to reject differences" (p. 71).

From the marginalization of people with disabilities as less than status quo, toward full acceptance of people with differences, the evolution of society's perception of disability is ongoing. Human rights laws provide important guiding principles regarding the acceptance of all people, but in many aspects of community life—the workplace, living environments, schools—people with disabilities continue to struggle for equal access and respect. Yet disability as a fundamental human experience is missing from our critical consciousness (Snyder, Brueggemann, & Garland-Thomson, 2002). Stories, and the context in which these stories are presented, can provide an important medium for change, drawing disability to the fore alongside other aspects of human diversity.

Three Essential Questions for This Chapter

1. In what ways have books changed over the course of your life? Reflect on things you might find today in titles for young people that were absent in the past.
2. What gaps have you been aware of in literature? In what ways have you seen your life reflected in available resources? Is this predictive of the experiences of other people you know?
3. In your previous schooling, have you had opportunities to critically examine the social and political messages of books? In what ways have your previous teachers encouraged you to assess classroom literature, and offered the opportunity for positive and negative feedback about these texts?

CHAPTER 1

The History of Characters with Disabilities in Children's Texts

The Evolution of Disability

The conceptualization of the term *disability* has evolved in a manner similar to the development of other social constructions, such as gender and ethnicity (Asch & Fine, 1988). Yet, while disability is "as fundamental an aspect of human diversity as race, ethnicity, gender, and sexuality," it is "rarely acknowledged as such" (Couser, 2006, p. 399). "Disability," say Jaeger and Bowman (2005), "is ordinary. Yet disability is rarely considered as a societal issue in a thoughtful and humane manner" (p. ix). "Despite the prevalence of disability in this society, disabled persons tend to be invisible" (Asch & Fine, 1988, p. 1). Addressing null curriculum—what schools "do *not teach*" (Eisner, 2002, p. 97) in terms of disability—has been one way to highlight disability issues that have been silent, and that have mirrored a pattern in early critical theorizing where "people of Color and women" were "ignored and marginalized" (Willis et al., 2008, p. 2).

One treatment absent from classic literature involves multiple perspectives in the presentation of a character with a disability. In her contemporary children's book *The Crazy Man*, Porter (2005) demonstrates how unidimensional viewpoints have clouded Emaline's mother's vision with regard to Angus, a former patient in a mental institution:

> The man said Angus
> was the best gardener they ever had.
> Mum looked at the man. Then
> she looked at Angus. "Oh," she said,
> like she'd never thought about
> Angus knowing how to do anything
> except be crazy. (p. 83)

Disability as a Social Construction

It is important to note here that the employment of the term *social construction* in the context of this book indicates my belief that the depiction of characters with disabilities arises as a product of our particular society, corresponding to Crossley's (2005) definition that a "relatively straightforward use of the term 'social construction' occurs in those instances where we wish to indicate that some part of the social world ... is better explained in social rather than biological or (individual) psychological terms" and "does not imply that everything is a social construct" (pp. 296–297).

Such usage of *social construction* relates to ideas about cultural, historical, and social influences on writing, where one can see language as a site of discursive struggle (Luce-Kapler, 2004). This use of *social construction* also links to theories of the conceptualization of race and gender and how such constructions relate to disability theories in which a distinction is made between "'disability,' a bodily configuration, and 'handicap,' a set of social relations or meanings assigned to a particular bodily configuration" (Klages, 1999, p. 2). Social constructionist theories of the body demonstrate how "dominant ideas, attitudes, and customs of a society influence the perception of bodies" (Linton, 2006, p. 174). In her master's thesis, Christina Minaki (2011) discusses at length how societal exclusion related to her cerebral palsy "resulted from systemic negativity" toward her disabled embodiment, and how "it was the response to disability that was a problem" (p. 1).

Lev Vygotsky's work, although best known for its underpinning of the theory of social constructivism, has also contributed to social constructionism, a closely related idea in the sense that people work together to construct understanding. A difference between these theories is that social constructivism focuses on individual learning as a result of group interactions, while social constructionism acknowledges that "meaning is not discovered but constructed" (Crotty, 1998, p. 42) and that society's artifacts, including language, represent human construction at work. Vygotsky asserted that deafness and blindness are shaped by the reactions of others and the social context in which a person operates. These social dynamics are of primary importance, beyond the condition itself, because these dynamics mediate how the person is included—fully or partially—into society (Moll, 2014).

According to social constructionist thinking, the term *disability*, used to signify "a physical or psychological condition considered to have predominantly medical significance," is "an arbitrary designation" (Linton, 2006, p. 162). This identification of the flexibility surrounding the labelling of disability corresponds with definitions of disability as a social construction alongside gender, sexuality, and race (Asch & Fine, 1988; Mitchell & Snyder, 2000; Sherry, 2008). Priestly's (2001) statement that "the principal factors shaping disabling experiences reside not within the body but within the wider society," yet "disability also involves embodied experiences and expressions of agency" (p. 242), reminds us that disability may occur both within the individual body and as cultural interpretations of the body's interaction with the world. "If we think of disability as located in societal barriers, not in individuals, then disability must be seen as a matter of social justice" (Davidson, 2006, p. 126).

Interpretations of diagnoses based on the medical model of "normal" almost always signal "ignorance, confusion, lack, absence, and ineptitude"; this is evidenced in the manner in which "ableist metaphors" rampantly slip into everyday speech and scholarly discourse (May & Ferri, 2008, p. 117). Such metaphors of disability, including the use of *upstanding* for admirable and *looked down upon* for rejected, are used because disability is an abstract concept, "not necessarily a 'scientific' or 'natural' truth" (Dolmage, 2008, p. 105), and because "Western society places a premium on wealth, youth, physical strength, and attractiveness" (Rubin, 1988, p. ix).

Disability was once regarded very differently. A social process of disabling arrived with industrialization, replacing the concept of "ideal"—a construct dating back to the 17th century—with the concept of "normal" (Davis, 2006, p. 4). Rather than moving toward perfection by approximating a particular essence or quality, respecting the potential diversity of humankind and agreeing that the ideal could never be attained, the word *normal* sharply emphasizes dualistic categories of *good* and *bad*. Brueggemann and Lupo (2008) cite Adorno in noting that there can only be *normal* as long as there is *abnormal* (p. ix).

While disability is as ordinary and fundamental an aspect of human diversity as race, ethnicity, gender, or sexuality, it is rarely acknowledged as a societal issue (Couser, 2006; Jaeger & Bowman, 2005). The goal of revisionary projects is to open and participate in aspects of culture that have historically been denied (Said, 2005). Such is the goal of disability studies, where schooling for democracy and critical citizenship addresses "questions of Otherness generally fashioned in the discourse of multicultural education, which in its varied forms and approaches generally fails to conceptualize issues of race and ethnicity as part of the wider discourse of power and powerlessness" (Giroux, 2005, p. 89).

The need to develop awareness of a lack of understanding with regard to people with disabilities is an important concept (May & Ferri, 2008), as it connects to topics that have previously been absent from school curricula. Texts such as Mary Anne Prater and Tina Taylor Dyches's (2008b) *Teaching About Disabilities through Children's Literature* offers teachers specific lesson plan ideas connecting to contemporary American children's books, and further recommended titles appear in their article "Books That Portray Characters with Disabilities: A Top 25 List for Children and Young Adults" (Prater & Dyches, 2008a).

However, the voices of people with disabilities are critical to school resources. We need to be reading about ourselves, as well as exploring our own identities, in a variety of literature. Canadian author Jean Little reports that, as a young girl bullied at school, "I was gradually learning that if you were different, nothing good about you mattered" (Little, 1987, p. 36). In high school, a home economics teacher reacted to Little's visual impairment: "You should be in an institution.

I'm paid to teach normal students; not abnormal ones" (Little, 1987, p. 150). An emphasis on difference leading to the segregation of people with disabilities was a common trait of Canadian education prior to the 1970s, when inclusionary practices became more common (Smith, Polloway, Patton, Dowdy, & Heath, 2001). Yet, "disability is not simply about diversity. It is also about commonality—not a commonality of embodied experiences but a commonality of purpose, in the struggle for a more inclusive society" (Priestly, 2001, p. 240). Schools, with their current interest in supporting "universal design" frameworks for learning (Orkwis & McLane, 1998), are working toward embracing both commonality and diversity.

Literary texts have "rarely appeared to offer disabled characters in developed, 'positive portraits'" (Mitchell & Snyder, 2000, pp. 15–16), creating "constructed oppression" where oppression describes acts that prevent people from "being more fully human" (Freire, 1983, p. 42). "In our modern society, after many years of social progress about disabled people's rights to be accepted … one might expect a more enlightened approach to the treatment of disability in cultural works" (Keith, 2001, p. 249). Books for adults that dislodge past stereotypes include David Foster Wallace's (1996) *Infinite Jest*, a satirical futuristic look at North America wherein a group called the Wheelchair Assassins appear as Québécois separatists.

While the novel form is generally, as L. J. Davis (2006) indicates, a "proliferator of ideology … intricately connected with concepts of the norm" (p. 15), it may be possible to change the impact of classroom literature by strategically adding particular contemporary titles and altering the way images and stories are presented, offering the potential for disability to teach that life can be reinvented (Riley, 2005). Literature can thus be a vehicle to address diversity (Rueda, 1998), fuelled by a critical literacy pedagogy that moves social justice ideals into classroom study.

Definition of Disability in the Context of This Book

A working definition of the word *disability* was required in this research for the purpose of having a finite list of categories within which to locate and explore Canadian children's and young adult literature. For this reason, I adapted ideas from Smith, Polloway, Patton, Dowdy, and Heath (2001), who identify that, in Canada, the majority of jurisdictions in education include the following categories of exceptionality: "learning disabilities, speech or language impairments, intellectual disabilities, emotional/behavioral disorders, multiple disabilities, auditory impairments, orthopedic impairments, other health impairments, visual impairments, autism … and traumatic brain injury" (p. 7). These categories reflect the choices made in uncovering particular titles to include in this book.

A number of picture books and novels were considered for the annotated bibliographies, but discarded as the concept of disability presented wasn't quite in line with the above definition. One such title was Paul Marlowe's (2010) *Knights of the Sea*, although the subtitle's reference to a "spoon addiction" was tempting.

Another was K. L. Denman's (2011) *Stuff We All Get*; however, the sound-colour synesthesia described as one of Zack's characteristics did not seem to qualify as any kind of impairment.

It is important to note that attention deficit hyperactivity disorder (ADHD) is not consistently approved for government education funding in Canada under the above categories of exceptionality, and thus it was not included in this literature review, although a book about a boy who demonstrates severe behavioural problems (Beth Goobie's [2012] *Jason's Why*) is included in chapter 4. Books about gifted individuals were also omitted from the study sample, although consideration was given to Rudman's (1995) suggestion that

> although intellectual, artistic, creative, or leadership talents are not disabilities, gifted people can be perceived as having disabilities because these people are sometimes treated in destructive ways by the rest of society. Most heroes in fantasies and fairy tales are gifted in one way or another; but it is more difficult to find children in stories about everyday life who are gifted and whose talents are respected, not instruments that invite punitive behaviour. (p. 318)

Rosemarie Garland Thomson (1997) reframes disability as another cultural construction of bodies and identity alongside race, gender, ethnicity, and sexuality. She also explains disability in more universal terms: "The fact that we all will become disabled if we live long enough is a reality many people ... are reluctant to admit" (p. 14). Perhaps the most accurate rendering of the word is from people who view themselves as disabled, because they alone can personalize a meaning within lived contexts. Disability is thus not an absolute term, nor should it define the person to whom it is attached, although it is commonly used in these ways. I am utilizing the word *disability* within this work because it is widely accepted in the contexts of education and social justice, although the term is currently being replaced in many contexts by the word *exceptionality* or other phrases, such as *differently abled*.

In Oppel's (2007) fantasy novel *Darkwing*, Dusk, an arboreal glider with physical properties different from the others of his clan, asks his sister, "Is different wrong?" (p. 83). *Darkwing*'s author speaks through this dialogue, asking readers to explore this question for themselves, and in the course of the story, the answer is complicated. As readers discover, Dusk is both penalized and lauded for his differences—once the other gliders discover that he is, in fact, a more evolved and therefore physically advanced form of their species.

Historical Patterns and Trends

Classic texts about characters with disabilities contain particular patterns and themes that are not represented in the sample of Canadian books I collected for study. The patterns and themes from classics provide a source of information on how people with disabilities were viewed at the time these books were written, and demonstrate how changes in contemporary books reflect societal changes. There appears to be a tendency in classical literary representations for adults to offer disabilities as punishments for particular characters and use them as plot devices rather than realistic accoutrements to characterizations.

Hays (1971) discusses how lameness in ancient as well as 20th-century texts has been described as symbolic of, or a euphemism for, a genital wound that, in turn, symbolizes a social disability. Rose (2006) talks about how texts surviving from ancient Greece equate deafness with diminished cognitive ability as well as impaired verbal communication. Baynton (2006) explores how, prior to the 1860s, deafness was described as a scourge that isolated its bearer from the Christian community, and after the 1860s, deafness was depicted as isolating the bearer from the national community.

The tendency to ascribe negative stereotypes to characters with disabilities has been linked to societal assumptions. Freire (1998) reinforces how people have a tendency to affirm that what is different from themselves is inferior, a sentiment he describes as intolerance. Another viewpoint attributes stereotypes about disability to hidden anxieties about the possibility of disablement happening to us or someone close to us. Longmore (1987) states that what we fear, we often shun or try to destroy. Pinker (2002) goes further to reflect on brain research that may identify genetic predispositions related to response to difference.

What critical study there is regarding disability in early children's literature describes patterns similar to the trends identified in classic texts for adults. A general consensus in the research is that folktales manifest the disabled body as an embodiment of evil. Classic fairy tales portray physical differences as metaphors for characters' inner qualities. Disability and illness were used as metaphors in the didactic, warm family stories of the 19th-century novel, and were employed to bring the character through a period of trial into a happy-ever-after ending. The authors of 19th- and early 20th-century novels tended to kill or cure their disabled characters with fictive ease. In addition, authors of Victorian prose often used illness and accident to accomplish the "taming" or "civilizing" of female adolescent characters (Keith, 2001).

Researchers have also noted patterns in the popularity of particular disabilities in early fiction, as well as societal viewpoints about disability. Between 1920 and 1955, polio and blindness tended to outweigh all other disabilities referenced in classic fiction, a trend partially related to the prominence of these exceptionalities in English-speaking society at that time. According to Keith (2001), in the 1940s and '50s, blindness in stories was reflected in excess of its actual occurrence because of the metaphorical possibilities of blindness that have interested storytellers—the idea that by not seeing the material world, one is able to see its essence.

In the classics Keith studied, the following ideologies were pervasive:

1. there is nothing good about being disabled;
2. disabled people have to learn the same qualities of submissive behaviour that women have always had to learn: patience, cheerfulness, and making the best of things;
3. impairment can be a punishment for bad behaviour, for evil thoughts, or for not being a good enough person;
4. although disabled people should be pitied rather than punished, they can never be accepted;
5. the impairment is curable. If you want to enough, if you love yourself enough (but not more than you love others), if you believe in God enough, you will be cured. (2001, p. 7)

Keith's discussion emphasizes standard historical responses to disablement, and her exploration of societal assumptions about disability reflects R. G. Thomson's (1997) work. Thomson outlines how the assumptions of society offer a rationale regarding the interpretation of a character with a disability: "Disabled literary characters usually remain on the margins of fiction as uncomplicated figures or exotic aliens whose bodily configurations operate as spectacles, eliciting responses from other characters or producing rhetorical effects that depend on disability's cultural resonance" (p. 9). Thomson also discusses how representation relies on cultural assumptions to fill in missing details—a factor that benefits the plot through its very economy, and may explain the missing discussions of characterization of disability in reviews and academic papers: "When literary critics look at disabled characters, they often interpret them metaphorically or aesthetically, reading them without political awareness as conventional elements ... of traditions" (pp. 9–10).

Historically, then, characters with disabilities were produced as stereotypical portraits, whose purpose in novels was to advance the plot and whose interpretation relied on cultural assumptions. Within early texts, disability is presented as a punishing condition that isolates characters from happiness and societal acceptance, although impairments are often presented as curable through individual desire and heartfelt displays of religion. I conjecture that historical sociocultural contexts have informed authors' depictions of characters with disabilities, although few studies have been conducted to measure this phenomenon.

Contemporary Trends

Past Limitations

Before examining contemporary patterns and themes in children's literature depicting characters with disabilities, it's important to consider past practice. In the last half of the 20th century, although writers aimed for greater realism, according to recent research they still found it hard to imagine a character moving toward a happy life as a grown-up disabled person. Such lack of imagination is contrary to advances in medical science, which imply that many people born with impairments can expect to lead full and rewarding lives. Keith (2001) indicates that "many writers of the new wave of books in the 1960s, 1970s and beyond have been unable to create a disabled character who is not weighed down with feelings of inadequacy and self-hatred" (p. 212). Keith's identification that authors rarely presented the prospect of a positive future for book characters with disabilities mirrors a statement by Canadian author Jean Little, who says, "Why couldn't any of these authors imagine a happy ending that was honest? Did they, deep down, believe that you could not remain disabled and have a full, joyful life?" (Little, 1990, p. 9). Similar sentiments are offered by Deborah Kent, who states that in her childhood reading materials, "I longed to find proof that disability need not bar me from all of the pleasures and perils that other girls regarded as their birthright" (Kent, 1987, p. 47).

Current Research Findings

Contemporary depictions of disability no longer tend to rest on the miracle cure, but death, according to Keith, unfortunately remains a popular option. Current explorations in critical studies of children's literature provide further discussion of patterns, although such studies are limited. Dyches and Prater's studies build upon their own previous work as well as the work of other researchers who focus on single categories of disability represented primarily in contemporary American children's texts. In one study, Dyches and Prater examine children's fiction published between 1999 and 2003 that qualified for the Dolly Gray Award, which recognizes literature that characterizes developmental disabilities. Their findings indicate that most characters are realistic, positive, and dynamic, and the researchers suggest that "current fictional children's books that characterize people with developmental disabilities are generally more positive than they have been in the past" (Dyches & Prater, 2005, p. 215), although this is implicitly a biased sample on which to make those assumptions.

The investigation of fiction about characters with disabilities in terms of single categories—research that focuses exclusively on developmental disabilities (for example, Down syndrome)—may reflect the history of disability studies in contrast to its recent evolution as a comprehensive entity. While there have been people with disabilities throughout history, only in modern times have people with diverse exceptionalities allied themselves as a united physical minority.

Limited research regarding biography and autobiography implies that change in representations of the oppressed and culturally displaced may be occurring through literature that reflects real experiences. Kelley Jo Burke's (2010) dramatic play covering the first five years of her evolving relationship with an autistic son—in addition to interviews with other parents of children on the autism spectrum and leading experts in the field—was recently published by Hagios

Press under the title *Ducks on the Moon: A Parent Meets Autism*. Luke Jackson's (2002) title *Freaks, Geeks and Asperger Syndrome: A User Guide to Adolescence* and Naoki Higashida's (2013) *The Reason I Jump* are both first-person accounts of adolescents with autism. Mariatu Kamara's (2008) gut-wrenching *The Bite of the Mango* narrates Kamara's own story, including what happened in her birthplace, Sierra Leone, when at the age of 12 her hands were amputated by rebel boy soldiers. Her need to find a voice and her belief that her life has value culminate as Kamara embarks on a UNICEF speaking tour. Minaki (2011) points out that "Mariatu's own hand-less body was far better able to function when left without useless, ableist devices" as, in her case, prosthetics served as an "oppressive representation of normalcy" (p. 119). Minaki goes on to suggest that "Mariatu, like Taylor in *Wild Orchid* (Brenna, 2005), insists on reclaiming her agency and the legitimacy of her own altered body" (p. 121).

Keith indicates: "As a disabled woman, I too look at the world differently and there are issues and ideas, apparently invisible to others, which are very real to me" (Keith, 2001, p. 9). Daniel Tammet's (2007) insightful non-fiction book *Born On a Blue Day: Inside the Mind of an Autistic Savant* can offer readers much about Tammet's unique brain-based perspectives on the world, much as Temple Grandin's (2012) non-fiction title *Different—Not Less* explores the stories of adults with autism, Asperger's, and ADHD. Sarah York's (2012) semi-biographical adult novel *The Anatomy of Edouard Beaupré* chronicles the life of the Saskatchewan-born "Willow Bunch Giant," just as Sandra Richmond (1983/2009) has fictionalized her own teenage experiences of paralysis in the older young adult novel *Wheels for Walking*.

The Value of Stories

It is also possible that a past lack of access to literacy in marginalized populations may have limited the production of particular voices in autobiography. With current computer technology and other means of communication, people whose voices went previously unheard are able to offer intimate discourse about their lives and experiences. The National Film Board's 2006 production of *Shameless: The ART of Disability*, directed by Bonnie Sherr Klein, is an example of contemporary films that are available. Another production is *FASD "Realities and Possibilities": The Myles Himmelreich Story*, a film created by the Saskatchewan Preventions Institute (2009) to support awareness of Fetal Alcohol Spectrum Disorder.

It is through differing perspectives of individuals that we make up a collective whole, and thus it is important that our educational curricula reflect the stories of the students we teach, seeking to nurture inclusive landscapes both inside, and outside, our classrooms. As Robert Coles (1989), a professor of psychiatry and medical humanities, stated about the value of story: "It's what we all carry with us on this trip we take, and we owe it to each other to respect our stories and learn from them" (p. 30). Stories about exceptionality are emerging to fill in spaces where previously they have been absent.

In some cases, the topic of exceptionality has been viewed as part of multiculturalism because of the need to address prejudices and biases related to students with disabilities. The philosophy of inclusive education, however, goes beyond the idea that mainstream groups need books to help understand the *Other*. Inclusive education implies that books about disability, for example, relate on multiple levels to the lived lives of the students we teach, and should therefore be part of our classroom curricula.

Christina Minaki, a writer with cerebral palsy, confides, "Eventually, it hit me that if I wanted to avoid being seen as 'courageous' for the wrong reasons (simply for getting out of bed and living the full and productive life we are meant to enjoy), the solution is to use my writing as a vehicle of my activism, to portray the lives of people with disabilities as lives lived by people of purpose, dignity, resilience and focus" (Minaki, 2009, p. 13). In a similar vein, Janz (2004) states in the author's note for her semi-autobiographical historical novel *Sparrows on Wheels* that it was originally written as a master's thesis to demonstrate what life was like growing up in the pre-integration era, when the education of people with disabilities occurred primarily in "special" schools.

The Evolution of the Reflection of Characters with Disabilities

Dresang (1999) discusses the developmental stages of literature about children with disabilities, indicating:

> When books about young people with disabilities first started proliferating in the 1970s and 1980s, an exclusively positive portrayal of characters represented the group. This seems to have been intended to redress the very negative images that were often present in the past. Neither stance allowed for depth of character development, but over time the portrayals were enriched and diversified. The lens of Radical Change assists in identifying books where authors include perspectives uncommon in books of previous times. Characterizations that reflect previously unheard voices and the presentation of inner emotions in youth who speak for themselves offer the inclusion of "issues not considered acceptable for children in the past." (Dresang, 1999, p. 134)

In this way, boundaries related to literary content are also reconfigured, another aspect of Radical Change worth consideration. Dresang notes that "collectively these books allow young people to experience a wide variety of mental and physical challenges, to draw conclusions of their own, and to begin to comprehend the diversity that exists among previously marginalized people" (p. 135). Dresang also addresses the idea that changing boundaries occur with "subjects previously forbidden, settings previously overlooked, characters portrayed in new, complex ways, new types of communities" and "unresolved endings" (p. 173).

Future Predictions

Perhaps we will move into the use of a split word, dis/ability, to foreground able possibilities, or evolve into a more comprehensive usage of the word *exceptionality*. It appears that differences already appear in the characterizations of children's literature that offer more positive potential for renditions of complex lives than in past literary portrayals. Most certainly we shall see more blending of categories of difference, with considerable space for cultural uniqueness and ability alongside minority sexual orientations. As more people begin to tell their own personal stories, in fiction and in non-fiction, with assistive technology supporting authors in ways beyond past practice, the field of fiction will no doubt have more authentic characterizations from which to draw. Filax and Taylor's (2014) title *Disabled Mothers: Stories and Scholarship by and about Mothers with Disabilities* is one example of writing that challenges cultural norms and assumptions. In addition to more inclusion in available titles, I suggest that more diversity will appear across genre categories. Where once notably confined to realistic fiction, characterizations that include differences related to ability will predictably appear in all genres, fully actualizing the idea that anyone can be a protagonist in any kind of book.

A consideration of Radical Change books is only one part of the equation for educators. Another part is the usability of books in classroom communities. Teachers must recognize not only the importance of introducing diverse perspectives through literature, but also the flexibility of books about characters with disabilities in supporting curricular themes beyond an isolated glance at "disability literature." As Minaki (2011) states, teachers—as well as society in general—need to learn to "use literature and all manner of artistic approaches to uproot normalcy's hold, instead of further entrenching it" (p. 137). In addition, teachers must be prepared to negotiate their way through the potential for controversy that some of these books carry because of Radical Change characteristics. To prepare for this negotiation, teachers must consider personal agency, as well as their role as educators in a changing world.

Three Essential Questions for This Chapter

1. What books can you list that include characters with disabilities? Are these characters involved as primary or secondary characters? Are the stories told mainly from the first or third person, or are there varied points of view in the books you know? Is the character's disability just part of a dynamic portrayal

or is it a large aspect of a flatter profile? What might your reflections here suggest about literary portrayals of characters with disabilities?
2. What is your own personal philosophy about the role of education? How might you envision the place of school resources, including literature for children and young adults, within this philosophy?
3. Reflect further on the work of Paulo Freire. Illustrate ways that stories might actually change the world.

CHAPTER 2

Critical Literacy and the Value of Shared Reading as a Teaching Context

Rationale for Sharing Stories with Children

"Read it again!" my four-year-old son would beg, bent on hearing *The Very Hungry Caterpillar*, Eric Carle's (1969) bright and predictable picture book, one more time before bed.

"It's time to go to sleep now" was my typically weary response as I thought of the dishes left to do, the laundry piling up, and various other household chores I had put on hold for later.

"But you promised two ones, and I need that book again."

"If I read that one again, I'll fall asleep," I answer.

"I won't," he hints, darkly. "I'm not ever goin' to sleep."

So I grudgingly begin to read the desired volume, and smile as the power of language helps us put aside our day, and glory in ideas and images. Before long, he is tucked under the covers, hands cradling his beloved toy—a child-sized plush caterpillar based on Carle's design and fittingly named Protector.

When I think about why reading matters, I think about the way that books protect us from a world happening too much at once. They bring us learning in manageable pieces, and can simply be shut when desired. I remember the delight I took in holding my own children close when they were toddlers and emergent readers, sharing pictures and text that pleased the eye and ear. The bond that was created during shared reading experiences was, and is, very strong. My children are now adults and I still share reading materials with them, eliciting their critical evaluations of popular texts and, on occasion, unpacking a story around the dinner table.

It's all about us: what touches the heart in what we are reading; what we fail to understand; and what we understand only too well. Because of the connections we make to what we read, and, through this, to each other, we have become an important reading club, my family and I, just as my students and I became important to each other through books we shared in the classroom.

In my storied past, I have had many experiences with books, hour after hour entranced by plot and character. Childhood memories of books my mother read to me at my repeated request: Alcott's (1868) *Little Women,* Sidney's (1880) *Five Little Peppers and How They Grew,* and a book I have been unable to locate in contemporary times: *Mouse Mountain.* With a head start through the absorption of book language through parent-child reading, I quickly became an independent reader, relishing the witty scrapes of Montgomery's (1908) *Anne of Green Gables* and the delicious sensitivities in White's (1939) *Charlotte's Web.* As I entered my teen years, repetitions of L'Engle's (1962) *A Wrinkle in Time* and Zindel's (1968) *The Pigman* offered solace, drumming a steady and accepting rhythm to accompany coming of age. Throughout this entranced reading, I became the characters offered to me in books—Anne, Meg, Lorraine—finding their joys and troubles to be very much like my own. And somehow, in perspective, my own troubles seemed just a little lighter.

Marshall (1998) emphasizes how reading books about individual differences is an important tool in building communities that understand and respect diversity. Paley (1979) suggests that coming to terms with one kind of difference prepares us for understanding other kinds of differences. While much has been written about cultural and gender sensitivity, little attention has been provided to books that include characters with disabilities.

Derman-Sparks suggests something very particular to the importance of reading about diversity: that children begin very early to notice and categorize differences, develop attitudes about themselves and others, and assume societal stereotypes about their own person and others in general (Derman-Sparks & ABC Task Force, 1989). She further emphasizes the teacher's obligation to address, rather than ignore, issues of individuality. One way of doing so is through teacher-led explorations of a diverse literature collection that respectfully encompasses a variety of differences among characters.

Evaluation of Children's Literature

When faced with choices for classroom resources or home libraries, educators and parents are well advised to consider a number of questions. How well do the materials reflect the lives and interests of young people in their own context? How well do the materials reflect the lives and interests of young people in the world? Further, what literary qualities are present in the works that make them stellar examples of literature in the field?

As we ask questions about the evaluation of literature, we must also think about the purpose of sharing stories with children. We want them to see themselves in literature, but we also want them to experience the world—Galda's (1998) idea of the potential of books as mirrors and windows. In addition, we hope that literature will serve as a strong model for language structures that will support the development of syntax—the grammar of language—and semantics—vocabulary—as well as phonological awareness, phonemic awareness, and phonics. By offering listeners or readers a model of linguistic patterns, we are supporting their writing development as well as their reading ability.

Reviews and Book Awards

Traditional elements of children's fiction can also be grounds for scrutiny. Exploring characterization, plot, setting, theme, style and point of view, as well as illustrations, are jobs for children as well as adults, as assessment belongs to everyone. While the number of independent book reviews of children's literature seem to be dwindling in local newspapers, reviews also appear in the *Canadian Children's Book News* and online. A good source of review information on Canadian titles is the online *CM Magazine* (www.umanitoba.ca/cm/).

Canadian book awards also spotlight worthy titles. Noteworthy awards include the Governor General's Literary Awards for children's literature—text and children's literature—illustrated book; the Geoffrey Bilson Award for historical fiction; the John Spray Mystery Award; the Marilyn Baillie Picture Book Award; the Monica Hughes Science Fiction and Fantasy Award; the Norma Fleck Award for non-fiction; and the TD Canadian Children's Literature Award. The Canadian Children's Book Centre offers information on various awards as well as its own catalogue of reviews and starred titles (see www.bookcentre.ca/award). Many provinces support children's literature through juried competitions and readers' choice awards, and these can be accessed through individual websites or by contacting provincial arts boards for further information.

The Governor General's Literary Award for Children's Literature: Children's Text was, until 2015, generally awarded to a novel for older children, although occasionally a picture book triumphed, as in the 1999 win for Gilmore's (1999) picture book *A Screaming Kind of Day*. The Governor General's Literary Award for Children's Literature: Children's Illustration used to be awarded to a picture book for younger children. In 2008, a graphic novel—*Skim*—was one of the four short-listed books nominated for the Children's Text category, with Mariko Tamaki as the author. Unfortunately, however, the illustrator, Jillian Tamaki, did not receive a nomination, and when one considers the connections between pictures and text in a graphic novel such as this, one wonders at a clear distinction between *writer* and *illustrator* in regards to graphic novels. In an attempt to prevent future inequities of this nature, the categories have since been revised to include one for illustrated books where both writer and illustrator share the award.

Critical Literacy

Brazilian educator Paulo Freire's ideal is that education be transformative. In Freire's view, change to the individual results in social change, moving communities and societies along a forward path. Rather than depositing knowledge into the minds of students, it is, he says, the role of teachers to pose problems for students to consider—and critical literacy offers one approach to draw such ideology into classrooms through literary studies. Storytelling and written text offer fuel for transformation, as both contain evocative messages that teach as well as entertain.

Notions of critical literacy as a classroom approach have been emerging since Freire's theoretical groundwork regarding the need for a critical stance with respect to literacy, a heightening of interest in the topic occurring in the late 1980s and early 1990s. The term *critical literacy* has come to refer to a wide range of educational philosophies, and although no single definition has emerged, critical literacy is generally conceived as an approach to reading pedagogy that positions critical approaches to the text alongside pragmatic, text-meaning, and coding practices. Critical literacy thus involves an awareness of how, why, and in whose interests particular texts might work. Alan Luke and Peter Freebody, two Australian researchers who discuss critical literacy at length, focus on strategies for talking about, rewriting, and contesting the contents of texts in the scope of literacy teaching (Luke & Freebody, 1997).

Other researchers discuss the shifts in individual consciousness that students may experience in critical literacy approaches, looking at the impact on the identity development, beliefs, and actions of readers. In order to facilitate identity-related explorations, educators must pay particular attention to differences in gender, cultural background, and ability when selecting representative texts. Much has already been written by previous researchers foregrounding gender and multicultural elements in children's literature. The discussions in chapters 3 to 6, referencing particular contemporary Canadian children's novels, are intended to assist understandings of noteworthy patterns and trends with respect to the representation of disability.

Lewison, Flint, and Van Sluys' (2002) framework of the four dimensions of critical literacy is important as we demonstrate the ways in which texts offer opportunities for teachers and parents to engage students in critical literacy discussions. Three of these four dimensions include disrupting the commonplace, interrogating multiple perspectives, and focusing on sociopolitical issues, and these perspectives are all evident to varying degrees within the children's literature listed in this text.

The fourth dimension—taking action and promoting social justice—emerges as we consider the author portraiture, and discover that particular authors have reasons for writing particular books toward the goal of changing the world. Such a discovery encourages children to think of their own writing as having potential in taking action and promoting social justice—a dimension of critical literacy that is most effectively approached through a consideration of authors along with their texts, rather than the texts in isolation.

A consideration of the perspectives of authors who create classroom texts is also important if children are to understand that real people have written the texts at hand. The author portraits included in chapters 4, 5, and 6 offer an opportunity to hear from three authors in anticipation of a resonance that reflects the influences of individual authorial practice. As well as supporting readers, these portraits support writers through the delineation of aspects of the writing process. Heffernan's (2004) work is inspirational in this regard as he describes a class of primary students whose writing was bland and unmotivated until he began sharing riskier texts and encouraging critical conversations.

The idea that language both arises and shapes social practice is a powerful one with regard to social justice perspectives, where the belief is that educators have a responsibility to offer classroom experiences that allow students to examine and then transcend a given text, comparing and contrasting aspects of that text to their understanding of reality. Diversity in regard to resources is imperative in cultivating the understanding of multiple perspectives. Classroom strategies that require students to learn critical reading practices, along with basic decoding, text-meaning, and pragmatic skills and strategies, form the basis for addressing current issues, connecting, in Freire's (1983) words, a reading of "the word" to a reading of "the world." In addition, within a critical literacy framework, student writers are encouraged to view writing as social action. As Minaki (2011) states, "Writers are educators, and writing is important, powerful work" (p. 143).

Elements of Freire's philosophy are seen in the call for critical literacy approaches that evaluate the legitimacy of curricular resources as well as propose learning as transformational to both the individual and the society. In this text, critical literacy implies a type of transcendence, where changes within the individual result in changes to the surrounding social fabric. Sensitivity to social context is foregrounded through a consideration of social considerations alongside the more traditional decoding and encoding established as core practices of literate individuals.

The social considerations under scrutiny in relation to this book involve the representation of characters with disabilities in past and contemporary children's novels, as well as the classroom practices that encourage students to read and reflect upon the messages included in these books. Discussing the absence as well as the representation of characters with disabilities in classroom texts is an example of how critical literacy can engage students to read "the world," as well as "the word," through Freire's "pedagogy of love" that involves acts of critical reflection. Critical literacy is thus an appropriate framework through which to discuss books about characters with disabilities.

Critical Literacy Applied

A previous study of mine examining Canadian novels portraying characters with disabilities identified that these characterizations rarely include other aspects of difference, such as minority sexual orientations or cultural backgrounds (Brenna, 2010b). This study illuminated other interesting patterns in the depictions of characters with disabilities within the Canadian children's novels that comprised the study sample, intriguing in the manner in which they reflect the exclusion as well as the inclusion of particular elements of the human condition.

This previous body of study texts excluded many elements of Radical Change (Dresang, 1999), with the exception of *changing perspectives* that appeared through the depiction of characters with disabilities, as well as some aspects related to *changing boundaries* and a few rare examples of *changing forms and formats*. This finding regarding the limited inclusion of Radical Change elements supports Dresang's theory of the way that changes in literature for young people sprout up from the horizontal, root-like structure of the children's literature rhizome: "here and there ... connected yet heterogeneous, and in a nonlinear manner" (p. xviii).

While including a number of Canadian settings, mentioning many provinces by name, the texts in my previous study did not make mention of Alberta, other than indirectly through a reference to a "western province," and none of Canada's territories—Yukon, Nunavut, or the Northwest Territories—were given specific illumination. In contrast, Ontario was mentioned 12 times, with seven of these references directed toward Toronto. This finding has implications for a consideration of place in classroom resources, offering educators insight into particular patterns that may be reflected in ways other than the restricted view that published fiction may provide. Whether place names in texts are a result of author location or the use of particular place names arises from marketing and involves the targeting of a particular audience remains to be discovered.

The texts in my previous study sample also gravitated toward intermediate and young adult audiences, with only two novels specifically targeted at junior readers—ages 8 to 11. In addition, fantasy and mystery novels were genres only minimally addressed, with realistic and historical fiction offering standard frameworks within the study sample. It is important that educators designing curriculum for children in the 8 to 11 age group be aware of the lack of children's fiction presenting characters with disabilities and attempt to accommodate inclusion in other ways.

Another factor emerged from my previous study in regards to how texts were presented in library database descriptions, where ableist language was noted on a number of occasions. For example, the Edmonton Public Library's catalogue uses the phrase "suffers from" in the description of Asperger's syndrome for Taylor in my own novel *Wild Orchid* (Brenna, 2005), as well as Fetal Alcohol Syndrome for Billy in *The Moon Children* (Brenna, 2007). In addition, Pauline in Carter's (2001) *In the Clear* is described as a "victim" of polio. On the back cover of Walters's (2000) *Rebound*, the central character, David, is described as "confined to a wheelchair."

Overall, the books in my previous study sample did not reflect what Keith (2001) described as the "kill or cure" mentality of authors writing about characters with disabilities in traditional texts, nor did they illustrate a predominance of particular disabilities, unlike the prominence of polio and blindness in classic literature, the latter reflected in excess of its actual occurrence (Keith, 2001). The books in the study sample also included a strong representation of first-person narrators that had disabilities.

The view of critical literacy supported by my previous study relates to particular classroom resources, a vision of why these resources are important, and a perspective on how these resources might fit into educational frameworks. Critical literacy offers one approach to literacy education that combines understandings of both "the word and the world" (Freire, 1983, 1991). In addition to including classroom texts that reflect all people, promoting Freire's "pedagogy of love" (1983; 1991; 1998), a critical literacy approach to these texts will support students in developing the skills they need to independently evaluate the copious amounts of textual materials offered as part of our digital age.

Critical literacy, conceptualized within the curriculum commonplaces of teacher, learner, milieu, and subject matter (Schwab, 1978), combines traditional work regarding reading and writing with the practice of critical, social thinking. A practice of critical, social thinking is presented in Lewison, Flint, and Van Sluys' (2002) four-dimensions framework regarding critical literacy: "(1) disrupting the commonplace, (2) interrogating multiple viewpoints, (3) focusing on sociopolitical issues, and (4) taking action and promoting social justice" (p. 382). Further exploration of aspects of these dimensions, in relation to particular titles, is included in the following four sections.

Disrupting the Commonplace

This dimension may be encouraged as teachers ask students to consider aspects of children's books that may not be initially recognized by children as stereotypes. One element of critical literacy that encompasses the portrayal of characters with disabilities is attention to issues regarding diversity within characterization. Asking students whether characters with disabilities are presented accurately, fairly, and respectfully, or whether these characters are represented at all in the work students are reading, foregrounds attention to stereotypes. Trends in classic fiction where characters with disabilities lacked opportunities for full and happy lives offer a compelling backdrop for classroom explorations of contemporary texts in terms of changing societal perspectives regarding people with disabilities.

Specific books that involve characters with a disability may be particularly helpful in encouraging readers to consider how a disruption of the commonplace has occurred within literary texts. In Porter's (2005) intermediate-age novel *The Crazy Man*, Em learns to see Angus, a man stigmatized by mental illness, in a more personal way, as do other members of the community. In her author portrait included in Chapter 5, Pamela Porter discusses a public presentation regarding *The Crazy Man*, after which many people wanted to share their stories of oppression and misunderstanding related to mental illness.

Rainey in Waldorf's (2008) young adult novel *Tripping* quickly establishes that only one of her distinguishing features is the use of a prosthetic leg. Her character defies a pattern involving disability as a plot device, and provides readers with a new way to consider the momentum of a fictional character with a disability. The growth of Rainey's character during the course of the novel, as well as her first-person narration, are elements of disrupting the commonplace to consider in discussions of this title.

In addition to presenting a single book about characters with disabilities as a study opportunity, teachers are encouraged to use literature about characters with disabilities alongside other classroom texts. Books portraying characters with disabilities should thus be integrated alongside other classroom resources, recognizing that "critical literacy should not be viewed as the best or only way of reading, especially when considering the importance of pleasure; that is, the value of purely aesthetic experience" (McDaniel, 2006, p. 155). Ideally, a focus on the characteristics of books beyond the commonplace will support students in their own writing as well, and teachers can assist students in drawing what they learn from one process into others. A study on the links between the reading of critical literacy texts and students' own writing can be found in Heffernan (2004).

Interrogating Multiple Viewpoints

This is another dimension of critical literacy that can be supported by a focus on texts about characters with disabilities, as well as their authors, rendering opportunities for students to consider contrasting points of view. For example, Gilmore's (1995) junior novel *A Friend Like Zilla* includes alternate viewpoints on a girl with intellectual disabilities. The alternate viewpoints are presented through considerations of Zilla's treatment by her mother, by her new friend Zenobia (Nobby), and by various members of her friend's family, including an uncle who demonstrates distinct prejudices against Zilla on the basis of her intellectual functioning. The excerpt that follows is told from Nobby's point of view and offers a scene in which Zilla and Nobby overhear Uncle Chad and Aunt Alice talking about Zilla.

> "... I simply cannot understand why Audrey encourages Zenobia to play with that girl."
> My back prickled.
> "Chad, really," cried Aunt Alice.
> "Seriously, Alice, do you think Zenobia ought to spend so much time with Zilla?"
> "Chad, what an awful thing to say!"
> Zilla's eyes were wide. I had to distract her.
> "I'm merely saying what everyone's thinking, Alice. After all she can barely read. Of course, we all feel sorry for her, one has to feel sorry for someone like that, but still ..."
> Zilla made a strangled noise. She half climbed, half dropped from the tree then ran to the farmhouse. (Gilmore, 1995, p. 94)

Through their relationship with Zilla, both Nobby and Uncle Chad learn to perceive the world, and each other, in a different way.

In addition to its support for disrupting the commonplace in terms of the stigma around mental illness, Pamela Porter's intermediate novel *The Crazy Man* (2005) also interrogates multiple viewpoints. This book reflects the idea that the four dimensions of critical literacy "are interrelated—none stand alone" (Lewison, Flint, & Van Sluys, 2002, p. 382). Em, the young female protagonist in *The Crazy Man*, absorbs the different reactions of the town to Angus, a man stigmatized by his previous hospitalization for mental illness. Within the context of this novel, readers are able to examine, just as Em does, a range of opinions regarding Angus, and decide for themselves whose opinion most matches their own.

In Sylvia McNicoll's (1994) intermediate novel *Bringing Up Beauty*, Kyle is depicted as a strong protagonist through the manner in which he grows and changes during the course of the story. At first, Kyle is drawn into despair because of his diabetes-induced blindness, but he pushes forward in the actualization of hopes and dreams that include a budding romance with Liz. However, Kyle also performs as an iteration of classic texts where characters with disabilities are either "cured or killed." In Kyle's case, just as he envisions a possible future with Liz, he dies. Tensions between these two patterns in characterization are interesting with respect to the consideration of multiple viewpoints concerning characters with disabilities. In addition, within the novel, the responses of other characters toward Kyle provide alternate examples of the way other members of society may perceive people with disabilities.

Focusing on Sociopolitical Issues

This is a dimension of critical literacy that appears in relation to notable exclusions in classroom texts. Previous research with Canadian novels (Brenna, 2010b) illuminates how characters with disabilities lack a specific ethnicity, religious framework, or minority sexual orientation. Only 6 of 64 characterizations, for example, were depicted as having ethnic or religious diversity, and in most of these cases, references were made very briefly regarding the character's family rather than in direct discussion of the character. In addition, none of the characters with disabilities were portrayed as LGBT, although a small number of the books did include gay or lesbian characters without disabilities.

In addition to previously discussed choices regarding the characterization of multiple "differences," my previous study (Brenna, 2010b) illustrates how characters with disabilities were almost entirely presented as single entities within the fiction in the study sample—rarely do two or more characters with disabilities occupy the same text. One other concerning pattern in the data is that positive portrayals of single fathers were clearly absent from the books in the study sample. While a number of the characters with disabilities were raised by supportive single mothers, the two single fathers presented in the study sample were portrayed negatively. This depiction of single fathers as they relate to characters with disabilities is a sociopolitical trend to monitor.

Sociopolitical issues also arise in the manner in which readers may interpret particular characters. Dopey Colvig, the antagonist of Iain Lawrence's (2006) Governor General's Literary Award–winning intermediate historical fiction novel *Gemini Summer*, is an interesting character to scrutinize. A reading of Dopey's character, according to reviews of the book (Bloom, 2006; Bryan, 2006; Bush, 2006; Huntley, 2006; Mouttet, 2007; Snyder, 2007), has been unproblematic, with no mention made of Dopey's characterization.

Dopey's portrayal, however, resting on the weight of atypical physical characteristics to explain negative behaviour, offers a chance for readers to explore the performativity of classic fairy tale elements in a contemporary text. Such performativity may impede critical thinking with regard to Dopey's depiction; alternatively, if his character were introduced in a special education context, it would surely raise questions regarding fair representation. The rendering of Dopey as a plot device, emerging as a stereotypical representation of a child with disabilities, has slipped under the radar of book reviewers, and is well worth further exploration with students in classroom settings. Further discussion regarding Dopey appears later in this chapter.

Taking Action and Promoting Social Justice

This may be the most complicated aspect of critical literacy to discuss due to its resolve toward demonstrated activity. Certainly characters who take this sort of stance may be identified in various works, most notably friends of characters with disabilities who speak up in their regard, and older texts such as Elizabeth Helfman's (1993) *On Being Sarah* demonstrate this.

An examination of the reasons why particular authors write about characters with disabilities may offer further understanding of the purposes for writing. The portraits of the authors in this text, included in chapters 4, 5, and 6, offer individual perspectives on a view of literature as transformative.

Teaching critical literacy in classrooms is an example of this category as well. Marshall (1998) emphasizes how encountering books about individual differences is an important tool in building communities that respect diversity. Sharing books with children can involve careful discussions of characterization, identifying stereotypes as well as personal reflections regarding the author's choices in character development. While much has been written about cultural and gender sensitivity, it is also imperative to pay attention to books that include characters with disabilities.

James A. Banks's (2014) discussion in *An Introduction to Multicultural Education* focuses on culture as a manifestation of diverse racial, ethnic, social class, and language groups. It is possible, however, to extend Banks's work to considerations of the portrayal of disability, in which disability is simply another construction alongside other differences, including ethnic background. Banks (2014) argues that true multicultural education goes beyond mere content integration. His model of the dimensions of multicultural education is as follows:

1. content integration,
2. the knowledge construction process,
3. prejudice reduction,
4. an equity pedagogy,
5. an empowering school culture and social structure. (p. 36)

Through content integration, teachers can ensure that examples, data, and information concerning a variety of ability groups are presented to illustrate the key ideas within a subject area or discipline. Unlike ethnicity, where content integration has been a prime focus over the past years, especially in subjects such as social studies and English language arts (Banks, 2014), inclusion of disability in classroom resources has been extremely limited.

The knowledge construction process, however, when linked to equity pedagogy, has offered a stronger avenue for ability considerations. Classrooms are or should be designed to support differentiated instruction (Tomlinson, 2008), and through this teaching method, examples of alternate ways of knowing are evident. What was once evident only in one-room schoolhouses where students, grouped by age, were directed toward different tasks, is now prevalent in classrooms operating through multiple, flexible grouping strategies.

In terms of prejudice reduction, schools have tended toward reactionary programs where behaviourism is applied in cases where bullying or other negative behaviours are apparent. More recently, an upward shift in attention related to literature can be noted, where books and other resources have been used to support dialogue and understanding. However, while applied in some capacity to various categories of difference, including ethnicity, gender, and sexual orientation, a lack of available titles of quality literature may be a factor preventing a similar trajectory in regards to disability. Books with Aboriginal characters are also well behind representations of other ethnicities in Canadian literary resources for children, and this will be an aspect of Radical Change (Dresang, 1999) to watch and encourage.

Teachers who embrace a philosophy of equity may offer different things to different students, increasing learning opportunities by responding to student strengths, needs, and interests. Schools that operate toward a culture of empowerment invite structural changes within the school framework "so that students from all groups will have an equal opportunity for success" (Banks, 2014, p. 41). While Banks's work is directed toward differences in social class and racial, cultural, gender, and language groups, it is the kind of thinking that is easily applied to diverse ability groups as well. In addition to planning and individualizing instruction, a social consciousness of this nature also demands differentiated assessment practices (Wormeli, 2006). Banks's equity continuum exemplifies how children's literature portraying characters with disabilities has shifted from acknowledgement of differences to transformative critical thought.

The following rubric (Figure 2.1) may be used to assist readers in identifying and discussing characters with disabilities, facilitating a deeper understanding of these characters, as well as encouraging thoughtful comparisons between books and life.

Book Title _____ Author _____

Publication Date _____

Genre _____ Character's Name _____

Main or Secondary Character _____

Setting _____

Identification of Disability	Language Related to Disability	Evaluation of Character with Disability	Growth and Development of Character with Disability	Relationships between Characters	Relationships between Character with Disability and Reader
character's disability described without accuracy	outdated and/or negative language used to describe the disability	character is uninteresting	character does not grow or develop during the course of the story	character with disability does not establish meaningful relationships	readers have few opportunities to identify with character
character's disability described with some accuracy	outdated and/or negative language used to describe the disability along with inclusion of information regarding setting/time of the story to contextualize this language	character is somewhat interesting	character displays some growth and development during the course of the story	character with disability establishes relationships that are somewhat meaningful	readers have a number of opportunities to identify with character
character's disability described accurately	current and/or neutral language used to describe the disability	character is very interesting	character displays marked growth and development during the course of the story	character with disability establishes relationships that are very meaningful	readers have many opportunities to identify with character

FIGURE 2.1: Exploration of Characters with Disabilities in Children's Fiction
Brenna, 2010b

Chapter 2   Critical Literacy and the Value of Shared Reading as a Teaching Context

This rubric can deepen responses to books where stereotyping may occur and offer a method of comparison between books of equal literary value. Senior students, along with their teachers, should be encouraged to invent rubrics of their own.

Sample Text for Classroom Discussion: Iain Lawrence's *Gemini Summer*

Gemini Summer (2006), Iain Lawrence's Governor General's Literary Award–winning juvenile fiction novel, offers a strong example of a literary text rich with possibilities for critical literacy extensions by middle elementary students (Brenna, 2010a). The plot revolves around brothers Beau and Danny's seemingly idyllic pursuits until Beau is killed in an unusual accident involving a neighbourhood bully, prophetically named Dopey Colvig. Dopey is presented as an inherent villain based on his physical differences, as well as the concise narration of his inexplicable dislike for Danny. Whether his depiction as Marx's repressed/the Other rests on the historical context of the novel and related stereotypes about disability, or on patterns of folktale literature which resound in the storyline, young readers will benefit from assistance from teachers in their interpretation of Dopey's presence within the novel to unpack and extend their responses.

As the novel's human monster, Dopey—son of Creepy—lives at the northern end of the Hollow, near the shortcut the boys use on their way to and from the heights and the local school. "Not one person in Hog's Hollow found a single thing to like about Creepy ... But Dopey was worse," having a "huge, empty head with no brains inside it," and talking in "grunts and howls—that no one but Creepy could understand. He was too stupid to go to school, and so he never left the Hollow" and "for no reason at all, he hated Danny River, and he guarded his end of the Hollow like a troll, lurking on the paths through the cottonwoods, waiting for Danny to pass" (p.13).

Readers are given clear descriptions of the character's large head, his inability to speak intelligibly, and his larger-than-average-sized body, along with narration defining him as "stupid." His presentation in the story continues on par with the indelibly wicked troll under the bridge in the classic folktale *Three Billy Goats Gruff*:

> They were crossing the bridge when Dopey Colvig leapt out from the bushes, holding a stick as stout as a rolling pin. Feet apart, hands at his side, he stood right at the fork in the trail. He was half again as wide as Beau.
>
> He made those sounds, those hoots and groans that only Creepy could understand. His great hollow head with its pudding of a face watched them like an owl's. (p. 60)

On Halloween night, Danny and Beau see into the Colvig house: "The living room was brightly lit, the curtains drawn to all but a crack in the middle. They could see the flicker of the television set, and a big round shadow on the curtains, cast by what must have been either a pumpkin or Dopey's head" (p.73). Although mild attempts at humour are made related to Dopey's head size, there is little sympathy for this character, and no explanation for his behaviour other than stereotypical connections to aggression, size, and intellectual capacity, heightened by references to trolls and ogres.

Thomson (1997) describes how literary texts have tended to strip disabled characters of normalizing contexts, allowing them to be engulfed by a single stigmatic trait. This is clear in the depiction of Dopey, whose rhetorical effect within the novel depends on disability's cultural resonance, just as the novel itself relies on an uncomplicated characterization of Dopey to support plot requirements. Certainly, in *Gemini Summer*, Dopey does his job very well. As the classic monster of our repressed fears, Dopey Colvig is inherently dangerous, and, in the end of the book, driven away by reason.

Children in the intermediate age range, for whom this book is intended, may not independently grapple with Dopey's characterization and its significance in terms of a representation of difference. An important role for educators is to introduce characters like Dopey to readers in a way that favours their understanding of the patterns on which the characters are based, and evaluate an author's choices in this regard. In this way, readers are assisted in avoiding the possibility that such stereotypical patterns add to belief systems about people with disabilities. Such patterns could be contextualized within the historical setting of *Gemini Summer*, or could be discussed in terms of relationships drawn between the novel and its roots in folk literature. A good companion read is David Ward's (2011) *Between Two Ends*, where a young boy enters a translation of the Arabian Nights on behalf of his father.

Risky Texts
The notion of "risky texts" originated with Simon and Simon (1995) to reflect children's and young adult literature that deals explicitly with complicated social issues such as racism and war, clearly aspects of Radical Change in terms of the changing boundaries we can identify in contemporary texts. Bearing witness to historical atrocities—as well as direct exploration of ideas beyond the status quo—may be emotionally uncomfortable for readers, but sensitively structured classroom reading situations can assist readers in considering important yet difficult topics. Damico and Apol (2008) describe the kind of testimonial response that may be supported through imagination exercises where readers are invited to engage deeply with dilemmas of literary characters; this outcome is characterized by historical engagement, emotional investment, and a collectivist orientation. Such testimonial responses would operate alongside, rather than replace, more standard practices, such as personal response, textual response, and critical response.

Educators might frame a testimonial response activity in relation to texts about characters with disabilities in a variety of ways, including guided imagery into a particular scene or scenes, resulting in a discussion of the question, "How would I feel if this happened to me?" Applied to the situation of Ruby Jean, for example, a young woman with Down syndrome in Gina McMurchy-Barber's poignant realistic novel *Free as a Bird* (2010), students could be led to envision a time when they, like Ruby Jean, felt like outcasts. The fact that Ruby Jean endures every manner of abuse elevates the reading age of this title; however, because she uses simplified language as narrator, the details of her situation are often implied rather than fully disclosed.

How adults assist students in selecting texts, what needs to happen before, during, and after potentially troubling readings, and what considerations apply to the inclusion or exclusion of a risky text in a collection are all important topics for exploration. The benefits of leading students through critical analysis of complex classroom material apply to the obvious circumstance that children will encounter much in the digital world that offers uneasy exposure, if not actual risk to health and safety. Kelly (2010) offers a discussion of critical media education that emphasizes the social construction of media representations, inviting readers to critically engage with media through careful examinations that heighten rational interpretation and response.

Michael W. Smith and Jeffrey D. Wilhelm's (2002) study with a diverse group of young men, narrated in *Reading Don't Fix No Chevys*, identifies how progressive curricula and instruction might help boys engage with literacy and all learning in more productive ways. The adolescents in the study repeatedly commented on being drawn to the "edgier" texts (p. 146), citing the more subversive content as making reading enjoyable. This edginess was linked to controversy, in that controversial topics in reading offered more fuel for thought. According to notions of Radical Change theory (Dresang, 1999), changing perspectives in children's and young adult literature are resulting in more authentic and serious subject matter. Elaine M. Will's (2013) graphic novel *Look Straight Ahead* is an example of a resource that pulls no punches when discussing 17-year-old Jeremy Knowles' descent into mental illness. Similarly, Sharon McKay and Daniel Lafrance's graphic novel (2013), based on Sharon McKay's novel (2009) *War Brothers*, is authentic and devastating in its depiction of child soldiers in Uganda.

Other examples of risky texts for adolescents abound. In Heather Waldorf's *Tripping* (2008), a young woman travels across Canada after high school with a group of young people. The fact that she wears a prosthetic leg hinders neither her self-concept nor her love life, although the teen sexuality in this title is interesting, as few literary characters with disabilities are described with sexuality intact. In my own book *Wild Orchid*, the fact that the adult protagonist Taylor Jane slips briefly into an (unconsummated) affair with a married man has garnered minor negative feedback. A scandalized woman cornered me briefly at a book launch, indicating that I should have created more supportive characters around Taylor because of her disability. Biklen and Bogdan (1977) surveyed a range of classic literature to determine how individuals with disabilities were presented, and one of the themes that emerged was that these characters were nonsexual, appearing as incapable of sexual activity or interest.

Books considered but ultimately not included in the annotated bibliographies here comprise stories of addiction, cutting, and other forms of self-harm. While not exactly a disability under the definition embraced by this book, it could be argued that addictions and negative forms of behavioural response to life circumstances are disabling in a number of ways, and as educators work to engage and support students in varying situations, the following young adult titles may be helpful:

- Wendy Phillip's *Fishtailing* (2010), a verse novel that deals with bullying through the story of four teens caught in a web of violence;
- Robert Rayner's *Scab* (2010), the title a reference to the protagonist, a boy who has been bullied long term;
- Cheryl Rainfield's *Scars* (2010), a title that grittily presents the life of a teen survivor of sexual abuse who resorts to cutting for emotional relief;
- Monique Polak's *Scarred* (2007), another book dealing with cutting, this time to relieve pressure in a competitive skater;
- In *Not Your Ordinary Wolf Girl* (2013), Emily Pohl-Weary navigates difference through a popular theme in contemporary young adult literature: werewolves;
- Sylvia McNicoll's *Dying to Go Viral* (2013) also navigates difficult territory as it relates the story of a young girl reliving the last week of her life; and
- Diane Tullson's *Blue Highway* (2004), where a teenage alcoholic causes a fatal accident in the community.

Three Essential Questions for This Chapter

1. Define "disability." Consider and reflect upon what may have influenced your definition. Do you think this term has the same meaning today as in the past? Discuss.
2. Research the history of school inclusion in Canada for students with disabilities. Create a timeline that demonstrates key aspects in the progression toward full inclusion.
3. What do you predict in terms of the future of children with exceptionalities in school and community settings?

CHAPTER 3

Contemporary Canadian Picture Books

Introduction to Picture Books in Canada

As Gail Edwards and Judith Saltman (2010) state in their seminal volume *Picturing Canada: A History of Canadian Children's Illustrated Books and Publishing*, there has been a distinct shift from picture books as products directly intended for children to works that will delight all ages. Notions of equity and appeals to social justice are evident in the most recently published group of picture books, although many publishers may still gravitate toward conservative topics for the purpose of sales. In comparing titles portraying disability (see the annotated bibliographies in chapters 3, 4, 5, and 6), it appears that characters with differing abilities appear much more prominently in novels for children and young adults than they do in picture books.

The blurring of age-related boundaries in terms of picture book audiences is a positive step toward supporting older readers of differing abilities. Two of my recent studies (Brenna, 2012a; Brenna & Bell, 2014) explore case studies where unique individuals require accessible texts. In the former, a 94-year-old previously avid reader with dementia recovered enjoyment in reading through picture books in which illustrations and topics of personal interest assisted with reading comprehension. In the latter, a 16-year-old with multiple challenges, including vision impairment and intellectual disabilities, demonstrated increased enthusiasm for reading related to particular illustrated titles within his range of comprehension.

Classroom libraries that contain a variety of ability-appropriate texts are worthy of consideration as supports for all students. In particular, the position of picture books as resources beyond the primary grades is something to ponder. These books allow for the exploration of print and meaning within a context supportive for readers with various difficulties. Supportive visuals, large print, and spare sentences increase the accessibility of these texts to struggling readers as well as readers with a variety of disabilities. Further research is recommended to support the availability of picture book materials for older readers in diverse classrooms and communities. Publishers would also do well to consider the potential of crossover titles—work that appeals to a variety of age groups—and market these titles accordingly.

A recommendation that intergenerational picture books be made available to adults and young adults in a *general* section of the community library, rather than a *children's* section, may enhance the use of these books in varied populations. Sections of the library labelled "Quick Reads," in conjunction with previously existing areas for magazines, may serve to respectfully widen the resources available to adult readers of various abilities. Various websites suggesting picture book titles for adult audiences can be located by using "picture books and adults" as a search phrase.

Further investigation of the responses of elderly readers and older readers with disabilities to picture books is suggested as a way to deepen the potentiality of available resources for unique populations (Brenna, 2012a). The dearth of current research in terms of literacy resources for all people offers a provocative call for further study, and one that cannot be ignored if we view literacy as an important and ongoing aspect of human existence.

Summary of Picture Books Portraying Characters with Disabilities

Previous Studies

I have long noted how differences related to ability are absent in curricular resources and classroom landscapes. In a recent study conducted with two graduate students (Emmerson, Fu, & Brenna, 2013), a group of 20 award-winning Canadian picture books, published between 1995 and 2012, were examined on the basis of content analysis derived from Dresang's conceptualization of Radical Change (1999). While the books demonstrated the three various aspects of Radical Change proposed by Dresang—changing forms and formats, changing perspectives, and changing boundaries—only four of them portrayed characters with disabilities: two through illustrations, and two through the text. The low number of books published since 1995 portraying characters with disabilities matches a statement by Jaeger and Bowman (2005): "Disability is ordinary. Yet disability is rarely considered as a societal issue in a thoughtful and humane manner" (p. ix). If the landscape of picture books for children is to offer authentic examples of Galda's (1998) transformative "windows and mirrors," it will take some creative problem-solving on the part of educators and parents, as well as some new work from writers.

Canadian findings corresponded with the fact that only 1 of 19 Caldecott-winning books in the United States presented a character with a disability, according to a study within a similar time frame. The Schneider Family Book Awards, supported by the American Library Association to specifically recognize titles presenting disability in characterization, has spotlighted seven winners between 2004 and 2013. The Dolly Gray Award—another American award program—has gone further, specifically recognizing picture books and novels presenting developmental disabilities such as autism.

Of the two Canadian Governor General award-winning titles for illustration, *Virginia Wolf* (Maclear, 2012) deals with the potentiality of childhood depression, while *Ten Birds* (Young, 2011) explores physical difference through an abstract narrative about supposedly flightless birds. Of the two award winners for text, *Ghost Train* (Yee, 1996) depicts a physical disability in the central character, while *A Screaming Kind of Day* (Gilmore, 1999) relates the story of a little girl whose hearing impairment is just one aspect of her characterization. During a period when most Governor General's Literary Award–winning picture books earned prizes in the illustration category, it is important to note that the only two picture books that won a Governor General's award for children's literature (text) within the time period studied presented characters with disabilities. This is possibly a sign that juries recognized the originality of such portrayals, allowing these books to contend alongside longer chapter books.

A study regarding a wider Canadian sample explored evidence of picture books in local bookstores portraying characters with disabilities (Emmerson, Fu, Lendsay, & Brenna, 2014). However, only one of the 252 fiction picture books surveyed in a prominent bookstore included a representation of a character with a disability, and this depiction involved a chronic illness; no titles were found in a second store.

Current Explorations and Comparisons
The current examination of Canadian picture books in this text offers rather different findings than a previous exploration of Canadian novels for young people (Brenna, 2010b). Patterns and trends in the sample of 21 picture books suggest that there is currently a shift toward more ethnically diverse characters who also have a disability, unlike the earlier study (Brenna, 2010b), in which characterizations that included a disability did not include considerations of minority culture alongside the disability. In addition, a number of the picture book titles were in genres that straddled the line between fantasy and realism, contradicting earlier findings related to the prevalence of solid realistic fiction as a genre within which characters with disabilities were most likely to be portrayed (Brenna, 2010b).

Combined disability traits, where characters may have more than one disability, are not evident in the current sample, and this would be a predicted pattern for future research to trace. In addition, studies following picture books presenting characters with disabilities in terms of children's responses are suggested: what supports for inclusion and fuel for critical literacy discussions might these books convey? Further research comparing picture books between and among countries is also suggested.

As these picture books are shared with children, it is important for adult facilitators to assist conversations related to portrayals of disabilities. The following questions may be helpful in providing opportunities to deepen what Louise Rosenblatt (1978) would call a "transaction" with the text, in terms of connections to self, other texts, and the wider world:

1. What character reminds you of yourself or someone you know? In what ways?
2. Are there other books or characters in books that remind you of this one?
3. Do you think there are people in the world like this character? Can you talk about why you think this?

Reader Response

Rosenblatt's (2005) work reminds us that readers make meaning from texts within a socio-cultural context. Both the text and the reader contribute to the responses that relate to an experience with literature. By encouraging a variety of modes of response, students can explore comprehension through drama, art, creative writing, and other means toward developing and representing understanding. Wilhelm (1998), for example, advocates that drama can work as a kind of scaffold in terms of student comprehension and deep inquiry into texts.

A number of the books included in this chapter's annotated bibliography are appealing to older readers due to their complex subject matter, and for this reason, age ranges are not included as part of the annotation. These titles include Nan Gregory's (1995) *How Smudge Came*, where the protagonist is an adult woman living in a group home. Through Ron Lightburn's illustrations, a reader is able to interpret one of Cindy's characteristics as Down syndrome.

Another Canadian picture book worth noting is Sheree Fitch's *Pocket Rocks* (2004), illustrated by Helen Flook. The character of young Ian suggests traits of people with Asperger's Syndrome, including naivety, fine-motor difficulties, emotional "meltdowns," sensitivity to smells, a unique perspective on things, unusual and perhaps obsessive interests, and the need for school assistance and supported stress breaks. The book is an uplifting tale about the power of stories, and emphasizes without didacticism the benefits of self-management strategies.

Missing Voices

While there has been considerable research on gender and multicultural diversity with regard to classroom texts in general (Finazzo, 1997; Galda, 1998; Gilbert, 1997, 2001; Rueda, 1998), little treatment has been given to the characterization of ability (Keith, 2001), although there are select discussions of the treatment of particular disabilities within contemporary fiction (Dyches & Prater, 2000; Dyches, Prater, & Cramer, 2001; Greenwell, 2004; Kalke-Klita, 2005; Mills, 2002; Pajka-West, 2007). Picture book illustrations are highlighted as a particular lens for studying the inclusion of characters with disabilities in children's material

(Matthew & Clow, 2007). Another avenue for study involves how books about characters with disabilities may be evaluated and used with children (Dyches & Prater, 2000; Landrum, 2001; Smith-D'Arezzo, 2003). Because these studies tend to focus predominantly on American children's literature, further applications of research on Canadian materials are recommended.

Dyches and Prater's (2005) work with content analyses suggests that when developmental disabilities are portrayed, they are conceived as either autism spectrum disorder or intellectual disability within a rich and dynamic character profile. Although the dynamic nature of newer portrayals is significant of a positive trend in characterization compared with their 2001 study, the majority of characters presented were male. This is an interesting pattern in American titles. Another recent study examining American graphic novels indicated that people with disabilities are represented within the graphic novel form, however these portrayals most frequently fit a negative and stereotypical image (Irwin & Moeller, 2010).

In Irwin & Moeller's (2010) study, 30 graphic novels—randomly selected from the Young Adult Library Services Association's Great Graphic Novels for Teens 2008—were scrutinized. Of the 30 books, 12 included at least one character with a disability. Those portrayals most frequently fit a negative stereotypical image, and characters were all defined by their disability. In terms of representations within stereotypes, more females than males were described as pitiable, and only males were depicted as evil. Irwin and Moeller (2010) also noted that no characters with disabilities were included in the group settings within the graphic novels they examined. This study, although of limited sample size, adds to previous research suggesting that increased realistic presentations of people with disabilities are required in illustrated texts for all ages.

Annotated Bibliography of Canadian Picture Books Portraying Characters with Disabilities

Award-Winning Picture Books

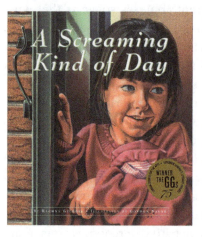

Gilmore, R., & Sauve, G. (Illustrator). (1999). *A screaming kind of day*. Markham, ON: Fitzhenry & Whiteside.

Scully, a little girl with hearing aids, experiences anger and redemption on a rainy day. This is a visually stunning book with an evocative text where a hearing impairment is simply one aspect of a richly characterized child. For ages four and up. Governor General's Literary Award winner (text).

Maclear, K., & Arsenault, I. (Illustrator). (2012). *Virginia Wolf*. Toronto, ON: Groundwood Books.

A young girl tries to cheer up her sister Virginia, who is feeling blue and wolfish. With possible connections to childhood depression, this title offers an image of depression without stigma. For ages four and up. Governor General's Literary Award winner (text).

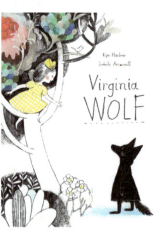

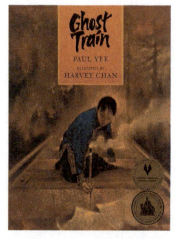

Yee, P., & Chan, H. (Illustrator). (1996). *Ghost train*. Toronto, ON: Groundwood Books.

Choonyi, born with one arm, reunites with her late father through dreams and drawing. For ages eight and up. Governor General's Literary Award winner (text).

Young, C. (2011). *Ten birds*. Toronto, ON: Kids Can Press.

In this counting book, ten seemingly flightless birds use inventive strategies to cross a river. For ages three and up. Governor General's Literary Award winner (illustration).

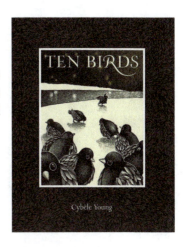

Other Canadian Picture Books

Chartrand, J., Nolan, D., & Chambers, J.M. (Illustrator). (2009). *I want to be in the show.* Winnipeg, MB: Pemmican Publications.

A First Nations boy is born with one foot turned inwards and eventually becomes an NHL hockey player. For ages six and up.

Cottin, M., Faria, R. (Illustrator), & Amado, E. (Translator). (2008). *The black book of colors.* Toronto, ON: Groundwood Books.

This book describes basic colours using both English print and Braille, and the illustrations are textured on black pages rather than coloured. The emphasis is on *seeing* in unique ways—through touch, taste, sound and smell—shifting the focus from viewing blindness as a disability to simply considering it as a difference. For ages five and up.

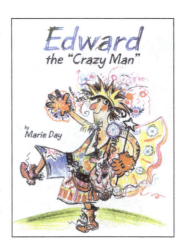

Day, Marie. (2002). *Edward the "crazy man."* Toronto, ON: Annick Press.

A story of friendship between a boy and a homeless artistic man with schizophrenia. For ages six and up.

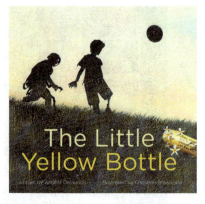

Delaunois, A., & Delezenne, C. (Illustrator). (2011). *The little yellow bottle.* **Toronto, ON: Second Story Press.**

Two children are seriously injured when they pick up a sparkling yellow bottle previously dropped by bombers. For ages eight and up.

Domney, A., & Crawford, A. (Illustrator). (2011). *Splish, splat!* **Toronto, ON: Second Story Press.**

Two painters who are deaf accidentally splatter paint around a room they are working on while signing to each other. For ages four and up.

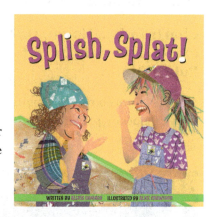

Epp, M., & Chrisholm, M. (Illustrator). (2007). *Hope and the dragon.* **Mississauga, ON: Aspirations Publishing Inc.**

Written by an 11-year-old with cancer, this book explores a dream about fighting a dragon that occurred during surgery. For ages seven and up.

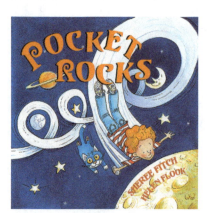

Fitch, S., & Flook, H. (Illustrator). (2002). *Pocket rocks.* **Victoria, BC: Orca Books.**

Ian finds a rock that helps him cope with the daily challenges of having a learning disability. His rock collecting is validated by a visiting storyteller. For ages four and up.

Gregory, N., & Lightburn, R. (Illustrator). (1997). *How Smudge came.* **Markham, ON: Red Deer Press.**

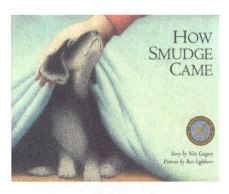

In the group home where Cindy lives, no dogs are allowed. How she befriends a puppy and finds an opportunity for him to live at the hospice where she works offers opportunities for critical discussions about decision-making and independence. A picture book for older readers where the disability—Down syndrome—is portrayed in the illustrations rather than the text. For ages five and up.

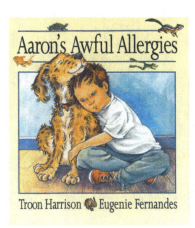

Harrison, T., & Fernandes, E. (Illustrator). (1996). *Aaron's awful allergies.* **Toronto, ON: Kids Can Press.**

Aaron loves animals but becomes allergic to them. For ages four and up.

Hodge, D., & Brassard, F. (Illustrator). (2007). *Lily and the mixed-up letters.* **Toronto, ON: Tundra Books.**

Lily has dyslexia and struggles in school. For ages six and up.

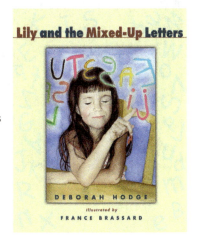

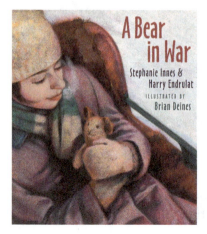

Innes, S., Endrulat, H., & Deines, B. (Illustrator). (2012). *A bear in war.* **Toronto, ON: Pajama Press.**

A true story about a girl with polio who sent her teddy bear to her father on the battlefield during World War I. For ages five and up.

Khan, R., & Fernandez, L., Jacobson, R. (Illustrators). (2001). *King of the skies.* **Toronto, ON: Scholastic/North Winds Press.**

A boy with a physical disability flies kites in annual competitions in Pakistan. For ages four and up.

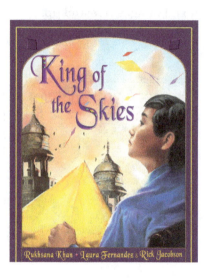

Levert, M. (2005). *Eddie Longpants.* **Toronto, ON: Groundwood Books.**

Eddie is bullied for being different because he is extremely tall. One day, his height proves useful. For ages four and up.

Mitchell, K., & Upjohn, R. (2010). *Patrick's wish*. Toronto, ON: Second Story Press.

Patrick's hemophilia leads to him becoming HIV positive. This biography is told in the style of a photo journal. For ages eight and up.

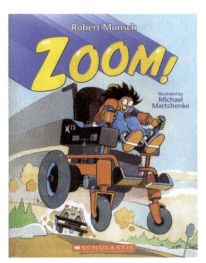

Munsch, R., & Martchenko, M. (Illustrator). (2012). *Zoom*. Markham, ON: Scholastic Canada.

Lauretta's new high-speed wheelchair earns a speeding ticket, but saves the day. For ages four and up.

Newhouse, M. (2010). *The Weber Street Wonder Work Crew*. Toronto, ON: Tundra Books.

The neighbourhood kids—including one youth in a wheelchair—use their skills to make the community shine. For ages four and up.

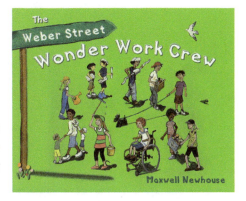

Rivard, E., & Delisle, A. (Illustrator). (2011). *Really and truly.* **Toronto, ON: Owlkids Books.**

Charlie wants to make his grandpa, who has dementia, smile again. For ages four and up.

Three Essential Questions for This Chapter

1. Spend some time in the children's section of a public library; locate at least three picture books that you think would be appropriate for older readers as well as the typical ages that picture books usually target. How would you use these books with an older audience?
2. Select a picture book that is new to you from the annotated bibliography. After you read it, list at least four age-appropriate response activities for students related to the book in the following categories: drama; art; creative writing; and music.
3. Read a graphic novel that is new to you. How is a graphic novel different from a picture book? How is it different from a regular novel? What characteristics do all three forms of book have in common?

CHAPTER 4

Contemporary Canadian Junior Novels

Introduction to Junior Novels in Canada

Issues Related to Age-Appropriate Reading

Attention to wide diversity in reading levels in children up to Grade 3 has encouraged the production of chapter books in Canada for ages six and up. Instead of being relegated to picture-book sections of the library, younger children are now able to sample various forms and formats, including early chapter books, more difficult chapter books about junior characters, and age-appropriate graphic novels. While not replacing the value of adult read-alouds, where children hear material with vocabulary slightly beyond what they can decipher on their own, "just right" novels that utilize words in children's listening and speaking vocabularies are highly supportive of independent reading.

A difficulty in providing age-appropriate reading for younger age categories is that authors must also rise to the challenge of producing literary work. A similar challenge is faced in the production of high interest–low vocabulary (hi-lo) books for older struggling readers. Shorter sentences and simple vocabulary can make characters appear stilted and flat, and authentic dialogue is difficult to achieve with constraints on a text's level of difficulty. Even the use of punctuation is challenging—dashes, for example, can often be a drawback to comprehension for less fluent readers.

Only 10 books were identified as appropriate for the junior fiction annotated bibliography in this chapter, compared with many more novels for older age ranges. In considering age range, titles aimed at audiences generally younger than nine were selected for this section, although, due to the diversity of reading skills and interests, no distinct upper age limits have been provided.

It may be that the difficulty of writing authentic stories in easy formats constrains authors here. It may also be that authors hesitate to include disability references in titles for younger readers. I conjecture that the latter carries weight because the number of picture books portraying characters with disabilities is also scant compared to the huge number of picture books produced in Canada. Illustrations can be used in picture books to convey ideas without the necessity of added words in the text, and so if picture book authors were interested in including disability as a character trait, the job might not rest with the text alone. Perhaps both picture books and junior novels are currently short of characters with disabilities because stereotypes continue to disconnect the idea of people with disabilities to happy lives. This is one direction Radical Change in children's literature might take—filling a gap in available titles for younger readers—to afford a representative picture of society.

Patterns and Trends

Of the 10 junior novels presented here, there is a slightly higher number of female characters with disabilities than male characters, and the types of disabilities range from writing disabilities to post-traumatic stress to developmental disabilities, severe behavioural disabilities, orthopaedic disabilities, blindness, cerebral palsy, mental illness, and epilepsy. Seven of the novels involve a protagonist with a disability, while three of the books involve either a friend of the protagonist (in two cases) or the protagonist's parent (in one case). Interestingly, the latter deals with a girl whose mother has a mental illness, somewhat predictive of the comparatively high number of books in the older intermediate age range where young characters deal with a mother's mental health challenges.

A book that appeared as a Canadian leader in its exceptionally strong characterization of a little girl whose hearing impairment is only one aspect of her identity is Rachna Gilmore's (1999) picture book *A Screaming Kind of Day*. This title was the winner of the 1999 Governor General's Literary Award for Children's Literature in the text category, where it competed with two other picture books, a young adult novel and an intermediate-age collection of short stories. *A Friend Like Zilla* (1995) is an earlier title of Gilmore's, also invoking Radical Change through its characterization of a young woman with an intellectual disability. What inspired Gilmore to develop work that pushed the envelope in terms of characterization? A portrait of this remarkable writer follows, adapted from a doctoral dissertation where extensive interview data was included (Brenna, 2010b).

Author Portrait: Rachna Gilmore

Rachna Gilmore was born in India in 1953 and lived in Bombay until the age of 14, when her family moved to London, England. After achieving her Honours Biology degree from King's College, London, she decided to do some travelling because the United Kingdom did not appeal as home—it felt "too racist and closed" (Brenna, 2010b). Canada appealed for a number of reasons, including its international reputation for accepting diversity. In addition, Rachna was drawn to Prince Edward Island because, as a child, she had adored Lucy Maud Montgomery's Anne of Green Gables books and the image their setting projected. "I was interested in books … that had to do with belonging" (Brenna, 2010b, p. 151).

In Prince Edward Island, Rachna married, and completed a Bachelor of Education degree. While raising two daughters and creating pottery, Rachna contemplated becoming a writer, inspired as a child by the literate character of Jo in Louisa May Alcott's (1868) *Little Women* and the books Rachna had begun to read to her own children. Other than setting aside scraps of paper containing ideas, the writing dream wasn't actualized until Rachna turned 30. Her first book, *My Mother Is Weird*, was published in 1988, and since then Rachna has published numerous works, including the Governor General's Literary Award–winning picture book *A Screaming Kind of Day* (1999, see Rachna Gilmore's website at http://www.rachnagilmore.ca for more information).

Rachna's books are sold internationally and have been translated into many languages, including French, Danish, German, Korean, Spanish, Urdu, Bengali, and Chinese. In 1990, Rachna and her family moved to Ottawa, where Rachna continues to "plark"—the term she's coined to describe her writing process, a mixture of play, work, and lark. One characteristic of her work that has been noted by reviewers is the attention she gives to minor as well as major characters. She explains this by stating:

> I do think that being a "visible minority"—detestable term, but one I'll use here for want of a better one—puts you in the fringes of life at times, and so perhaps that's why I'm interested in the other people who appear to be in the fringes of life. In *Of Customs and Excise*, for instance, I was quite aware, after writing that first story, that I wanted to explore and get inside, and understand and give voice to, the characters that were in the fringes of that first story. Subsidiary characters, who aren't subsidiary in their own lives—because we're all central in our own lives, and we all have nuanced and layered stories to tell. (Brenna, 2010b, pp. 143–144)

I first encountered Rachna's writing in her Governor General's Award–winning picture book *A Screaming Kind of Day* (1999), whose heroine is a little girl with a hearing impairment. I then read her junior novel *Mina's Spring of Colors* (2000), and appreciated its multicultural references; here is an author, I thought, who is cognizant of characters that have been previously marginalized in fiction. My theory was reinforced when I discovered that her first junior novel, *A Friend Like Zilla* (1995), portrayed a young woman with a developmental disability.

Writing Process

In terms of her writing process, Rachna walks outside to:

> ... work out ideas ... I love the magic of trusting that seemingly disparate elements work together, that you can make the pieces fit eventually. There is reason, in the fantasy world, for everything ... *Sower of Tales* is all in

> an imaginary world ... it started with an image of an old woman bending down and planting seeds, and I thought to myself, "She's planting stories!" and a chill ran down my spine; it felt so right. (Brenna, 2010b, p. 148)

Rachna's description of the underpinnings to her writing process relates to what fantasy writer Ursula Le Guin (2004) discusses when she advises writers to trust themselves, trust the story, and trust the reader. Embracing the idea of trust in a developing character doesn't, according to Rachna, devalue the importance of research. After Rachna had written the basic first draft of *A Screaming Kind of Day* (1999), she had to work out a number of things, including specifics regarding deaf culture and choices regarding how Scully would communicate, just as with Zilla she needed to find out more about developmental disabilities. Similarly, "For *Atlantis Time*," she said, "I visited Santorini, because it has many artifacts and ruins from the Minoan culture which seem to have many similarities to the culture of Atlantis, described by Plato" (Brenna, 2010b, p. 150). Before Santorini, Rachna had not specifically travelled to a research site related to a book's setting, but she indicated that place has always informed the visual images in her fiction.

With respect to Zilla, a girl with an intellectual disability in the junior novel *A Friend Like Zilla* (1995), Rachna reports that:

> I didn't set out with the idea of writing a book about a girl with intellectual disabilities. She just happened to be that way ... the genesis of the story was one day when I was in Gatineau Park with my daughters, feeding seagulls, and I suddenly had this image in my head of two kids feeding seagulls, one of them younger and one of them a lot older ... so immediately I thought that this was going to be set near the ocean. On the drive home, I thought about it some more and I initially thought ... the story was going to be about a friendship between an older woman and a younger girl. (Brenna, 2010b, pp. 150–151)

As Rachna began to work out how the second character was really an older girl, not an older woman, it became possible that she might have an intellectual disability.

> This may seem to people who are concerned about getting the facts absolutely right ... as unorthodox, but I tend to do my research after I've written my first draft ... I had noticed that a lot of stories that are written about children with disabilities tend to focus on the disability and there's not often much of a story there, so I wanted it to be a good story ... So I wrote the story first, and then I did the research. (Brenna, 2010b, p. 151)

Acceptance and Inclusion

Acceptance has become a major theme in much of Rachna's work for children; in *A Friend Like Zilla* (1995) for example, Uncle Chad is disdainful of Zilla because of her intellectual disability. In return, Nobby despises her uncle for his narrow thinking. Both Nobby and Uncle Chad learn to see the world, and each other, in a different way due to their relationship with Zilla. The inclusion of characters with disabilities in Rachna's work appears to be mindful of the diverse world we live in, and the idea that stories should represent that diversity.

Counterstories and Social Justice

Lindemann Nelson (1995) suggests that a counterstory is what is told in reaction to a story that seeks to reinforce the status quo. In terms of the genesis of Scully, a character who is hearing impaired in the picture book *A Screaming Kind of Day* (1999), Rachna explains:

> I was having a conversation with someone about children with disabilities, and what I got thinking on the drive home was about how we tend to think of children with disabilities in terms of what they can't do, rather than what they can do ... And the character of Scully came to me on the drive ... and I could hear her voice and what she was saying. And I knew that she was this enormously lively, strong, energetic girl with not a trace of self pity, and her mother was a very strong woman who had great respect for her and was not going to let her daughter get away with anything. Scully was ... mischievous ... a handful ... she's absolutely going to use whatever she can, including her so-called disability, to her advantage! I was quite captured by her, and so when I got home I started to jot down notes. (Brenna, 2010b, p. 153)

Here, Rachna is essentially offering a story about children with disabilities, and their families, that may run counter to public sentiment. As she considered the character of Scully further, she added:

> And one day as I was walking down my street I noticed that there was a sign saying Deaf Children Area. I'd walked down that street lots of times before and never noticed this sign. I thought, "Oh, someone on this street has a child who is hard of hearing ... I wonder who it is." And as I continued to do my research and got in touch with an organization of parents with children who were hard of hearing, I realized that two or three occupants ago, the people who lived in my house—I recognized their name on my list—had a child who was hard of hearing. This child had lived in the house that I lived in! (Brenna, 2010b, p. 154)

Rachna addresses the idea of isolation by generalizing that "... every child feels this—we all have some way in which we feel the 'other.' And I've learned that. Because when you come into a society where there is racism ... or you have a disability ... there's a tendency to think that your particular suffering is the worst kind ... And when you grow older you realize you're not the only one—every single person experiences this in some way or another" (Brenna, 2010b, pp. 154–155). Perhaps in her writing, Rachna is consciously developing the "safe thread" she herself has located in books, a connection, based in social justice, that facilitated her development of self-identity, that encouraged her writing passion, that carried her from one continent to another and in and out of her own storied past.

In her book *Peripheral Visions*, Catherine Bateson (1994) says, "Until you are at home somewhere, you cannot be at home everywhere." Possibly the safe threads in Rachna's work encourage readers to feel at home, to connect to a character who may represent the person they are or the person they would be, allowing them to feel comfortable within the spaces the book provides. Or perhaps Rachna's work offers readers the kind of "world"-travelling Maria Lugones talks about when she describes how outsiders practice a "loving way of being and living" (1987, p. 3) by entering into a foreign world.

Summary

I suggest that Rachna Gilmore's portrayal of characters with disabilities emerged consciously, offering readers rich depictions that are more than happy accidents or opportunities developed as a result of Radical Change trends (Dresang, 1999). As educators consider Rachna's storied past alongside her children's books, we are offered motivation for including these books in classrooms where "some children never learn to feel at home, to feel they really belong ..." (Paley, 1992, p. 103). Aspects of Rachna's work may function to assist children in taking action and promoting social justice, just as she herself has taken action in the work she has created that disrupts the commonplace, interrogates multiple viewpoints, and focuses on sociopolitical issues—all various dimensions of critical literacy (Lewison, Flint, & Van Sluys, 2002).

Annotated Bibliography of Canadian Junior Novels Portraying Characters with Disabilities

Cassidy, S. (2012). *Seeing orange*. Victoria, BC: Orca.

Through the story of a lost cat, we meet seven-year-old Leland, a boy who has trouble writing and concentrating. While he initially only earns negative comments from his Grade 2 teacher, he gets rave reviews on his artwork, and the heart of this story is how a boy finds his gifts. This is a book that might just inspire teachers as well as children. Leland also appears in two other titles: *Slick* and *Windfall*. For ages six and up.

Description: realistic fiction; themes include lost pets and school challenges.

Read-ons: Leland can be favourably compared with another Grade 2 student in Judy Blume's classic *Freckle Juice*, as well as characters in Sheree Fitch's picture book *Pocket Rocks,* Addison Addley from Melody DeFields McMillan's series by the same name, and Jack Gantos's Joey Pigza titles. The power of the imagination is also a theme found in Susin Nielsen's junior novel *The Magic Beads*.

Citra, B. (2010). *After the fire*. Victoria, BC: Orca Books.

Eleven-year-old Melissa dreads the summer she will spend with her mother and younger brother at a remote lakeside cabin in BC until a new friendship adds excitement and a chance to see her own family from a new perspective. Alice—a girl whose secrets build until finally Melissa discovers some sad truths about Alice's family—introduces Melissa to an imaginary world called Dar Wynd and offers her a chance to demonstrate some good decisions. How Melissa and her younger brother recover from the undefined but very evident post-traumatic stress brought on by a fire in their previous home makes for a sensitive story. For ages eight and up.

Description: realistic fiction; themes include friendship, family, and recovery from traumatic events.

Read-ons: Students will find strong connections between the treehouse where Alice has created an imaginary world called Dar Wynd and the magical kingdom in Katherine Patterson's *Bridge to Terabithia*. Melissa's family situation is similar to Billy's in Bev Brenna's *The Moon Children*, as both children appear in lower socio-economic situations, and seek summer fun while their single-mom wage earners worry about costs. Parallels can also be noted between the setting in *After the Fire* and Kit Pearson's *A Handful of Time*.

Gilmore, R. (1995). *A friend like Zilla*. Toronto, ON: Second Story Press.

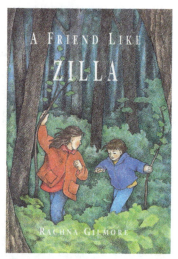

The setting is a summer cottage on Prince Edward Island where Nobby, short for Zenobia—a young girl from Ottawa—is holidaying with relatives. The cottage owner has a 17-year-old daughter, Zilla, whose developmental disabilities elicit stereotypical reactions from Uncle Chad. As Zilla becomes Nobby's friend, "it was sort of neat how we fit together," Nobby relates. "Like puzzle bits. Zilla could do things I couldn't, like cook and find clams and berries and stuff. But I could read and draw and think up ideas." Through her friendship with Zilla, Nobby learns to understand the complexities of people, including her Uncle Chad, who, until this point in her life, she has vilified. For ages eight and up.

Description: realistic fiction; themes include friendships and considerations of diversity.

Read-ons: *Lily's Crossing* by Patricia Reilly Giff, Myrna Neuringer Levy's *The Summer Kid*, and Kate DiCamillo's *The Tiger Rising* make good connections through their exploration of developing friendships. Betsy Byars's *Summer of the Swans*, along with *The Summer Kid*, also offers opportunities to compare and contrast notions of ability and disability.

Goobie, B. (2013). *Jason's why*. Markham, ON: Red Deer Press.

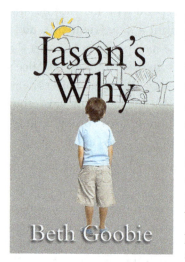

This is the fictional story of nine-year-old Jason, transitioning into a group home when his mother can't cope with his behaviour or her own out-of-control life. The first-person point of view is personal and poignant, and the text, while simple enough for young readers, is also accessible to older struggling readers without being patronizing. Jason's story is one rarely encountered in children's books and offers an authentic picture of what happens when a child goes into care. Through the support of workers at his group home and school personnel, Jason learns that it's okay to make mistakes. During the course of the story he also discovers strategies to help himself control his negative behaviour. The ending isn't "happily ever after," but it's true to life. For ages eight and up.

Description: realistic fiction; themes include overcoming challenges and dealing with trauma. Suitable for all ages, including adults learning to support youth in crisis.

Read-ons: Becky Citra's *The Way Home* and Betsy Byars's *The Pinballs* are other novels for this age group dealing with disrupted home lives and foster care. Impulsivity is also introduced in the depiction of Aaron, a secondary character in Anna Kerz's title *The Mealworm Diaries*; Aaron's story is continued in *Better than Weird*.

Guest, J. (2011). *Triple threat.* Toronto, ON: James Lorimer.

Thirteen-year-old Matt Eagletail welcomes a summer visit from his friend John "Free Throw" Salton, who shares his love of basketball and intends to coach the summer league from his position in a wheelchair. An injury offers Matt the opportunity to see what using a wheelchair is like, and he begins to appreciate his friend's skills all the more. Matt's archrival also has a team in the league, and discovering who triumphs becomes the high point of the book. For ages eight and up.

Description: realistic fiction; themes include competitive sports, bullying, and honesty.

Read-ons: Loris Lesynski's *Crazy About Basketball* (a collection of poems) and Eric Howling's *Hoop Magic* make good sports connections. Books where characters play wheelchair basketball include Ainslie Manson's *Roll On: Rick Hanson Wheels Around the World*. *Wheelchair Challenge* is a production in VHS by the National Film Board that also spotlights students with disabilities who compete in sports.

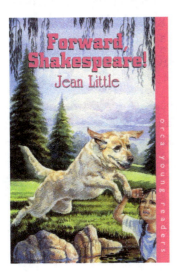

Little, J. (2005). *Forward, Shakespeare!* Victoria, BC: Orca Books.

This simple junior novel is narrated from the third-person perspective of a dog protagonist. Shakespeare is a seeing-eye pup, trained to be a rescue dog and assigned to Tim, an angry, blind teen, who is staying at the Seeing Eye residence in Morristown, New Jersey. As Shakespeare accompanies Tim on his journey back to Guelph, Ontario, and a healthy, hopeful future, there are a few amusing turns in the plot, including the scenario of two guide dogs accidentally switched with each other. For ages seven and up.

Description: realistic fiction for ages seven and up, especially suitable for older, reluctant readers; themes include self-acceptance, self-confidence, and overcoming obstacles.

Read-ons: Jean Little's prequel, *Rescue Pup*, explores Shakespeare's training as a seeing eye dog. Another helpful canine is depicted in Christina Minaki's *Zoe's Extraordinary Holiday Adventures*. Other texts told from an animal's point of view include particular selections from Tiffany Stone's poetry book *Floyd the Flamingo and his Flock of Friends*, Avi's *The Good Dog*, Glenda Goertzen's *The Prairie Dogs*, and Beverly Cleary's *Ribsy*. Another connection is the non-fiction title *Working Like a Dog: The Story of Working Dogs through History* by Gena K. Gorrell. Barbara Smucker's *Jacob's Little Giant* is an additional junior title that explores self-confidence, and Jean Little's first novel, *Mine for Keeps*, would offer great connections regarding the relationship between a little dog and Sally, a 10-year-old with cerebral palsy.

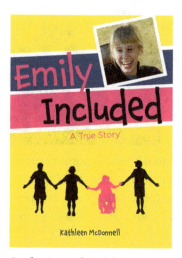

McDonnell, K. (2011). *Emily included: A true story.* **Toronto, ON: Second Story Press.**

This is a detailed version of the true story of Emily Eaton, an Ontario girl with cerebral palsy who won the right to attend her neighbourhood school. In 1995, the Supreme Court of Canada ruled against local courts and school boards who wanted Emily in a segregated setting, ending a three-year battle by Emily's family and setting a strong precedent in favour of inclusionary education. This is a book that explores Canadian history related to the school inclusion of children with special needs, and covers a great deal of territory. For ages eight and up; educators may find the historical facts here very engaging.

Description: historical fiction; themes include inclusive education, educational support, and lobbying for change.

Read-ons: Liam O'Donnell's *Food Fight* and Mike Deas's *Dalen & Gole* are two graphic novels where characters take on important causes. A look at residential schools can also be found in Nicola Campbell's *Shin-chi's Canoe* and in Gina McMurchy-Bower's title for more mature readers, *Free as a Bird*.

Minaki, C. (2007). *Zoe's extraordinary holiday adventures*. Toronto, ON: Second Story Press.

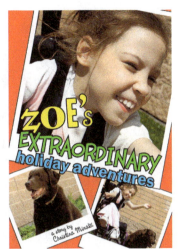

As this junior novel begins, Zoe and her Labrador retriever Ella are not having the kind of adventures Zoe craves, and Zoe wishes she didn't have to use a wheelchair. To make matters worse, when her friend Anna is absent from school, Zoe is embarrassed by the way other kids treat her. Cultural themes are prominent in the story as the class explores seasonal holidays, further emphasizing differences and universal connections. For ages eight and up.

Description: realistic fiction; themes include self-discovery and self-acceptance, as well as multiculturalism.

Read-ons: Elizabeth Helfman's *On Being Sarah* presents another girl who yearns for adventure and uses supports for a physical disability, as does Jean Little's *Mine for Keeps*. Beverly Cleary's Ramona books offer a similarly spunky heroine, beginning with *Ramona the Pest*. Multicultural themes for similar age groups are found in Rachna Gilmore's *Mina's Spring of Colors* and *Christmas at Wapos Bay* by Jordan Wheeler and Dennis Jackson.

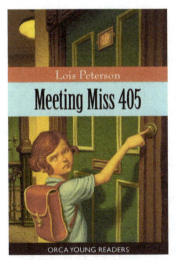

Peterson, L. (2008). *Meeting Miss 405*. Victoria, BC: Orca Books.

Tansy's mother has depression and is unable to care for her. Tansy's father therefore hires a neighbour, Miss Stella, to babysit. Tansy's approach to diversity is initially narrow; she is insensitive to a boy at school with a peanut allergy and another boy with a skin disease. How she learns to see the world a little differently, as well as make a new friend, is at the heart of this book. For ages eight and up.

Description: realistic fiction; themes of bullying, loneliness, discrimination, and friendship.

Read-ons: Another boy who doesn't want to stay with a babysitter is Luke in Bev Brenna's *Spider Summer* (available as a free PDF at www.beverleybrenna.com). Another initially difficult relationship between a child and an older person can be found in Susin Nielsen's *Mormor Moves In*.

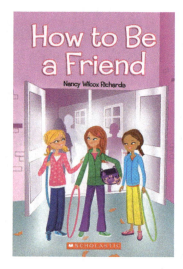

Richards, N.W. (2011). *How to be a friend.* **Toronto, ON: Scholastic Canada.**

Lexie Peters is afraid of life in her new Grade 3 classroom. Because she has epilepsy and has to wear a helmet outside and eat a special diet, she worries about bullying. Although she does have a run-in with a boy who teases her, this is a supportive environment and she finds she likes it here, especially once she figures out how she's going to meet the challenge her teacher sets out of doing a random act of kindness. For ages seven and up.

Description: realistic fiction; themes include friendship and self-advocacy.

Read-ons: *The 18th Emergency* by Betsy Byars has a character similar to Lexie in anxiety level. Other connections can be found in simple books about new friendships, including titles from Barbara Park's Junie B. Jones series. Another book about friendship is Barbara Wersba's *Walter: The Story of a Rat*.

■ Read-on Bibliography

Avi. (2001). *The good dog.* Toronto, ON: Aladdin.
Blume, J. (2014). *Freckle juice.* New York, NY: Atheneum.
Brenna, B. (1998). *Spider summer.* Toronto, ON: ITP Nelson.
Brenna, B. (2007). *The moon children.* Calgary, AB: Red Deer Press.
Byars, B. (1970/2000). *Summer of the swans.* New York, NY: Scholastic.
Byars, B. (1977). *The pinballs.* New York, NY: Harper & Row.
Byars, B. (1993). *The 18th emergency.* New York, NY: Viking Press.
Campbell, N. (2008). *Shin-chi's canoe.* Toronto, ON: Groundwood Books/House of Anansi Press.
Citra, B. (2013). *The way home.* Toronto, ON: Second Story Press.
Cleary, B. (1964/2007). *Ribsy.* New York, NY: HarperTrophy.
Cleary, B. (1968). *Ramona the pest.* New York, NY: Morrow.
Deas, M. (2011). *Dalen & Gole: Scandal in Port Angus.* Victoria, BC: Orca Book Publishers.
DeFields McMillan, M. (2008). *Addison Addley.* Victoria, BC: Orca Book Publishers.
DiCamillo, K. (2001). *The tiger rising.* Cambridge, MA: Candlewick Press.
Fitch, S., & Flook, H. (Illustrator). (2004). *Pocket rocks.* Victoria, BC: Orca Book Publishers.
Gantos, J. (2000). *Joey Pigza loses control.* New York, NY: Farrar, Straus and Giroux.

Giff, R.P. (1997/1999). *Lily's crossing.* New York, NY: Doubleday/Bantam.
Gilmore, R. (2000). *Mina's spring of colors.* Markham, ON: Fitzhenry & Whiteside.
Goertzen, G. (2005). *The prairie dogs.* Markham, ON: Fitzhenry & Whiteside.
Gorrell, K.G. (2003). *Working like a dog: The story of working dogs through history.* Toronto, ON: Tundra Books.
Helfman, E. (1993). *On being Sarah.* Morton Grove, IL: A. Whitman.
Howling, E. (2013). *Hoop magic.* Toronto, ON: James Lorimer & Company.
Jackson, D., & Wheeler, J. (2006). *Christmas at Wapos Bay.* Regina, SK: Coteau Books for Kids.
Kerz, A. (2001). *Better than weird.* Victoria, BC: Orca Book Publishers.
Kerz, A. (2009). *The mealworm diaries.* Victoria, BC: Orca Book Publishers.
Lesynski, L. (2013). *Crazy about basketball.* Toronto, ON: Annick Press.
Levy, N.M. (1991). *The summer kid.* Toronto, ON: Second Story Press.
Little, J. (1962). *Mine for keeps.* Boston, MA: Little, Brown.
Little, J. (2004). *Rescue pup.* Victoria, BC: Orca Book Publishers.
Manson, A. (2012). *Roll on: Rick Hanson wheels around the world.* Vancouver, BC: Greystone Books.
McMurchy-Bower, G. (2010). *Free as a bird.* Toronto, ON: Dundurn Press.
Minaki, C. (2007). *Zoe's extraordinary holiday adventures.* Toronto, ON: Second Story Press.
Nielsen, S. (2004). *Mormor moves in.* Victoria, BC: Orca Book Publishers.
Nielsen, S. (2007). *The magic beads.* Vancouver, BC: Simply Read Books.
O'Donnell, L. (2010). *Food fight.* Victoria, BC: Orca Book Publishers.
Park, B. (1992). *Junie B. Jones.* New York, NY: Random House.
Patterson, K. (1977/1987). *Bridge to Terabithia.* New York, NY: HarperTrophy/ Harper Collins/ Harper & Row.
Pearson, K. (1987/2007). *A handful of time.* Toronto, ON: Puffin Canada.
Silverthorne, J. (1996/2007). *The secret of Sentinel Rock.* Regina, SK: Coteau Books.
Smucker, B. (1987). *Jacob's little giant.* Markham, ON: Viking Kestrel.
Stone, T. (2004). *Floyd the Flamingo and his flock of friends.* Vancouver, BC: Tradewind Books.
Wersba, B. (2005). *Walter: The story of a rat.* Asheville, NC: Front Street.
Wheeler, J. & Jackson, D. (2005). *Christmas at Wapos Bay.* Regina, SK: Coteau Books for Kids.

Three Essential Questions for This Chapter

1. Explore Rachna Gilmore's website: www.rachnagilmore.ca. Read at least three books by this author. What characteristics do her books have in common? For what reasons might you share these books with young people?
2. Explore a published writing program or consider how writing is taught in a classroom familiar to you. What activities occur to assist students in

developing a first draft? How do these activities compare to Rachna Gilmore's writing process described in this chapter?
3. Select a junior novel that is new to you from the annotated bibliography. After you read it, list at least four age-appropriate response activities, in the following categories, that students could do that are related to the book: drama; art; creative writing; and music.

CHAPTER 5

Contemporary Canadian Intermediate Novels

Introduction to Intermediate Novels in Canada

Patterns and Trends

Serious themes run through many of the new Canadian intermediate-age novels for ages nine and up, offering evidence of Dresang's (1999) theory of Radical Change in books for young people. Books such as Maggie de Vries's (2011) *Somebody's Girl*—included here as a connecting read for some of the titles portraying characters with disabilities—deals in a straightforward manner with adoption and the complex feelings that may arise in blended families. Numerous other titles deal explicitly with diversity through characterizations of minority viewpoints. While previous titles for this age group may have shied away from dealing directly with disability topics, many of the books spotlighted in this chapter offer a sensitive but clear approach toward identifying ability differences that children may experience in themselves and others.

Some patterns and trends emerge in the group of intermediate-age novels included in this chapter's annotated bibliography, compiled on the basis of portrayals of characters with disabilities. It is interesting to note the titles with blended genres, as in Lawrence's (2006) *Gemini Summer*—historical fiction with magic realism threaded through. K.C. Dyer's (2002) Seeds of Time series is another combination form, framed in the fantasy genre with historical fiction a key aspect of its content. Such blending of genres could be an aspect of Dresang's (1999) Radical Change in operation, and more examples of this will quite possibly follow in coming years.

Of the 50 intermediate-age titles included here, 28 are realistic fiction (with one series of three titles included), 8 are fantasy (including one series of three titles by the same author, which also have historical content), 7 are historical fiction (with one title involving magic realism as well), and 4 are steampunk (as a series of four titles by one author) while 3 titles can be classified as magic realism.

About a third of the characters who have disabilities are primary characters, with two-thirds operating as secondary characters. As many of the books have more than one secondary character with a disability, this ratio is not unusual. What is particularly interesting are the numbers of different disabilities included. Whereas in the past particular disabilities, such as polio and blindness, took precedence in the children's literature where disability was included (Keith, 2001), there are no patterns toward isolated "favourites" as far as types of disabilities included in the books described in this chapter. This group of 50 intermediate-age books includes examples of almost every category of exceptionality described by Smith, Polloway, Patton, Dowdy, and Heath (2001), including learning disabilities, speech or language impairments, intellectual disabilities, emotional or behavioural disorders, auditory impairments, orthopaedic impairments, other health impairments, visual impairments, autism, and traumatic brain injury. The only category not well represented is multiple disabilities, with one character clearly demonstrating more than one disability. One example is Twig, in Jean Little's (2000) novel *Willow and Twig*, who is hearing impaired and demonstrates behavioural challenges likely related to the prenatal substance abuse described in his past.

In terms of disabilities included, one troubling pattern involves the five titles that deal with children—three girls and two boys—who have mothers who are currently mentally ill. The children involved in these stories have varying degrees of caregiving responsibilities related to their mothers. That mothers would be singled out as family members through which to identify mental illness is possibly coincidental, or possibly related to societal stereotypes about men, women, and mental illness. In an additional title, Jeff Rud's (2008) *Paralyzed*, Reggie's father confides that he at one time quite possibly had an anxiety disorder, but it was clearly isolated to a short period of time and treated expediently.

The idea that mental illness is a source of entertainment, while certainly not at all explicit in these titles, may run alongside the favouring of mental health above other themes in characterization in terms of the historical impact of society on book production. The American Psychological Association discusses this topic under the name *asylum tourism* (http://www.apa.org/monitor/2014/02/asylum-tourism.aspx), and it would be interesting to pursue this idea with a closer look at the inclusion of characters with mental health challenges.

In only one novel is physical difference used as a trope for evil, as part of the fairy-tale underpinnings of Iain Lawrence's (2006) *Gemini Summer*. In one other novel, Rachel Dunstan Muller's (2009) *The Solstice Cup*, a character's mean-spiritedness seems to have emerged along with her physical disability. In general, however, the characters with disabilities in this group of books are presented as complex individuals who navigate their challenges with varying degrees of ease, and seem to be just as authentic in terms of their depiction as any group of characters in other titles for readers in this age group.

Critical Literacy Suggestions

Individual titles lend themselves to explicit teaching and critical discussion regarding prejudice against those with disabilities. With her direct writing style, Deborah Ellis's *No Ordinary Day*, (2011), the story of a young Indian girl, offers both a picture of what it is like to be shunned for one's differences as well as how prejudice is communicated socially. From early childhood, Valli has learned to fear the "monsters"—those with the physical signs of what she later learns is a disease called leprosy. Ellis does not shy away from the horror sometimes felt by people who face others with differences. In the early pages of *Camp Outlook* (2014), Brenda Baker's protagonist parallels this discomfort toward others with disabilities. Such discomfort is also seen in the community in Pamela Porter's title *The Crazy Man* (2005), in the self-loathing at first felt by Pauline in Anne Laurel Carter's *In the Clear* (2001), and by Mike in Bruce McBay and James Heneghan's (2003) *Waiting for Sarah*. In Liane Shaw's *The Color of Silence* (2013), Alex does not really see Joanie, a girl essentially imprisoned by the limitations of her body, at first. How Alex grows and changes in perceptivity is a strong theme of this book.

It is clear that many of the authors of books portraying characters with disabilities intended for intermediate age-ranges are attempting to use their books as a teaching vehicle. All of the books mentioned in the previous paragraph support characters who grow and change in their perceptions about difference through the course of their respective novels. In Shaw's (2013) book, for example, Alex learns to think about Joanie as a rich and complicated person as she begins to understand Joanie's methods of communication.

Commonly, Canadian books portraying characters with disabilities for this age group contain references to school situations where children are teased on the basis of their differences. Josh is persecuted because of his dyslexia in Jenny Watson's *Prove It, Josh* (2013). Both Travis and Chantelle are bullied in Glen Huser's *Stitches* (2003). Rose, a girl with severe learning disabilities, must cope with teachers who tell her she is "retarded" and "lazy" in Barbara Haworth-Attard's (2002) *Irish Chain*. Darrell Connor suffers criticism from a particular classmate for her physical difference in K.C. Dyer's *Secret of Light* (2003). Unlike the group of titles where characters with disabilities grow in understanding of others, the titles where a classmate bullies a protagonist do not offer equal opportunities for growth and change in the bully.

Other intermediate books included in the annotated bibliography in this chapter contain evidence of stereotyping that will offer interesting debate for critical literacy discussions. In Jeff Rud's (2008) novel *Paralyzed*, a high school middle linebacker is unable to perform on the field after an incident that hospitalizes an opposing teammate. While Reggie's post-traumatic response is soon recognized, his coach's initial criticism involves the statement, "Reggie, I've seen better tackle attempts from the junior girls' volleyball team." Another coach, a marginal character in Spring's (2008) *Breathing Soccer*, offers only a substitute position on the team to Lisa, a strong player, due to the medical information presented on her registration form. His close-minded response to diversity doesn't end with medical issues, and later in the book he is heard using other kinds of negative slurs, criticizing two girls for running slowly: "What do you girls think—that you're married?" (p. 73).

Kids in the titles spotlighted in this chapter appear ruthless when it comes to accepting another kid with a disability. In both *Addy's Race* (Waldman, 2011) and *Breathing Soccer* (Spring, 2008), classmates stigmatize Addy and Lisa, even avoiding Lisa's birthday party with last-minute excuses. Each girl has one close friend, in both cases another outsider like themselves. Addy's friend is Lucy, a large girl who enters sports only to please her domineering mother. Lisa's friend is Beth, an overweight girl who is loyal to the core. Both Addy and Lisa suffer bullying by shallow, "popular" girls in their respective schools.

Other titles promote ableist thinking in more indirect ways, where good and bad characters use stereotypical language indiscriminately and without question. In Rachel Dunstan Muller's (2009) fantasy *The Solstice Cup*, Breanne criticizes her sister's moral coaching in a number of ways, reprimanding, "Don't be retarded" (p. 3) and calling her "an old lady" (p. 8), then later telling her she has "a defective brain" (p. 13). In addition to Breanne's treatment of her sister, a man with a physical difference is continually referred to in language that is anything but people first: "There's that hunchbacked piper guy" (p. 59). The book's narrator later describes this character: "He was a strong man, in spite of his deformity" (p. 71). Similar ableist descriptions are used about Breanne herself: "too bad she's a cripple" (p. 67), says Nuala, one of the fairies who seems to prize physical beauty above all else.

In Jamieson Findlay's (2011) book *The Summer of Permanent Wants*, 11-year-old Emmeline can speak after her coma, but the words are so jumbled she is "scared that she would be thought weird, *retarded*, for the rest of her life" (p. 81). And so she keeps silent—at least for a time. The people and animals she and her grandmother meet on their journey along the Rideau Canal in Ottawa are such that Emmeline forms new perspectives on non-verbal communication and desires with a passion that her story be heard, lest she be thought of as just a "blank" (p. 88). One poignant moment occurs when Em shares her medical ID bracelet with Tom, a new friend. "If only her bracelet listed all the things she *could* do, and not just her problems. She could draw and paint quite well, everybody said ... She could do karate, too. Most of all, she could play the violin. In fact, she heard music everywhere." (p. 117).

Radical Change in Action

In terms of comparisons to Dresang's (1999) Radical Change theory about the evolution of children's books, the variety and depth of characterizations involving disability in this collection of books published within the last 20 years, with many primary characters emerging from first-person perspectives, are striking innovations. One particularly interesting finding in terms of the publication dates of these 50 books is that 34 of them have appeared in the last decade, with only 16 of them appearing in the span from 1995 to 2004. It appears as if authors and publishers are becoming more comfortable with aspects of difference involving ability, and that readers of intermediate age groups have access to more texts than ever before that depict authentic characters representative of real life in terms of ability/disability.

A title for the intermediate age range that reflects all aspects of Dresang's theory is *The Crazy Man* by Pamela Porter (2005), winner of the 2005 Governor General's Literary Award for children's text. It is realistic historical fiction in a verse-novel format, speaking directly to readers through the first-person perspective of Emaline, an 11-year-old who becomes disabled in a farm accident. The novel explores mental health, a subject only recently common in books for this age range. Through the story of Angus, a farm hand, readers are introduced to various perspectives while, in the end, free to develop their own opinions of Angus and the prairie community of Souris. What is it in Pamela Porter's background that has inspired such themes? What follows in terms of a portrait of this inspirational Canadian author is adapted from interview data presented in my doctoral dissertation (Brenna, 2010b).

Author Portrait: Pamela Porter

Pamela Porter was born in New Mexico in 1956 and lived in various American states before moving to Canada with her husband. She and her family now live on Vancouver Island in British Columbia. Pamela has four published books of poetry for adults—*Stones Call Out* (2006), *The Intelligence of Animals* (2008a), *Cathedral* (2010), and *No Ordinary Place* (2012), in addition to three intermediate novels—*I'll Be Watching* (2011), *The Crazy Man* (2005), *Sky* (2004)—and a picture-book: *Yellow Moon, Apple Moon* (2008b). Her undergraduate degree is from the Southern Methodist University in Dallas, Texas, where she met her husband; Pamela also has a Masters of Fine Arts, specializing in creative writing, from the University of Montana.

When she began to write *The Crazy Man* (2005), she and her husband had been spending part of each summer in Weyburn, Saskatchewan, working on the family farm. A photo of Pamela on her online member profile for the Writers' Union of Canada shows her alongside a chestnut gelding, a light breeze ruffling her short hair, smiling into the sunshine. She has a fondness for stray animals, feeling a kinship with any human or animal who's had a tough time. These connections seem to underpin the kind of resilience portrayed in her characterizations of Emaline and Angus in her intermediate novel *The Crazy Man*—two characters who have indeed had a "rough go of life," and yet emerge richer for the experience.

Pamela began her writing career as a poet, and sought the power of short line lengths and white space in what would become her Governor General's Award winning verse novel *The Crazy Man* (2005). This novel demonstrates the changing forms and formats of Dresang's (1999) notion of Radical Change in addition to changing perspectives and changing boundaries. Pamela had been thinking about the concept of verse novels when she was shelving books at her children's public school library, saw Karen Hesse's (1997) *Out of the Dust*, and realized that someone had already pioneered this form for young readers, paving the way for future titles.

Writing Process

In terms of characterization, Pamela reported that she sees

> a number of lives simultaneously. I joke with other fiction writers that one's characters live with you, stand over your bed and wake you up, sit at the table and watch you eat, and demand to be attended to. [As] E.L. Doctorow said, "Writing is an acceptable form of schizophrenia." (Brenna, 2010b, p. 161)

Pamela confided that after the characters start following her around and she commits to telling their story, she thinks about what she needs to learn in order to accomplish that.

> Sometimes I spend months just reading, though often I read with pen and paper close by in case I need to write down information ... that comes to me while doing the research. I also write down certain facts, place names, etc. that will be important. After I've done quite a bit of reading, I start to write. Sometimes I get to a point in the writing where I realize I need to take a break and go back and read some more. I might reread a book I'd already read, or I might go find another book on another aspect of the subject that will give me different information and insights. (Brenna, 2010b, p. 161)

The writing process Pamela favours is full of motion, backwards and forwards, inwards and outwards, considering place, as she weaves her way between real and imagined lives. "To my mind, it's all connected and part of the whole writing process," she says. "I don't make an outline though I do make lists, and I keep a lot in my head. When I finished writing *The Crazy Man*, I was really amazed at how much I kept in my head at one time. I think in normal daily life I can't keep so much in my head, but writing a novel seems to occupy a different space in my brain." Pamela's description of her "writing brain" is reminiscent of the entrancement that Rachna Gilmore, another Canadian author, talked about as she discussed her own engagement in a writing project (Brenna, 2010b, p. 162).

Acceptance and Inclusion

Pamela presented a session on the history of the Weyburn Mental Hospital for the University of British Columbia's Serendipity conference in January of 2009, combining archival photographs of life at the hospital with excerpts from her verse novel *The Crazy Man* (2005), in which a character from a similar mental hospital transitioned, in 1965, to life outside the institution. Following her talk, she reported that "many people came up to me with their own psychiatric hospital stories; I think it is a statement to the continuing stigma of mental illness or around an institution that treated, or mis-treated, the mentally ill ... it takes someone to give permission and a space to be able to talk about those things. I heard many more stories that day. I thought it was a risk to talk about the mental hospital at a conference for children's literature, but it seemed to open up doors to many old memories" (Brenna, 2010b, p. 162–163).

I mentioned Pamela's experiences at the conference to a relative who had grown up a few hours away from Weyburn. This relative's response included the reflection that when he was a youth in the late 1960s, the Weyburn Mental Institution often provided a source of ridicule. Kids would offer barbs such as, "What's wrong with you—are you from Weyburn?" Pamela conveyed that a poet friend also reported hearing similar epithets when she was young, things like "You're going to end up in Weyburn!" These comments related to another statement of Pamela's:

> My husband Rob has said that when he used to go on band trips across Saskatchewan, others would ask, "Where are you from?" And when he said "Weyburn," eyebrows would lift. Sometimes others would say, "Oh, Weyburn, eh?" as if to imply that the band group had come directly from the mental hospital. (Brenna, 2010b, p. 163)

The Saskatchewan town of Weyburn thus appears as a strong, shaping force within the rendering of *The Crazy Man* (2005), a novel that takes place in Souris, a fictional town in Saskatchewan, named after the river that runs in actuality through Weyburn. The Souris landscape includes a mental institution described in the book from the point of view of 11-year-old Emaline, the novel's narrator:

> There's me, walking home from Haig School
> at the very end of April, nineteen sixty-five.
> Our first hot spell. At the edge of town
> I have to pass the mental hospital
>   which looks like a castle
> behind a long line of caragana bushes
> towering way over my head.
> Joey and Jamie, twins from down the road,

> They run past that place every time. But me,
> I don't mind it. I just imagine
> I'm in England—me, Emaline Bitterman—
> and the queen lives there,
> and I walk by, calm as a cabbage. (p. 13)

Weyburn was one of two Saskatchewan towns to have a mental hospital back in Saskatchewan's early years. Built in 1920, the hospital's intention was to support men returning from the First World War, many of whom had what we might now recognize as post-traumatic stress disorder. Later, it supported Second World War veterans. Pamela discovered from long-time residents of Weyburn that this hospital "eventually became a dumping ground for unwanted persons of all ages. Since there were no social safety nets, there was no public, secure place to house the elderly with dementia, the developmentally disabled, anyone who had an illness which the prevailing medical establishment didn't know how to treat, such as epilepsy or obsessive-compulsive disorder, or any number of mental illnesses for which there are treatments today" (Brenna, 2010b, pp. 164–165).

In terms of stories about the Weyburn hospital, Pamela acknowledged how some people who worked there were proud of the roles they held, supporting patients through psychiatric nursing or working in the laundry or kitchen. Other people in town were frightened of the patients, although many of these patients did not have mental illnesses. "In those days, you didn't have to have a doctor's certificate to commit someone to 'the mental'; you could be admitted simply on the word of a family member, or sometimes, a neighbour" (Brenna, 2010b, p. 165).

Pamela was haunted by particular narratives, including one from a family friend who, as a boy, lived on a farm near the Weyburn mental hospital (Brenna, 2010b). This boy's father hired many of the patients but told him to stay away from them. "They were dangerous and not quite human," was the message the lad received from his father. One day when the boy was descending a staircase, one of the hired hands was ascending the stairs. The child felt frightened, especially when he got closer to the man. Then the hired man from "the mental" bent over and tied the boy's shoelace. Pamela said her friend knew then—at the age of five—that the man was human, and that his father was wrong. Pamela worked this story directly into her characterizations of Emaline and Angus in her novel *The Crazy Man* (2005). The excerpt that follows is all the richer for the backstory of its inception:

> I couldn't decide if I should go to the trouble
> to hobble all the way around
> to the front porch to avoid him,
> or if I should try to just slide past him
> there on the back step.
> Mum called again, looking down

> out of the window over the sink.
> So I started toward the back step. I got closer
>   to the crazy man.
> My hands gripped hard
> on the handles of my crutches.
> My good foot landed in front of the step
> where he sat eating off our blue plate
> with the chip on one side.
> All of a sudden he put his plate down
> on the ground, and he bent over
> and tied up my shoelace. (pp. 49–50)

Pamela wanted to write about the stigma of mental illness in this historical time period because today, in the 21st century, this stigma largely remains. She planned to characterize someone "who was labelled mentally ill just because he had been admitted to the hospital at one time ... wanted to talk about the notion of what is crazy ... who really is 'the crazy man' in the story." (Brenna, 2010b, p. 166). Readers will no doubt explore the response of the Souris community to Emaline and Angus as the crazy element in the novel.

Counterstories and Social Justice

The central story in the novel *The Crazy Man* is really what Lindemann Nelson (1995) would call a counterstory, in this case, to historical and contemporary stigma associated with mental illness. When asked about how inspiration to tell such a counterstory may have emerged, Pamela reported, "I've been thinking ... about where I got the idea to act out my counterstory and whether I had adult models. The answer is that the adults around me were frustratingly compliant with the status quo" (Brenna, 2010b, p. 167). When Pamela was about 10 years old, she was fascinated with the national news, which she had access to on television. She reports,

> I watched marches, and young Black girls nearly my age saying, 'We've waited 100 years for justice to come; we've waited 100 years to vote. Don't ask us to wait any longer.' I saw President Lyndon Johnson on television pushing for desegregation of schools and the voting rights act, and saying, 'We shall overcome.' It was a gutsy thing for him to say at the time. I remember watching Governor George Wallace of Alabama stand at the front steps of the University of Alabama and refuse to let young Black students enter. I hear parents talk about the 'junk food' of television, but it was my social education. (Brenna, 2010b, pp. 167–168)

Pamela speaks further about her derivation of the Weyburn hospital in the fictional book *The Crazy Man*:

> The presence of the mental hospital and the various reactions of members of the [Weyburn] community were all new examples of story and counterstory ... My professor at the University of Montana in my MFA program, Richard Hugo ... wrote a book on the craft of writing titled, *The Triggering Town*. In the book, Hugo says that the "triggering town" for a writer is the town you wander into, the town you've never been to before, but in which you soon realize you've lived all your life, you know the people in it and you know the griefs that the town bears, because it is your psychic town. I think Weyburn, because of the hospital and the people we visited who had known my husband all his life, became my "triggering town." I realized that Weyburn was in many respects a Southern town with its strict unwritten culture and its guilt and shame over the presence of the mental hospital, much like Southern towns I knew where the citizens had to deal daily with the guilt and shame of racial segregation. (Brenna, 2010b, pp. 169–170)

An early experience from 1968 was perhaps in Pamela's mind as well. When she was attending Robert E. Lee Junior High in Monroe, Louisiana, her mother had instilled in her the value of addressing elders as "Ma'am" and "Sir." The janitorial staff at the school were all African-Americans, and one day Pamela had said good morning to one of the janitors, an elderly man with a kind face. He replied that it was a nice day, and Pamela responded, "Yes, Sir, it is." A girl walking with her turned and said, "What you doin' callin' him 'Sir'?" Pamela knew that, in that culture, African-Americans were regularly called by their first names, but even at the age of 12, she found the practice unjust and had decided to speak to every one of her elders with respect. "I decided that if I was required to call my white elders 'Sir' or 'Ma'am,' then I would call every one of my elders 'Sir' or 'Ma'am.' And I did. I had the loveliest conversations with women standing at bus stops after their day working as housekeepers at my neighbour's houses. Those women always greeted me and told me what a nice child I was" (Brenna, 2010b, p. 171).

Summary

Perhaps *The Crazy Man* will elicit classroom explorations of tensions with respect to societal stigma about disability, much as the five o'clock news was a catalyst in its author's development; perhaps *The Crazy Man* will even become what one of Pamela's writing teachers, Richard Hugo, referred to as a "triggering town," opening a space for readers to recognize similar tensions among conflicting social forces in their own world (Hugo, 1979). The foregrounding of Pamela's storied past alongside her writing promotes the inclusion of *The Crazy Man* (2005) in classrooms where educators wish to develop "social actors who have a sense of their own agency as well as a sense of societal responsibility toward and with others and the society as a whole" (Bell, 1997, p. 3).

Annotated Bibliography of Canadian Intermediate Novels Portraying Characters with Disabilities

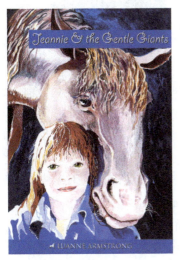

Armstrong, L. (2002). *Jeannie and the gentle giants.* **Vancouver, BC: Ronsdale Press.**

After her mother's breakdown from an undefined mental illness, 11-year-old Jeannie is placed in a foster home where she discovers horses, a dog she can tame, the outdoors, and friendship. When her mother is well enough to leave the hospital, Jeannie struggles with the idea of losing her new life. For ages nine and up.

Description: realistic fiction; themes include developing friendships, family relationships, mental health, and horse logging.

Read-ons: Becky Citra's *Missing* has a setting involving a young girl's experiences learning about horses, and an outdoor rural setting can also be found in Sonya Spreen Bates' *Thunder Creek Ranch*. In Maggie de Vries's *Somebody's Girl*, nine-year-old Martha spends Christmas with a foster child's family while her own adoptive mother is in hospital having a baby.

Baker, B. (2014). *Camp Outlook.* **Toronto, ON: Second Story Press.**

This story is about a 12-year-old whose much anticipated baby brother is born with Down syndrome. The book tackles the subjects of spirituality and social justice with sensitivity, offering a believable yet magical narrative about a summer church camp during which Shannon is irrevocably changed, and where other characters with disabilities have much to share. For ages nine and up.

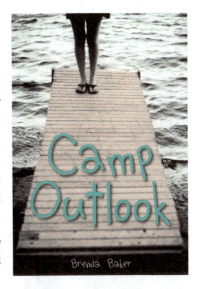

Description: realistic fiction; themes include developing friendships, spirituality, identity, and social awareness of people with differences.

Read-ons: Other summer camp stories include Pam Withers' *Camp Wild* and the graphic novel *Brain Camp* by Susan Kim and Laurence Klavan. Another clever girl who compares well to Shannon in *Camp Outlook* is Elizabeth in Sylvia McNicoll's *Bringing Up Beauty*.

Brenna, B. (2007). *The moon children*. Calgary, AB: Red Deer Press.

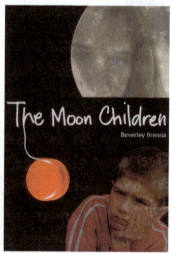

The Moon Children is a realistic fiction novel about a friendship between Billy, a boy with Fetal Alcohol Spectrum Disorder, and Natasha, an adopted girl from Romania. The story takes place in North Battleford, Saskatchewan, where Billy is planning to enter a community talent show with his amazing yoyo routine. He and his dad have practiced the tricks, but his father, an alcoholic, disappears and may not return for the contest—and Billy is not convinced he can perform without his dad. For ages nine and up.

Description: realistic fiction; themes include self-actualization and friendship.

Read-ons: Ann Cameron's picture book retelling of the north coast explanatory myth *How Raven Freed the Moon* is worth reading alongside *The Moon Children*, as it contains the story that helps Billy understand Natasha's need to share the weight of the heavy secret she has been carrying. *Joey Pigza Swallowed the Key* by Jack Gantos involves a boy who is also dealing with self-control issues. Powerlessness is a theme common to the Joey Pigza books as well as to others, including *The Pinballs* by Betsy Byars, Trilby Kent's *Medina Hill*, and *The 18th Emergency* by Betsy Byars. Kate di Camillo's *The Tiger Rising* and Pamela Porter's *The Crazy Man* portray friendships between people who also carry burdens and secrets.

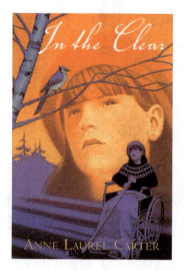

Carter, A.L. (2001). *In the clear*. Victoria, BC: Orca Books.

Pauline is a 12-year-old Ontario girl recovering from polio. The story is set in the late 1950s and begins when Pauline is at home from the hospital, using a leg brace, and refusing to consider old friends or a return to her past life. She even gives up on reading, and then, through secret encounters with *Heidi* and *The Secret Garden*, despairs that she will never realize that kind of happy ending. Slowly, she overcomes the idea that happy endings must always involve the overcoming of a disability, and begins to fashion for herself a different kind of happy ending. For ages nine and up.

Description: historical fiction that evokes time and place but also hinges on the universal; themes include friendship, self-actualization, and dealing with changes.

Read-ons: Spyri's *Heidi* and Burnett's *The Secret Garden* are recommended companion titles. Julie Johnston's Governor General's Award–winning *Hero of Lesser Causes* also deals with juvenile polio, as does the New Zealand published *Run* by Linda Aksomitis, while Bernice Thurman Hunter's title *A Place for Margaret* deals with tuberculosis. Other contemporary fiction with related themes includes Kit Pearson's *Awake and Dreaming*, whose protagonist uses reading as a source of support. *Home Free* by Sharon Jennings—another story about friendship and courage—also has references to classic literature. *The Mealworm Diaries* by Anna Kerz involves a young protagonist coming to terms with a different kind of loss. Maxine Trottier's historical fiction *Blood Upon Our Land: The North West Resistance Diary of Josephine Bouvier* presents a young Métis girl's search for personal identity.

Chandler, A. (2008). *Siena summer*. Vancouver, BC: Tradewind Books.

On a holiday to visit her mother's relatives in Italy, Angela befriends a neighbour's horse named Tempesta, and ends up as his jockey in an important race called the Palio. A secondary character in the book is the neighbour's daughter, Catarina, who has been thrown from the horse and is now using a wheelchair while she recovers from her injuries. In the course of the story, Angela helps Catarina overcome her new fear of riding. Angela also discovers that Tempesta is blind in one eye, which might be the reason for his skittishness, and a patch on the eye corrects the problem. Along with the story of the race, there is also a budding romance between Angela and another jockey named Tony, although Tony, it turns out, is not a good choice for Angela. For ages 12 and up.

Description: realistic fiction; themes include triumph over adversity, disability "cure", romance, and family relationships as well as horse-related adventure.

Read-ons: Other horse stories, such as Angela Dorsey's *A Horse Called Freedom*, will make good connecting reads. Books showing a horse's perspective, which could be used to compare or to inspire creative writing revisions in which Tempesta's story is told through first person, are Anna Sewell's *Black Beauty* and *The Winter Pony* by Iain Lawrence.

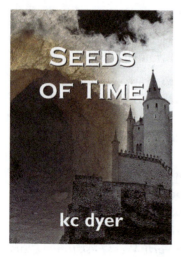

Dyer, K.C. (2002). *Seeds of time*. Toronto, ON: Dundurn Press.

Thirteen-year-old Darrell Connor is spending the summer at an oceanside British Columbia boarding school where she discovers a passage through time, through which she hopes to change her own circumstances—a motorcycle accident that, three years ago, took her father's life and severely damaged her leg, requiring the use of a prosthesis. Darrell's adventures in 14th-century Scotland are unique in that she arrives with the same physical disability, just a different type of artificial leg as dictated by the times. For ages 10 and up.

Description: fantasy; themes include self-acceptance and bullying as well as emphasizing the lessons to be learned from history.

Read-ons: This title and its two sequels connect well to other time slip novels including Lynne Kositsky's *A Question of Will*, Judith Silverthorne's *The Secret of the Stone House*, Lois Donovan's *Winds of L'Acadie*, Marsha Skrypuch's *The Hunger*, and Lynne Fairbridge's *Tangled in Time*, as well as Nicholas Maes' combination of futuristic science fiction and time travel in *Laughing Wolf*. Darren Krill's *The Uncle Duncle Chronicles: Escape from Treasure Island* involves characters that move into a fictional past. One other connecting fantasy is Barbara Nickel's *Hannah Waters and the Daughter of Johann Sebastian Bach*.

Dyer, K.C. (2003). *Secret of light*. Toronto, ON: Dundurn Press.

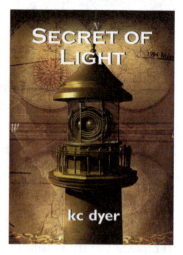

In this sequel to *Seeds of Time*, Darrell Connor's story continues as, along with new friends Brodie and Kate, she begins her first full year at the alternative art school Eagle Glen. The friends, along with stray dog Delaney, travel through the abandoned lighthouse to 15th-century Italy, where they encounter a young Leonardo da Vinci. When school bully Conrad Kennedy accidentally accompanies them, things don't go according to plan and he is left behind in the past. In these travels, Darrell's prosthetic limb is rendered as an elaborately carved, roll-toed paw, similar to a piano leg, but she bears the discomfort so that she can search further for a way to change her own past—to somehow alter the motorcycle accident that caused her injury and killed her father. For ages 10 and up.

Description: fantasy; themes include self-acceptance and bullying as well as emphasizing the importance of history.

Read-ons: As above, for *Seeds of Time*.

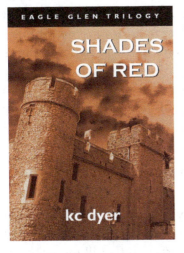

Dyer, K.C. (2005). *Shades of red*. Toronto, ON: Dundurn Press.

In this conclusion of the Eagle Glen trilogy, Darrell and her friends travel through a portal in the library, entering the period of the Protestant Reformation in England. In this context, Darrell's prosthesis transforms into a peg leg that has a hinged wooden foot. Modern issues of racism and discrimination are depicted as ages old through Darrell's experiences in the Court of King Henry VIII, where priests secretly offer safe passage to Jews targeted by the Church's brutal cleansing. In this title, Darrell learns what she has always known—that you cannot change the past—and comes to terms with her physical self in the present time. For ages 10 and up.

Description: fantasy; themes include self-acceptance and coming to terms with loss.

Read-ons: As above, for *Seeds of Time*.

Dyer, K.C. (2007). *Ms. Zephyr's notebook*. Toronto, ON: Dundurn Press.

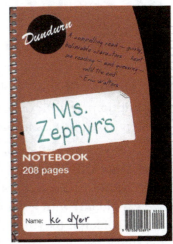

Much of the emotional buildup in this novel takes place in the children's ward of a fictional Evergreen County Hospital and revolves around three main characters: 15-year-old Logan, whose point of view is dominant in the story and who has Crohn's Disease; 14-year-old Cleo, whose "real" name is Jacqueline, and who has an eating disorder; and 11-year-old Kip, who is awaiting a kidney transplant. This complex story about identity and relationships unfolds through documents discovered by Logan in their hospital teacher's journal. Ms. Zephyr's school notebook contains letters from families, updates from the school, and assignments from the students themselves. Each of the three children deals differently with illness, and yet what they have in common becomes a tie that binds, even through what Logan fears is Cleo's next suicide attempt. For ages 12 and up.

Description: realistic fiction; themes prompt readers to explore what life is like with debilitating illness, and to recognize how barriers between people are erected and removed.

Read-ons: Paul Zindel's *The Pigman* offers a good companion read due to its presentation through the alternate voices of John and Lorraine and in terms of its close look at teen relationships. The desperate search for a friend provides a connection between K.C. Dyer's *Ms. Zephyr's Notebook* and Deborah Ellis's *Looking for X*. Natalie Babbitt's *Tuck Everlasting* offers a look at life choices through the theme of everlasting life. Other life choices are explored in Susin Nielsen's *Word Nerd* about a boy with a serious peanut allergy who seeks identity and acceptance, and Iain Lawrence's *Ghost Boy*.

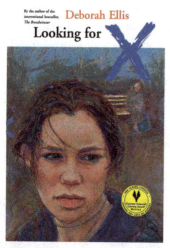

Ellis, D. (1999). *Looking for X*. Toronto, ON: Groundwood Books.

Eleven-year-old Khyber, living in downtown Toronto, embarks on a desperate search for a friend through first-person narration that illuminates her intelligence and resiliency in a life that looks bleak from the outside but from the inside has a fine balance of edginess, warmth, and adventure. Because of Khyber's strong, matter-of-fact voice, the scenes depicting her relationship with autistic twin brothers and the episodes with X, a homeless person, operate without sentimentality. One of the main plot lines in the novel is that Khyber's mother has decided to place David and Daniel in a group home, a plan to which Khyber is resistant. For ages 12 and up.

Description: realistic fiction; winner of a Governor General's Award for Children's Fiction (text); themes include family dynamics and dealing with change.

Read-ons: Jean Little's *Dancing Through the Snow* and Katherine Paterson's *The Great Gilly Hopkins* have girl protagonists with similar spunk. Cynthia Lord's *Rules* is another intermediate novel that explores the relationship of a 12-year-old girl with a younger brother who has autism. *No Place for Kids* by Alison Lohans is the story of two siblings on the run from social services through the sometimes terrifying, sometimes comforting, world of the urban homeless, while Martin Leavitt's *Tom Finder* deals with another type of escape. Sarah Ellis's *Pick-Up Sticks*, winner of a Governor General's Award for Children's Fiction (text), focuses on a mother/daughter relationship similar to the one between Khyber and Tammy. The subject of imaginary friends is also dealt with in Lesley Choyce's *Smoke and Mirrors*.

Ellis, D. (2011). *No ordinary day*. Toronto, ON: Groundwood Books.

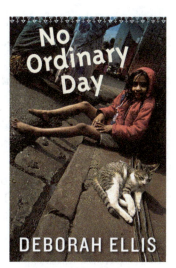

Valli is an orphan girl in India who stows away on a coal truck to escape an unbearable existence with a family that is not her own. Rejected by a brothel owner because of early signs of leprosy, Valli becomes a street person, eating and sleeping however she can. When she meets a doctor who diagnoses the disease, Valli is at first unsure whether she wants to stay in hospital for treatment with other "monsters"—the word that is used for people affected by Hansen's Disease. Her strong desire for learning is what sets her on the right track, and by the end of the book we get a sense that Valli will make a wonderful doctor herself someday. For ages nine and up.

Description: realistic fiction; themes include the power of self-determination and the importance of education.

Read-ons: Valli's quest for survival is paralleled in other titles, including Rick Revelle's title for slightly older readers, *I Am Algonquin*. Both books serve to counter a reader's lack of information with authentic information delivered from first-person narrative. Mary Razzell's book *Smuggler's Moon* offers information about a Canadian leper colony active in the early 1900s on the Pacific Coast.

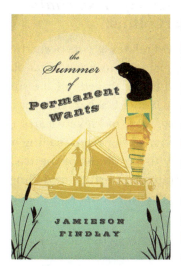

Findlay, J. (2011). *The summer of permanent wants*. Toronto, ON: Doubleday Canada.

Eleven-year-old Emmeline hasn't spoken in almost a year, affected by an illness-induced coma during a family vacation in Kenya. Her problem in remembering words is compounded by the stress of having them finally come out but in the wrong order, and at the beginning of the book, she is not speaking at all. She and her grandmother are starting a floating bookshop called *Permanent Wants* that will sail between real and imagined ports along the Rideau Canal, between Ottawa and Kingston, all summer long. Other characters who are differently abled include Aunt Tilley, who has also lost the power of speech, Belle/Bella, who is deaf, and other unique individuals who remind us that everyone has a story to tell. For ages 11 and up.

Description: magic realism; themes include self-acceptance and overcoming challenges.

Read-ons: Another fantasy novel about a girl on a journey is *Plain Kate* by Erin Bow, whose cat Taggle is reminiscent of Crow in Findlay's title.

Goto, H. (2002). *The water of possibility*. Regina: Coteau Books.

Twelve-year old Sayuri Kato, an avid swimmer, does not want to move from the city to a home in rural Alberta where her father has found a nursing job. Move they must, however, and one day after school, she and her little brother are transported through the root cellar to a woodland full of figures from Japanese folklore. When Keiji, who has serious asthma, becomes lost, Sayuri is assisted on her quest to find him while she also attends to the evil that has befallen Middle World. For ages nine and up.

Description: fantasy; themes include sibling relationships and dealing with prejudice.

Read-ons: This book is from a series called In the Same Boat, whose mandate was to offer Canadian kids titles in which they can see themselves. Other connections include Janet Lunn's *The Root Cellar* and Judith Silverthorne's *The Secret of Sentinel Rock*. Bev Brenna's fantasy *The Keeper of the Trees* also has a protagonist whose young friend has asthma and for whom protecting the environment becomes paramount.

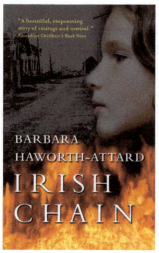

Haworth-Attard, B. (2002). *Irish chain*. Toronto, ON: HarperCollins.

This historical fiction novel relates events occurring alongside the Halifax explosion of 1917 as 12-year-old Rose Dunlea is enveloped in the tragedy of the surrounding community. Told by her teachers that she is "slow," "retarded," and "lazy," Rose has severe learning disabilities that have prevented her from reading or writing with ease. Yet, by using pieces of the Irish chain quilt, she demonstrates masterful storytelling, and offers exceptional leadership in the face of danger. For ages 10 and up.

Description: historical fiction; themes include self-acceptance and the value of storytelling.

Read-ons: Another title from Haworth-Attard—*Flying Geese*—makes a nice companion read as it also involves quilting as a life-affirming act, as does Deborah Hopkinson's picture book, *Sweet Clara and the Freedom Quilt*. The value of storytelling is explored in Marcus Sedgwick's *Floodland*, a futuristic fantasy where a young girl realizes that stories are how people survive, and how they remember who they are and where they are from. Jean Little's *The Belonging Place* identifies similar themes of growing up in transition, as does Alice Walsh's *A Sky Black with Crows*. Penny Draper's *Terror at Turtle Mountain* also focuses on Canadian disasters and is told from the perspective of a young girl whose self-doubts mirror Rose's. Dave Glaze's *Danger in Dead Man's Mine* is also a great companion read.

Haworth-Attard, B. (2010). *To stand on my own: The polio epidemic diary of Noreen Robertson.* Toronto, ON: Scholastic Canada.

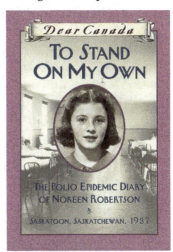

This fictional diary is a detailed and gripping account of an 11-year-old Saskatoon girl's experiences with polio. Noreen contracts the virus from a swimming pool, and spends time in quarantine before hearing that she will never walk again. She does make physical gains, however, thanks to her grandfather who explores new treatments of the time. For ages nine and up.

Description: historical fiction; themes include prejudice, bullying, and changing friendships.

Read-ons: Anne Laurel Carter's novel, *In the Clear,* is another historical title in first-person narrative for the same age group about a girl who also contracts polio. Many other titles from the *Dear Canada* series offer parallels in terms of characters dealing with locally contextualized challenges, and other novels by Haworth-Attard would make good comparison studies, including *Flying Geese*, a nice counterpart in terms of a girl's loneliness and struggle following a move from Saskatchewan to Ontario.

Horrocks, A. (2006). *Almost Eden.* Toronto, ON: Tundra Books.

Twelve-year-old Elsie deals with her mother's mental illness, isolated by feelings of guilt and confusion in the fictional Mennonite community of Hopefield, Canada. Serious subject matter is presented in a style younger readers can absorb regarding the course of the summer of 1970, when Elsie's mom is in the local mental institution taking shock treatments. The story follows Elsie's feelings of responsibility regarding her mother's breakdown, her relationship with Beth, her bossy older sister, and her forgetfulness of family responsibilities with regard to Lena, her younger sister, and her loss of faith in God. For ages 10 and up.

Description: historical fiction; themes include self-discovery and coming of age.

Read-ons: Lucy Maud Montgomery's *Anne of Green Gables* offers a comparatively spunky character who despairs at her own mistakes. Miriam Toews's

A Complicated Kindness is an adult crossover novel that portrays another Mennonite girl coming of age, although it is geared to older readers. Elizabeth Berg's *Joy School* is an additional crossover novel that serves the young adult market, and Katie, its protagonist, is a 12-year-old with striking similarities to Elsie. Martine Leavitt's *Heck, Superhero* and Susan White's *The Sewing Basket* also follow characters dealing with a parent's mental illness.

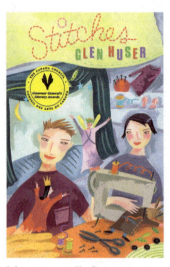

Huser, G. (2003). *Stitches*. Toronto, ON: Groundwood.

This book is set in the fictional Western Canadian town of Acton and explores the friendship between Travis, a boy in junior high school whose artistic talents direct him toward a future in sewing and design, and Chantelle, a classmate with a rare bone disease. Bullied since grade school, Travis perseveres in designing puppets and dreams of a place "where there are no Shon Dockers" and "where you could do what you wanted and no one would make fun of you. Where your best friend could be a girl. Where people wouldn't look away when they saw someone like Chantelle." Travis stands up for Chantelle when even his family calls her a "poor little thing," but, without anyone to prevent the bullying that eventually puts him in hospital, he decides to move to the city to attend art school where "no one seems to mind how different you are." The ending implies that someday Chantelle will also move away to the city, leaving a lasting impression that some problems can't be solved, just escaped. For ages 11 and up.

Description: realistic fiction, winner of a Governor General's Award for Children's Fiction (text); themes include self-discovery and self-acceptance, as well as bullying and the power to endure.

Read-ons: Katherine Paterson's *Bridge to Terabithia* offers connecting characters and themes, as does Christopher Paul Curtis' *Elijah of Buxton* about a pre-teen determined to become a "man's man" but struggling with emotional fragility. Lori Saigeon's *Fight for Justice* also deals with bullying.

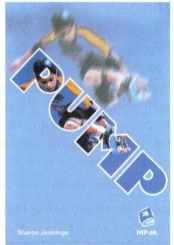

Jennings, S. (2006). *Pump*. Toronto, ON: HIP Books.

Twelve-year-old Pat loves to skateboard, but neighbours complain. When Pat and his friends advocate for a neighbourhood skateboard park, his new friend John supports the cause even though John himself uses a wheelchair since a bike accident with a drunk driver. For ages nine and up.

Description: realistic fiction in hi-lo format; themes include self-advocacy and pushing against stereotypes.

Read-ons: Liam O'Donnell's graphic novel *Ramp Rats* also follows kids who like to skateboard.

Johansen, K.V. (2007). *Torrie & the snake-prince.* Toronto, ON: Annick Press.

A 14-year-old orphan named Wren, who is a travelling pedlar, fights off goblin, griffin, and dryad attacks on her quest to rescue the Snake-Prince. Her club foot causes some difficulties on the journey, but she overcomes all challenges and her adventures occur fast and furiously, narrated by an unusual character named Torrie whose close perspective offers exactly the details readers need in this engaging romp of the imagination. For ages nine and up.

Description: fantasy; themes include good triumphing over evil and the power of friendship.

Read-ons: Jennifer A. Nielsen's fantasy *The False Prince*, first in a trilogy, offers similar humorous fantasy adventures, as does Margaret Peterson Haddix's *Just Ella*.

Lawrence, I. (2006). *Gemini summer.* New York, NY: Delacorte Press.

Magic realism transforms this poignant story about a boy's loss of his brother. Set in 1965 Hog's Hollow (a fictionalized Toronto suburb), tragedy strikes just when each member of the River family is bent on following a personal dream. After the death of Danny's brother, Beau, and Beau's eventual reincarnation as a dog, Danny vows to take Beau to Cape Canaveral to satisfy what had been his brother's dream as well as assuage his own guilt. The novel's antagonist, a boy who is initially blamed for Beau's death, is Dopey Colvig, a child depicted completely through atypical physical characteristics (a large head and absence of speech) suggesting autism or another developmental disorder. It is Dopey's unexplained violent antagonism to the brothers that offers good fuel for classroom discussion. For ages 10 and up.

Description: historical fiction and a winner of a Governor General's Award for Children's Fiction (text); themes include death of a sibling and following your dreams. Because this story is framed in fairy-tale imagery, Dopey Colvig, lurking like a troll under the bridge in the woods, appears as a believable figure of evil. An exploration of how this type of framing contributes to negative stereotypes about people with physical differences is a theme well worth exploring.

Read-ons: Susan Patron's *The Higher Power of Lucky* also involves a young protagonist recovering from a death—the death of her mother— through a runaway adventure with a dog, HMS Beagle. Another book that explores loss in the hopeful style of *Gemini Summer* is Katherine Paterson's *Bridge to Terabithia*. Other titles with stereotypical villains include Frieda Wishinsky's *Queen of the Toilet Bowl* and Colin Frizzell's *Chill*, as well as *The Proof That Ghosts Exist* by Carol Matas and Perry Nodelman. Fairy-tale imagery also frames the plot in *Broken* by Alyxandra Harvey-Fitzhenry, and Cynthia Nugent's *Francesca and the Magic Bike* includes the Dickensian technique of naming as representation of character.

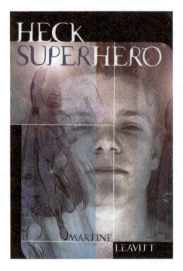

Leavitt, M. (2004). *Heck superhero*. Red Deer Press.

In this title, a 13-year-old boy deals with his mother's mental illness by trying to pretend things are okay, imagining himself a superhero. After they are evicted from their apartment, Hector spends four days on the street, not knowing where his mother is but certain that she is in a phase of illness Heck calls "hypertime." It is in this urban setting where Heck's new friendship with a boy called Marion teaches him the difference between imagination and another type of being gone that is permanent; Marion's own mental illness and eventual suicide force Heck to admit that he and his mother need help. For ages 10 and up.

Description: realistic fiction; themes include self-discovery and coming of age, as well as living with mental illness.

Read-ons: Dianne Linden's *Shimmerdogs* is a story for a similar age group about a young boy trying to cope in difficult circumstances. Sarah Ellis' *Odd Man Out* further explores stereotypes about mental illness as a young boy discovers facts about his deceased father. Tim Wynne-Jones's *Stephen Fair* follows a 15-year-old boy who is also struggling with terrifying events in his life before returning home to his mother. *Looking for X* by Deborah Ellis portrays another young protagonist spending a series of days on the street. *Slake's Limbo* by Felice Holman is another young adult novel about living on the streets, in this case, the interior of the New York subway; it connects, as well, to an intermediate graphic novel: Brian Selznik's *Invention of Hugo Cabret*.

Lekich, J. (2002). *Losers' club*. Toronto, ON: Annick Press.

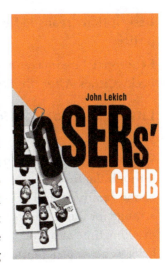

Alex Sherwood, a high school kid with cerebral palsy, becomes the leader of a group of so-called losers. When his father goes into hiding, Alex moves in with another friend whose family is also away, and the two boys become acquainted with a neighbour nicknamed "The Beast," Harry Beardsley, who is persuaded to act as their surrogate parent. Harry eventually decides to go and visit his own son, a boy who also has cerebral palsy. A bet regarding a Christmas display contest earns Alex the opportunity to save his friends once and for all from bully Jerry Whitman. Other than using his disability and his use of crutches for put-downs by other students, the author includes it as a very minor aspect of Alex's characterization. Metafictional elements appear in the narrator's habit of speaking directly to the reader. For ages 12 and up.

Description: realistic fiction; themes include bullying and making the best of difficult situations.

Read-ons: Titles connecting on the basis of their high-school humour include Don Trembath's *A Fly Named Alfred* and Gordon Korman's *A Semester in the Life of a Garbage Bag*. Ted L. Nancy's *Letters from a Nut* provide a good connection to a letter to Alex's dad in Chapter 2. Another title depicting physical disability as merely one aspect of characterization is Mary Downing Hahn's *Following My Own Footsteps*.

Linden, D. (2013). *On fire*. Saskatoon, SK: Thistledown Press.

Fourteen-year-old Matilda (Mattie) Iverly discovers a young man wandering out of the heart of wildfire country, who remembers nothing about his life. Over the course of time, as his mental illness is treated, his unhappy past returns. We see him in alternating chapters told through Mattie's first-person narrative, and then from Dan's own third person perspective. Mattie has Tourette Syndrome (TS), evident in many of her interactions with others, but not used as a single defining character trait. Readers unfamiliar with the condition will get an authentic sense of how TS feels from the inside through Mattie's descriptions. For example, she suggests that a tic feels like a sneeze that can be delayed, but that must eventually be released. For ages 11 and up.

Description: realistic fiction; themes include respecting differences and social justice.

Read-ons: Fire images also race through Frank O'Keefe's *Harry Flammable* and Becky Citra's *After the Fire*.

Little, J. (2000). *Willow and Twig.* Toronto, ON: Penguin Canada.

Willow is a 10-year-old girl caring for her four-year-old brother in Vancouver through the disappearance of their mother, drug-addicted Angel, and the death of the family friend where they have been living. Child and Family Services arrange for the children to fly to Toronto, to a grandmother Willow has not seen in a long time and who has never met Twig—a little boy who was born an addict, has attention problems, and is hearing impaired as a result of a beating. Uncle Humphrey, their grandmother's brother, who is blind, offers love and support, but Aunt Con is at first unfriendly and judgemental. The heart of the story is the bond between Willow and Twig, and how these children make the transition to their new home. For ages 10 and up.

Description: realistic fiction; themes include adapting to change and sibling relationships.

Read-ons: Julie Johnston's *Adam and Eve and Pinch-Me* (a Governor General's Award winner for children's text) also offers happy outcomes for a 15-year-old foster child, as does another intermediate novel by Jean Little: *Dancing Through the Snow*. Other parallels can be seen in Linda Holeman's historical fiction novel *Search of the Moon King's Daughter* as well as the fantasy novel *The Third Eye* by Mahtab Narsimhan. Another book about a character who is hearing impaired is *Missing Sisters* by Gregory Maguire, while Jean Little's *From Anna* is about a character with a visual impairment.

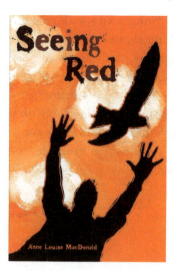

MacDonald, A.L. (2009). *Seeing red.* Toronto, ON: Kids Can Press.

Fourteen-year-old Frankie discovers he can dream the future, his only claim to fame, and yet even with this talent he cannot prevent disaster. Caught in confusing circumstances, Frankie presents feelings common to young people striving to control unpredictable situations. Descriptions of Joey, a kid with autism who Frankie babysits and eventually chaperones during riding therapy at a local stable, are rendered with care, as are other characters with special needs who shift in and out of the therapeutic riding context. Through the course of the novel,

Frankie explores his fears, including his fear of horses, as well as a developing friendship with Maura-Lee, a girl who also has extrasensory abilities. For ages 10 and up.

Description: realistic fiction; themes include self-acceptance, conquering fears, and friendships.

Read-ons: René Schmidt's *Leaving Fletchville* explores similar themes of friendship as well as racial prejudice, as does Ted Stenhouse's *Across the Steel River*. Jean Little's *Different Dragons* also involves conquering fears. Cora Taylor's *Julie*, Julie Johnston's *A Very Fine Line*, Robin Stevenson's *Impossible Things*, and Carol Matas's psychic adventure series beginning with *The Freak* explore situations where children identify themselves as having extrasensory perception and struggle with their gifts.

McBay, B., & Heneghan, J. (2003). *Waiting for Sarah*. Victoria, BC: Orca Books.

Following a serious accident, Mike is assisted in his transition back to high school in False Creek, Vancouver, by Sarah, a younger girl he believes has been sent to help him with a yearbook project. Mike's loss of mobility has created a bitterness that takes time to dissolve, but eventually Sarah wins his heart. It is then that Mike realizes she is actually the ghost of a young girl murdered by a teacher—and that it is up to him to prove Mr. Dorfman's guilt. For ages 14 and up.

Description: fantasy; themes include adapting to change and the power of friendships.

Read-ons: Another boy's relationship with a ghost is outlined in Lesley Choyce's *Smoke and Mirrors*. Kit Pearson's *Awake and Dreaming* takes a protagonist's responsibilities to a ghost one step further. Pat Hancock's *Haunted Canada: True Ghost Stories* offers another look at mysterious phenomena.

McMurchy-Barber, G. (2010). *Free as a bird*. Toronto, ON: Dundurn Publishers.

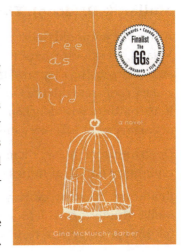

This novel offers the unique perspective of growing up with Down syndrome, told by protagonist Ruby Jean Sharp. A survivor of the residential Woodlands School in BC, and eventually adopted by an elderly couple, Ruby's unique narration briefly explores homelessness, abuse including sexual abuse, and injustice—with detail appropriate for older children. For ages 11 and up.

Description: realistic fiction; themes involve unique perspectives on the world and independence.

Read-ons: Another title that employs misspellings to convey a character's disability is Richard Scrimger's *Ink Me*.

Mercer, A. (2011). *Rebound.* Toronto, ON: James Lorimer.

This sports story is about C.J., a Grade 9 basketball player whose juvenile arthritis is diagnosed and treated during the course of the narrative. For ages 10 and up.

Description: realistic fiction in a hi-lo format; themes include supporting the team and courage amidst challenges.

Read-ons: Other basketball books for slightly younger audiences include Loris Lesynski's *Crazy About Basketball*, *Three On Three* by Eric Walters, and *Boot Camp* by Eric Walters, Jerome Williams, and Johnnie Williams III.

Mulder, M. (2011). *Out of the box.* Victoria, BC: Orca.

Thirteen-year-old Ellie is spending the summer in Victoria with her Aunt Jeanette while her parents sort things out; one of their challenges involves a potential mental illness in Ellie's mother, which she won't acknowledge. How Ellie navigates her mother's emotional dependency is one of the plotlines, in addition to a mystery involving a *bandoneón* found in her aunt's basement that leads her to a deeper understanding of Argentinian history. Ellie moves back with her parents at the end of the summer with new skills. For ages 10 and up.

Description: realistic fiction; themes include developing friendships, family relationships, the challenges of mental illness, and the previous military dictatorship in Argentina.

Read-ons: *Pick-up Sticks* by Sarah Ellis outlines the story of another complex mother-daughter relationship, while another title by Ellis, *Odd Man Out*, involves a boy's discovery, while staying with relatives, of his father's mental illness.

Muller, R.D. (2009). *The solstice cup.* Victoria, BC: Orca.

A pair of 13-year-old twins are spending time with an aunt and uncle in Northern Ireland, a location where five years ago Breanne was mysteriously involved in an injury causing a "sprain" that evolved into a permanent limp. Once again they come in contact with the Otherworld, and this time they are not so lucky. Drawn into a battle of wits, Mackenzie must save her sister and herself from seven years of enslavement to a faery mistress. For ages nine and up.

Description: fantasy; themes include the importance of freedom as well as the cautionary notion of things that seem too good to be true.

Read-ons: Another fantasy set in Ireland is O.R. Melling's *The Druid's Tune*. Mollie Hunter's classic fantasy *A Stranger Came Ashore* is an additional novel for this age group that rests on legend, also with a plotline involving otherworld creatures capturing human slaves. Norma Fox Mazer's *Ten Ways to Make My Sister Disappear* would make another good companion read.

Nelson, C. (2011). *Tori by design*. Winnipeg, MB: Great Plains Publications.

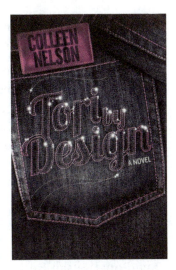

Fifteen-year-old Tori happily moves from Winnipeg to New York, quickly excited by a summer internship at the Fashion Institute of Technology—her dream job. Midway through the novel, she learns that her 40-year-old mother is pregnant, and eventually prenatal testing indicates that the baby has Down syndrome, something dealt with in a fairly cursory way and utilized as a plot twist to assist Tori in demonstrating a newly learned selflessness by offering to move with the family back to Winnipeg. For ages 11 and up.

Description: realistic fiction; themes include developing friendships and navigating challenges.

Read-ons: Another title involving a young fashion designer is Glen Huser's *Stitches*.

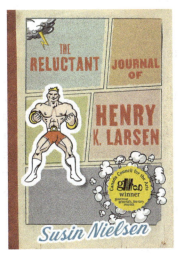

Nielsen, S. (2012). *The reluctant journal of Henry K. Larsen*. Toronto, ON: Tundra Books.

Thirteen-year-old Henry's first-person story appears through journal entries that detail events surrounding an older brother's suicide and a mother who is now in psychiatric care. Readers learn that Henry's brother Jesse was a bullied teen who formulated and actualized a plan to shoot his worst enemy at school, and then end his own life. How Henry processes his agonizing memories and learns to live with himself is part of the story; the other part involves the intriguing people he comes to know in his journey forward. While it is at times difficult to read about the devastating events that took place, this is also a tale filled with warmth and humour. For ages 12 and up.

Description: realistic fiction, winner of the Governor General's Literary Award for Children's Fiction (text); themes include developing friendships and dealing with challenges.

Read-ons: Other good connecting titles by Susin Nielsen include *Dear George Clooney: Please Marry My Mom* and *Word Nerd*.

Nugent, C. (2004). *Francesca and the magic bike*. Vancouver, BC: Raincoast Books.

A new friendship between 10-year-old Francesca and an elderly neighbour who is visually impaired blossoms into an adventure that moves them both into happier contexts. Augusta offers Frankie a chance to find a family heirloom while she guides Ron, Frankie's dad, into a healthier lifestyle that will convince social services he is a capable father. Riding Hippogriff, a bike whose "emotionally responsive metal" offers intuitive support, and with Augusta's dog Dan for company, Frankie sets out to find a ring that's been lost since Augusta's childhood—the recovery of which, in the end, brings two feuding sisters together again. For ages 10 and up.

Description: magic realism; themes include the power of imagination and family relationships.

Read-ons: Susan Patron's *The Higher Power of Lucky* has a protagonist of a similar age and character engaging in a remarkable journey. *Inkheart* by Cornelia Funk offers fantasy for this age group, also reminiscent of *The Bad Beginning* and other work by Lemony Snicket, Arthur Slade's *Jolted: Newton Starker's Rules for Survival*, and Roald Dahl's *The Twits* where the Dickensian technique of attaching names representative of characters is employed.

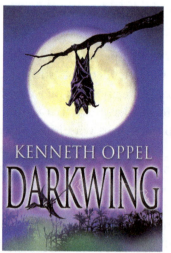

Oppel, K. (2007). *Darkwing*. Toronto, ON: HarperCollins.

Set in the Paleocene epoch, this is a prequel to Oppel's previous bat books (*Silverwing*, *Sunwing*, and *Firewing*). Dusk is the lead character and a youthful "chiropter" who at first is stigmatized for his physical differences by the other members of his clan, then respected as a more evolved form of the arboreal gliders. In a poignant conversation with his sister, Dusk asks, "Is different wrong?" and much of the storyline revolves around this theme. For ages 10 and up.

Description: fantasy; includes universal themes of belonging and self-discovery as well as an exploration of being different.

Read-ons: Good connecting books include: Monica Hughes's fantasy *The Guardian of Isis*, in which the gifted Jody is as much of an outcast from his community as Darkwing is from his; Lois Lowry's *Gathering Blue*, about a futuristic society that discards people with physical disabilities; Virginia Frances Schwartz's *Initiation,* a story of self-discovery set on the West Coast of North America during the 15th century; Sara Winthrow's *Bat Summer,* the story of Lucy, a girl who walks the line between reality and fantasy to save herself from a traumatic memory; and Patricia C. Wrede's look at exceptionality through the steampunk genre in *Thirteenth Child.*

Porter, P. (2005). *The crazy man.* Toronto, ON: Groundwood Books.

The setting of this verse novel is rural Saskatchewan, 1965, where the shadow of the local mental hospital looms large on the landscape. The story is told from the first-person viewpoint of 11-year-old Emaline following the farm accident that left her leg seriously injured, her dog dead, and her father gone—blaming himself for her tragedy. Her mother hires Angus, a previous resident of the mental hospital, as a farmhand, and both Emaline and Angus are the recipients of stereotypical remarks from neighbours. To many in the surrounding community, they seem reduced to "Hopalong" and "Subhuman." The friendship between Em and Angus transcends difference and offers each the power to shape their identity in ways beyond the physical. For ages nine and up.

Description: historical fiction verse novel, winner of the Governor General's Award for Children's Fiction (text); themes include friendship, dealing with loss, and acceptance of diversity.

Read-ons: Kristin Butcher's *The Gramma War,* Glen Huser's *Skinnybones and the Wrinkle Queen,* Bev Brenna's *The Moon Children,* and William Bell's *Alma* make good companion reads as they deal with changing family dynamics as well as deepening friendships at first unlikely to succeed. Karen Hesse's Newbery Award–winning *Out of the Dust,* with its similar style and setting, Cora Taylor's *Julie,* with its farm setting as well as a protagonist who must learn to deal with her own gifts and challenges, and Sharon Creech's *Love That Dog*—another verse novel—are three other connected titles. Colleen Sydor and Nicolas Debon's *Timmerman Was Here* is a picture book with a number of commonalities, relating the story of a young girl's relationship with a new boarder. Barbara Nickel's poetry collection *From the Top of a Grain Elevator* would also make a great companion read.

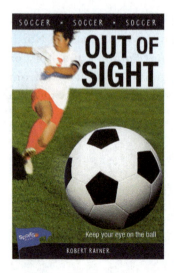

Rayner, R. (2011). *Out of sight*. Toronto, ON: James Lorimer.

Linh-Mai, a keen Grade 7 soccer player, finds out she requires glasses, but since they're shatter proof, she's allowed to stay on the team. Their goalkeeper, Brian, is not so lucky. He is eventually diagnosed with Leber's Disease, from which he will become legally blind. For ages 10 and up.

Description: realistic fiction; themes involve the importance of winning, and developing friendships, as well as how people are more than a single story.

Read-ons: Jean Little's *From Anna* also explores a character with a vision impairment.

Rivers, K. (2012). *The encyclopedia of me*. New York, NY: Arthur A. Levine Books.

Tink Aaron-Martin is a 12-year-old girl with twin older brothers, one of whom has autism. Family life revolves around Seb until an intervention promotes balance and safety. For ages 10 and up.

Description: realistic fiction; themes include humour and coming of age.

Read-ons: Susin Nielsen's *Word Nerd* has a similar affinity for language, as does Doris in Nancy Belgue's *Summer on the Run*. Comparisons to Tink's comic voice can be found in the short story anthology *Opening Tricks* edited by Peter Carver.

Rud, J. (2008). *Paralyzed*. Victoria, BC: Orca Books.

Reggie is a middle linebacker who's involved in controversy when an opposing player suffers an accidental spinal cord injury. Although a hearing finds him innocent of any wrongdoing, Reggie is plagued by memories, and the resulting anxiety requires the help of a therapist as well as a confession from his father, who has also experienced anxiety issues in the past. While Nate seems to be making a full recovery, this title introduces an important look at subjects all too common in contact sports. For ages 10 and up.

Description: realistic fiction; themes include father-son relationships and mental health.

Read-ons: Other titles in the Orca Sports series may provide good comparisons, as will Steven Sandor's *Replay*. Richard Brignall's *China Clipper: Pro Football's First Chinese-Canadian Player, Normie Kwong*, is a worthy non-fiction read about football, as is John Danakas's *Choice of Colours: The Pioneering African-American Quarterbacks Who Changed the Face of Football*.

Slade, A. (2009). *The hunchback assignments*. Toronto, ON: HarperCollins.

Fourteen-year-old Modo, a shape-shifting teen with a "hunchback," becomes a secret agent for the Permanent Association, battling the evil Clockwork Guild. An innovative title full of engaging adventure and humour. For ages 10 and up.

Description: steampunk fantasy; for themes, see next page.

Read-ons: See below.

Slade, A. (2010). *The dark deeps*. Toronto, ON: HarperCollins.

Secret agent Modo is back, this time to work with Octavia to uncover the underwater mystery of the Ictineo. For ages 10 and up.

Description: steampunk fantasy; for themes, see below.

Read-ons: See below.

Slade, A. (2011). *Empire of ruins*. Toronto, ON: HarperCollins.

Agents Modo and Octavia, along with Mr. Socrates, head to Queensland, Australia to discover the truth behind the God Face, competing with the evil Clockwork Guild. For ages 10 and up.

Description: steampunk fantasy; for themes, see below.

Read-ons: See below.

Slade, A. (2012). *The island of doom*. Toronto, ON: HarperCollins.

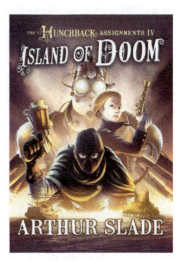

In this fourth and final book of the Hunchback Assignments steampunk series, an investigation takes agent Modo back to his origins. A theme that has carried throughout all four titles is the relationship between physical beauty and identity, with Modo continually searching for love and acceptance in spite of his "disfigured" face and body, a search that fuels his need to exchange one stereotypical mask for another in his repertoire of personas. Modo's intellect is clearly one quality that endears him to the people with whom he lives and works. This story is narrated from multiple third-person perspectives and is an energetic and complex adventure story. For ages 10 and up.

Description: steampunk; themes include perspectives on beauty, and good vs. evil.

Read-ons: Other books in the series include *The Hunchback Assignments*, *The Dark Deeps*, and *Empire of Ruins*. Another related title by Arthur Slade and

Christopher Steininger is the forthcoming graphic novel *Modo*. Other crime novels include Shane Peacock's *Becoming Holmes*, and Tim Wynne-Jones' *Blink & Caution*.

Spring, D. (2008). *Breathing soccer.* Saskatoon, SK: Thistledown Press.

Through a series of health challenges, Lisa learns to cope with her asthma while at the same time enjoying life—sports in particular. For ages 10 and up.

Description: realistic fiction; themes include developing friendships, family relationships, and dealing with health challenges.

Read-ons: other titles about soccer for this age range include Sarah Dann's non-fiction *Play Like a Pro: Soccer Skills and Drills* as well as Liam O'Donnell and Mike Deas' graphic novel *Soccer Sabotage: A Graphic Guide Adventure*.

Waldman, D. (2011). *Addy's race.* Victoria, BC: Orca Book Publishers.

Addy, a girl with a hearing impairment, navigates discord with a new classmate who has an even more profound hearing loss, while training for long-distance running.

Description: realistic fiction; themes include developing friendships and identity.

Read-ons: Eric Walters's *Run* is a fictionalized story about Terry Fox, and the inclusion of long-distance running as well as overcoming stereotypes will make it a good companion read for *Addy's Race*. For ages 10 and up.

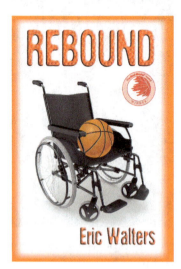

Walters, E. (2000). *Rebound.* Toronto, ON: Stoddart Kids.

Sean is a Grade 8 kid who is trying to rise above all the trouble he caused at school last year. His new friend, David, gives him some pointers about getting along with girls as well as basketball skills, and, in return, Sean learns to listen to David about his wheelchair use and his hopes of a complete recovery someday from the accident that paralyzed him. For ages 10 and up.

Description: realistic fiction; themes include living with disability and making choices.

Read-ons: Don Trembath's *Frog Face and the Three Boys* is also about kids who are trying to make positive behavioural choices. Diana Wieler's *Last Chance Summer* is a good stepping-stone into more literary reading, as it deals with similar issues through more in-depth characterization. Beth Goobie's *Kicked Out* offers another look at societal response to disability.

Walters, E. (2003). *Run*. Toronto, ON: Penguin Books.

It's 1980, and Terry Fox is undertaking his selfless act of running across Canada after an amputation due to cancer. This fictionalized account of the Terry Fox story brings details to readers through the voice of 14-year-old Winston MacDonald, its first-person narrator. Winston, a troubled teen, travels to Nova Scotia with his distant journalist father, and spends time with Terry Fox and Doug Alward during the Marathon of Hope. For ages 11 and up.

Description: historical fiction; themes include father-son relationships and the power of heroes.

Read-ons: Richard Scrimger's *The Nose from Jupiter* offers a zany look at a boy of a similar age with parents strikingly similar to Winston's, solving life's problems in an alternative way. *Run, Billy, Run* by Matt Christopher is another title about a boy who uses running to improve his life, and Katherine Paterson's *Bridge to Terabithia* includes a character that takes pride in his speed and endurance and who uses running as a way to gain respect. *Rebound*, also by Eric Walters, explores another perspective on physical disability. Titles that deal with imaginary friends include Lesley Choyce's *Smoke and Mirrors* and Deborah Ellis's *Looking for X*.

Walters, E. (2005). *Elixir*. Toronto, ON: Penguin Books.

The setting of this historical fiction novel is the Institute of Biological Research, University of Toronto, in the summer of 1921. The story traces events regarding Banting and Best's discovery of insulin through the first-person narration of Ruthie, a fictional 12-year-old girl who spends time at the Institute while her mother works there as a cleaning lady. Ruthie pities the experimental dogs, and joins demonstrators in hatching a plan for their release. A chance meeting with Emma, a young girl with diabetes, offers Ruthie another perspective, and then Ruthie has a decision to make. While Emma's character is a minor one, she has a powerful and heroic role to play within the context of this book and her cameo is evocative of a time and place before the treatment of diabetes. For ages nine and up.

Description: historical fiction; themes involve the ethics of science and animal rights.

Read-ons: Jerry Spinelli's *Wringer,* and *Crow Medicine*, the second in the "Wildlife Rescue" series by Diane Haynes, offer alternate perspectives on animal rights. Marsha Skrypuch's *The Hunger* offers two other perspectives on characters and weight loss.

Walters, E. (2009). *Special Edward*. Victoria, BC: Orca Books.

Edward is looking for a way to improve his high school grades without working, and he thinks a special education label might be the answer. The results are surprising; not only does he achieve this goal, he discovers that he actually does have some special learning needs, after all, that he has been hiding from his parents and teachers as well as from himself. For ages 11 and up.

Description: realistic fiction with a grade 3.5 reading level consistent with the Orca Soundings imprint; themes include acceptance of diversity.

Read-ons: Valerie Sherrard's *Speechless* provides another perspective on high school identity with a protagonist who attempts to escape an oratory assignment through a "protest of silence" that eventually helps him find his true voice. René Schmidt's *Leaving Fletchville* portrays a main character with similarly disruptive characteristics at school who also changes his behaviour through the course of the novel.

Watson, J. (2013). *Prove it, Josh*. Winlaw, BC: Sono Nis Press.

Josh is an 11-year-old boy with dyslexia who has recently come to live with his dad in Arbutus Bay, BC. Josh is struggling in school and ridiculed by classmates. Skills in sailing connect him to another newcomer to Vancouver Island, and the two compete in a race with high stakes, thanks to a bet Josh has made with a mean classmate; if Josh loses the race, he will have to read aloud at a Literacy Day library event. Thanks to a new friend who's had experience supporting a family member with a reading disability, Josh makes progress, and the book in all aspects feels like an authentic picture of reading challenges and support as well as a fast-paced sailing story about bravery and the sea. For ages nine and up.

Description: Realistic fiction; themes include facing challenges, courage, and developing friendships.

Read-ons: Billy in Bev Brenna's *The Moon Children* is also a grade five non-reader. Helen Ward's illustrated book *The Boat* deals with another kind of water rescue, and Robin Stevenson's *Dead in the Water* is another fast-paced sailing adventure, as are Curtis Parkinson's two novels *Storm-Blast* and *Sea Chase*. Lynn Manuel's *The Summer of the Marco Polo* is an additional title featuring a ship, albeit on the east coast.

Read-on Bibliography

Aksomitis, L. (2007). *Run*. Toronto, ON: Viking Canada/Penguin Group.
Babbitt, N. (1975). *Tuck everlasting*. New York, NY: Farrar, Straus, Giroux.

Bates, S.S. (2013). *Thunder Creek Ranch*. Victoria, BC: Orca.
Belgue, N. (2005). *Summer on the run*. Victoria, BC: Orca.
Bell, W. (2003). *Alma*. Toronto, ON: Doubleday.
Berg, E. (1997). *Joy School*. New York, NY: Random House.
Bow, E. (2010). *Plain Kate*. New York, NY: A. Levine/Scholastic Canada.
Brenna, B. (1999). *The keeper of the trees*. Vancouver, BC: Ronsdale Press.
Brenna, B. (2007). *The moon children*. Calgary, AB: Red Deer Press.
Brignall, R. (2010). *China clipper: Pro football's first Chinese-Canadian player, Normie Kwong*. Toronto, ON: James Lorimer.
Burnett, F.H. (1987). *The secret garden*. New York, NY: HarperCollins.
Butcher, K. (2001). *The gramma war*. Victoria, BC: Orca.
Byars, B. (1973). *The 18th emergency*. New York, NY: Viking.
Byars, B. (1977). *The pinballs*. New York, NY: Harper & Row.
Cameron, A. (1985). *How Raven freed the moon*. Madiera Park, BC: Harbour Publishing.
Carter, A.L. (2001). *In the clear*. Victoria, BC: Orca.
Carver, P. (Ed.). (1998). *Opening tricks*. Saskatoon, SK: Thistledown Press.
Choyce, L. (2004). *Smoke and mirrors*. Toronto, ON: Boardwalk/Dundurn Press.
Christopher, M. (1980). *Run, Billy, run*. Boston, MA: Little, Brown.
Citra, B. (2011). *Missing*. Victoria, BC: Orca.
Creech, S. (2001). *Love that dog*. New York, NY: HarperCollins.
Curtis, C.P. (2007). *Elijah of Buxton*. Toronto, ON: Scholastic Canada.
Dahl, R. (1981). *The twits*. New York, NY: Knopf.
Danakas, J. (2007). *Choice of colours: The pioneering African-American quarterbacks who changed the face of football*. Toronto, ON: James Lorimer.
Dann, S. (2013). *Play like a pro: Soccer skills and drills*. St. Catharines, ON: Crabtree.
de Vries, M. (2011). *Somebody's girl*. Victoria, BC: Orca.
di Camillo, K. (2001). *The tiger rising*. Cambridge, MA: Candlewick.
Donovan, L. (2007). *Winds of L'Acadie*. Vancouver, BC: Ronsdale Press.
Dorsey, A. (2004). *A horse called Freedom*. Markham, ON: Scholastic Canada.
Draper, P. (2006). *Terror at Turtle Mountain*. Regina, SK: Coteau Books.
Draper, S. (2010). *Out of my mind*. New York, NY: Atheneum.
Dyer, K.C. (2007). *Ms. Zephyr's notebook*. Toronto, ON: Boardwalk Books/Dundurn Press.
Ellis, D. (1999). *Looking for X*. Toronto, ON: Groundwood Books/Douglas & McIntyre.
Ellis, S. (1991). *Pick-up sticks*. Toronto, ON: Groundwood/Douglas & McIntyre.
Ellis, S. (2006). *Odd man out*. Toronto, ON: Groundwood/House of Anansi.
Fairbridge, L. (2000). *Tangled in time*. Vancouver, BC: Ronsdale Press.
Frizzell, C. (2006). *Chill*. Victoria, BC: Orca.
Funk, C. (2003). *Inkheart*. New York, NY: The Chicken House/Scholastic Canada.
Gantos, J. (1998). *Joey Pigza swallowed the key*. New York, NY: Farrar, Straus and Giroux.
Glaze, D. (2009). *Danger in Dead Man's Mine*. Regina, SK: Coteau Books.
Goobie, B. (2002). *Kicked out*. Victoria, BC: Orca Books.

Haddix, M.P. (1999). *Just Ella.* New York, NY: Simon & Schuster.

Hahn, M.D. (1996). *Following my own footsteps.* New York, NY: Avon/Camelot.

Hancock, P. (2003). *Haunted Canada: True ghost stories.* Markham, ON: Scholastic Canada.

Harvey-Fitzhenry, A. (2008). *Broken.* Vancouver, BC: Tradewind.

Haworth-Attard, B. (2001). *Flying geese.* Toronto, ON: HarperCollins.

Haynes, D. (2006). *Crow medicine.* (Jane Ray's Wildlife Rescue Series, 2). North Vancouver, BC: Walrus Books/Whitecap Books.

Hesse, K. (1997). *Out of the dust.* New York, NY: Scholastic.

Holeman, L. (2002). *Search of the moon king's daughter.* Toronto, ON: Tundra Books.

Holman, F. (1974). *Slake's limbo.* New York, NY: Aladdin.

Hopkinson, D. (1993). *Sweet Clara and the freedom quilt.* New York, NY: Knopf.

Hughes, M. (1981/2000). *The guardian of Isis.* Toronto, ON: Tundra Books.

Hunter, B.T. (1984). *A place for Margaret.* Toronto, ON: Scholastic Canada.

Hunter, M. (1975). *A stranger came ashore.* New York, NY: Harper Trophy.

Huser, G. (2003). *Stitches.* Toronto, ON: Groundwood.

Huser, G. (2006). *Skinnybones and the wrinkle queen.* Toronto, ON: Groundwood/ House of Anansi.

Jennings, S. (2003). *Home free.* Toronto, ON: Penguin Canada.

Johnston, J. (1992). *Hero of lesser causes.* Toronto, ON: Lester Publishing.

Johnston, J. (1994). *Adam and Eve and Pinch-Me.* Toronto, ON: Lester Publishing.

Johnston, J. (2006). *A very fine line.* Toronto, ON: Tundra.

Kent, T. (2009). *Medina Hill.* Toronto, ON: Tundra Books.

Kim, S., & Klavan, L. (2010). *Brain camp.* New York, NY: First Second.

Korman, G. (1985/2012). *A semester in the life of a garbage bag.* Toronto, ON: Scholastic Canada.

Kositsky, L. (2000). *A question of Will.* Montreal, PQ: Roussan.

Krill, D. (2006). *The Uncle Duncle chronicles: Escape from Treasure Island.* Montreal, PQ: Lobster Press.

Lawrence, I. (2000). *Ghost boy.* New York, NY: Dell Laurel-Leaf/Random House Canada.

Lawrence, I. (2011). *The winter pony.* New York, NY: Delacorte Press/Random House Canada.

Leavitt, M. (2004). *Heck, superhero.* Calgary, AB: Red Deer Press.

Lesynski, L. (2013). *Crazy about basketball.* Toronto, ON: Annick Press.

Linden, D. (2008). *Shimmerdogs.* Saskatoon, SK: Thistledown Press.

Little, J. (1986). *Different dragons.* Markham, ON: Viking Kestrel.

Little, J. (1997/2008). *The belonging place.* Toronto, ON: Puffin Canada.

Little, J. (2007). *Dancing through the snow.* Toronto, ON: Scholastic Canada.

Little, J. (2012). *From Anna.* Toronto, ON: Scholastic Canada.

Lohans, A. (1999). *No place for kids.* Montreal: Roussin.

Lord, C. (2006). *Rules.* New York, NY: Scholastic.

Lowry, L. (2000). *Gathering blue.* Boston, MA: Houghton Mifflin.

Lunn, J. (1994). *The root cellar.* Toronto, ON: Lester Publishing.

Maes, N. (2009). *Laughing wolf.* Toronto, ON: Dundurn Press.
Maguire, G. (1994). *Missing sisters.* New York, NY: Harper.
Manuel, L. (2007). *The summer of the Marco Polo.* Victoria, BC: Orca.
Matas, C. (1997/2007). *The freak.* Toronto, ON: Key Porter.
Matas, C., & Nodelman, P. (2008). *The proof that ghosts exist.* Toronto, ON: Key Porter Books.
Mazer, N.F. (2007). *Ten ways to make my sister disappear.* New York, NY: Scholastic.
McNicoll, S. (1994). *Bringing up beauty.* Toronto, ON: Stoddart Kids.
Melting, O.R. (1983). *The druid's tune.* Markham, ON: Puffin Books.
Montgomery, L.M. (1908/2000). *Anne of Green Gables.* Toronto, ON: Tundra Books.
Nancy, T.L. (1997). *Letters from a nut.* New York, NY: Spike/Avon Books.
Narsimhan, M. (2007). *The third eye.* Toronto, ON: Dundurn Press.
Nickel, B. (1999). *From the top of a grain elevator.* Vancouver, BC: Beach Holme.
Nickel, B. (2005). *Hannah Waters and the daughter of Johann Sebastian Bach.* Toronto, ON: Penguin.
Nielsen, J.A. (2012). *The false prince.* New York, NY: Scholastic.
Nielsen, S. (2008). *Word nerd.* Toronto, ON: Tundra Books.
Nielsen, S. (2010). *Dear George Clooney: Please marry my mom.* Toronto, ON: Tundra.
Nugent, C. (2004). *Francesca and the magic bike.* Vancouver, BC: Raincoast Books.
O'Donnell, L. (2008). *Ramp rats: A graphic guide adventure.* Victoria, BC: Orca.
O'Donnell, L., & Deas, M. (2009). *Soccer sabotage: A graphic guide adventure.* Victoria, BC: Orca.
Parkinson, C. (2003). *Storm-blast.* Toronto, ON: Tundra Books.
Parkinson, C. (2004). *Sea chase.* Toronto, ON: Tundra Books.
Paterson, K. (1977). *Bridge to Terabithia.* New York, NY: HarperTrophy.
Paterson, K. (1978). *The great Gilly Hopkins.* New York, NY: Crowell.
Patron, S. (2006). *The higher power of lucky.* New York, NY: Atheneum.
Peacock, S. (2012). *Becoming Holmes.* Toronto, ON: Tundra Books.
Pearson, K. (1996/2007). *Awake and dreaming.* Toronto, ON: Viking Books.
Porter, P. (2005). *The crazy man.* Toronto, ON: Groundwood Books.
Razzell, M. (1999). *Smuggler's moon.* Toronto, ON: Douglas & McIntyre/ Groundwood.
Revelle, R. (2013). *I am Algonquin.* Toronto, ON: Dundurn.
Saigeon, L. (2009). *Fight for justice.* Regina, SK: Coteau Books.
Sandor, S. (2013). *Replay.* Toronto, ON: James Lorimer & Co.
Schmidt, R. (2008). *Leaving Fletchville.* Victoria, BC: Orca Books.
Schwartz, V.F. (2003). *Initiation.* Markham, ON: Fitzhenry & Whiteside.
Scrimger, R. (1998). *The nose from Jupiter.* Toronto, ON: Tundra Books.
Sedgwick, M. (2001). *Floodland.* New York, NY: Delacorte Press.
Selznik, B. (2007). *The invention of Hugo Cabret.* New York, NY: Scholastic Press (Distributed in Canada by Scholastic Canada).
Sewell, A. (2001). *Black Beauty.* New York, NY: Scholastic. (Original work published 1877).

Sherrard, V. (2007). *Speechless*. Toronto, ON: Boardwalk Book/Dundurn Press.
Silverthorne, J. (1996). *The secret of Sentinel Rock*. Regina, SK: Coteau Books.
Silverthorne, J. (2005). *The secret of the stone house*. Regina, SK: Coteau Books.
Skrypuch, M. (1999). *The hunger*. Toronto, ON: Boardwalk Books.
Slade, A. (2008). *Jolted: Newton Starker's rules for survival*. Toronto, ON: HarperTrophy Canada.
Slade, A. (2009). *The hunchback assignments*. Toronto, ON: HarperCollins.
Slade, A. (2010). *The dark deeps: The hunchback assignments II*. Toronto, ON: HarperCollins.
Slade, A. (2011). *Empire of ruins*. Toronto, ON: HarperCollins Canada.
Slade, A., & Steininger, C. (pending publication) *Modo*. Toronto, ON: HarperCollins.
Snicket, L. (1999). *The bad beginning*. New York, NY: HarperCollins.
Spinelli, J. (1997). *Wringer*. New York, NY: HarperCollins.
Spyri, J. (1994). *Heidi*. (E. Hall, Trans.). London: Puffin Books. (Original work published 1880).
Stenhouse, T. (2001). *Across the Steel River*. Toronto, ON: Kids Can Press.
Stevenson, R. (2008). *Dead in the water*. Victoria, BC: Orca.
Stevenson, R. (2008). *Impossible things*. Victoria, BC: Orca.
Sydor, C., & Debon, N. (2009). *Timmerman was here*. Toronto, ON: Tundra Books.
Taylor, C. (1985). *Julie*. Saskatoon, SK: Western Producer Prairie Books.
Toews, M. (2004). *A complicated kindness*. Toronto, ON: Vintage Canada.
Trembath, D. (1997). *A fly named Alfred*. Victoria, BC: Orca.
Trembath, D. (2000). *Frog face and the three boys*. Victoria, BC: Orca.
Trottier, M. (2009). *Blood upon our land: The North West resistance diary of Josephine Bouvier*. Toronto, ON: Scholastic.
Walsh, A. (2006). *A sky black with crows*. Calgary, AB: Red Deer Press.
Walters, E. (1999). *Three on three*. Victoria, BC: Orca.
Walters, E. (2000). *Rebound*. Toronto, ON: Stoddart Kids.
Walters, E. (2003). *Run*. Toronto, ON: Viking Canada/Penguin Group Canada.
Walters, E., Williams, J., & Williams J. III. (2007). *Boot camp*. Victoria, BC: Orca.
Ward, H., & Andrew, I. (2005). *The boat*. Vancouver, BC: Simply Read Books.
White, S. (2013). *The sewing basket*. Charlottetown, PE: Acorn Press.
Wieler, D. (1986). *Last chance summer*. Saskatoon, SK: Western Producer Prairie Books.
Winthrow, S. (1998). *Bat summer*. Toronto, ON: Groundwood Books/Douglas & McIntyre.
Wishinsky, F. (2005). *Queen of the toilet bowl*. Victoria, BC: Orca.
Withers, P. (2005). *Camp Wild*. Victoria, BC: Orca.
Wrede, P.C. (2009). *Thirteenth child*. New York, NY: Scholastic.
Wynne-Jones, T. (1998). *Stephen Fair*. Toronto, ON: Groundwood/Douglas & McIntyre.
Wynne-Jones, T. (2011). *Blink & caution*. Sommerville, MA: Candlewick Press/Random House of Canada.
Zindel, P. (1968). *The pigman*. New York, NY: Harper & Row.

Three Essential Questions for This Chapter

1. Consider the following genres: realistic fiction, fantasy, historical fiction, steampunk, magic realism. Which is your favourite, or if not favourite, the one you most commonly read? Why? Which is the one you least commonly read? Why?
2. Describe books that you think fit Dresang's (1999) categories related to the evolution of books for young people in terms of changing forms and formats, changing perspectives, and changing boundaries. Consult a bibliography of Pamela Porter (such as www.umanitoba.ca/cm/profiles/porter.html) and identify books of hers that seem to fit these categories.
3. Select an intermediate novel that is new to you from the annotated bibliography. After you read it, list at least four age-appropriate response activities in the following categories that students could do that are related to the book: drama; art; creative writing; and music.

CHAPTER 6

Contemporary Canadian Young Adult Novels

Introduction to Young Adult Novels in Canada

Radical Change in Action

This chapter spotlights young adult novels for ages 12 and up. These books appear in a field where particular aspects of Radical Change are at work, moving serious subject matter further and further into central operations. As far as range, the young adult category contains titles such as Bobet's (2012) *Above*, a dystopian fantasy that includes a transgender character—unusual even in contemporary young adult fiction—although the political subject matter of *Above* does reflect other young adult titles in the field, including books like American author M.T. Anderson's (2002) *Feed*.

Bookstores have risen to the challenge of flagging edgy content by developing specific sections in addition to young adult shelves, and advertising those sections with definitive slogans such as McNally Robinson's shifting section of "PG 15s: Books for Older Teens." These are books with characters facing real world, serious challenges, and not all of them have happy endings. In addition to Canadian authors who deal with authentic and gritty subject matter for teens, crossover texts appear that extend material between adult and young adult audiences, elevating available subject matter into even more mature content. Elaine M. Will's (2013) graphic novel *Look Straight Ahead*, although not included in the annotated bibliography of this chapter because it is not specifically marketed to young adults, is clearly within both YA and adult territory with its focus on mental illness through a 17-year-old protagonist.

In a time when a wealth of everyday drama is available on the Internet, it is possible that teen readers will insist on more serious types of realism in their fictive worlds. However, it's also possible that agents, publishers, and booksellers are simply catering to a perception that particular texts sell more copies. More research in this area is important to pinpoint what Canadian young people are reading and want to read.

Patterns and Trends

When undergraduate students were asked to read the set of novels portraying characters with disabilities included in the annotated bibliography later in this chapter, their response indicated how as a whole these titles are serious and heavy, invoking reader sympathy but also—particularly where the mature themes involve abuse—a devastating sense of the difficulty of particular lived lives. Select books in the group were welcomed for even minor aspects of comic relief, and definitely for the kinds of hopefulness that certain authors conveyed. Susan Ketchen's (2012) *Grows That Way* was one such title, and one of the undergraduate research assistants who read these books as part of preparing this text emphasized her enjoyment of the sections on the Sasquatch that inhabited Ketchen's novel.

Fifty-three titles are spotlighted in this chapter as young adult novels containing characters with disabilities. It is interesting how the numbers of novels grow steadily from one age category to the other in this volume, with 10 junior novels located for this text, 50 intermediate novels, and 53 young adult novels. Almost all of the 53 young adult titles emerge in the genre of realistic fiction, with only a handful of fantasy, magic realism, and historical fiction titles, consistent with the other novels about characters with disabilities under scrutiny here. Even more pronounced in comparison with the group of intermediate novels is the discrepancy between books published from 1995 to 2004, and 2005 to 2014. The young adult novels offer a ratio of 10 to 43, favouring the last 10 years, where the intermediate novels count in at 16 to 34. Clearly Radical Change (Dresang, 1999) is at work here in terms of moving young adult fiction into print much faster than in years past, portraying voices previously unheard in terms of disability topics.

Another striking detail in the group of 53 young adult titles is the number of high interest–low vocabulary resources that are included. A half-dozen titles specified "hi-lo" vocabulary, while others appear in a range from easier to harder reading levels. It is possible that where particular disabilities are included in characterizations, authors and publishers consider that students with reading challenges may require easier material in terms of accessing age-appropriate content. For example, Paul Kropp's (2004) *Against All Odds*, involving a brother who has an intellectual disability, is written at about a grade 3.4 reading level, according to Kropp's website (http://www.paulkropp.com/highint.html).

As noted in the group of intermediate-age novels, particular disabilities included in this group for young adult readers cover the range of disabilities listed by Smith, Polloway, Patton, Dowdy, and Heath (2001), who identify that, in Canada, categories of exceptionality addressed by funding include "learning disabilities, speech or language impairments, intellectual disabilities, emotional/behavioral disorders, multiple disabilities, auditory impairments, orthopedic impairments, other health impairments, visual impairments, autism ... and traumatic brain injury" (p. 7). In this group of novels, however, there is scant coverage of characters with multiple dissabilities.

Particular syndromes noted in the YA group add a kind of authenticity to various titles, and these include Turner's syndrome in the trilogy by Susan Ketchen, concluding with *Grows That Way* (2012), and Van der Woude syndrome, in Richard Scarsbrook's *The Monkeyface Chronicles* (2010), books included in the annotated bibliography in this chapter.

Interesting trends within the group of YA books involve the appearance of wheelchairs when physical disability is included. In terms of physical disability, very few exemplifying features other than wheelchairs have been envisioned to represent difference. A close examination of the depiction of the characters who use wheelchairs might offer a range of possibilities in terms of characters' agency related to wheelchair use, and inspire thought regarding their inclusion. Are the wheelchairs introduced as "agents of restriction and imprisonment, instead of as tools of transport and freedom" (Minaki, 2011, p. 75)? This would be a critical point for young readers to ponder. Rainey's character in *Tripping* (Waldorf, 2008)—another book included in the annotated bibliography—has a prosthetic leg, appearing unique alongside other characters in this set.

In addition to problematizing the propensity of wheelchair use when depicting physical disability, there are also two other trends of note. One involves the high percentage of characters in this set with eating disorders—at least nine, at last count— equivalent to the numbers of characters using wheelchairs, if minor characters are included. Also worth discussion is that all of the characters with eating disorders are female. One other trend relates to mental illness, where at least 10 characters are depicted with challenges in this regard.

As with books in the other categories, in addition to the lack of attention to multiple disabilities, character portrayals also use disability as a rather exclusive form of difference, with authors somehow reluctant to characterize anyone with a disability as part of a minority cultural group or presenting LGBT characteristics. It is predicted that as radical changes continue to affect the evolution of children's literature, readers will discover more titles appearing that blend categories of difference.

It is possible that authors themselves, noting trends in the field, will conceive material to fill some of the evident gaps. This was the case as I developed my own trilogy of books about Taylor Jane Simon, a fictional character with autism spectrum disorder, in whose actualization I responded to particular trends I had noted. More about Taylor's conception appears in the author portrait that follows in this chapter, drawn from my doctoral dissertation (Brenna, 2010b).

Author Portrait: Beverley Brenna

As a classroom and special education teacher engaged with populations of children and young adults who were vibrant and interesting, I began to notice how few classroom resources mirrored the young people I knew who had disabilities.

After some initial and relatively futile searches for titles, and Canadian titles in particular, I determined a path toward doctoral research in this area. At the same time, I began crafting the characterization of Taylor Jane, a teen with autism spectrum disorder who would appear as the central character in my Wild Orchid trilogy.

After writing the first book of the Wild Orchid series, intended to be a standalone novel, I began to consider a novel related to a character with Fetal Alcohol Spectrum Disorder (FASD), as I had not ever seen FASD in any fictional portrayal at all. Following the completion of *The Moon Children* (Brenna, 2007), I returned to Taylor and completed the second book in the series (*Waiting for No One*—winner of a 2012 Dolly Gray Award), and then, after another break looking at a character with post-traumatic stress syndrome in my historical novel *Falling for Henry* (Brenna, 2011), I returned to Taylor for *The White Bicycle* (Brenna, 2012b), winner of a 2013 Printz Honour Award and shortlisted for a 2013 Governor General's Award. These titles contribute to my previous body of work involving character-driven novels for junior, intermediate, and young adult readers.

Writing Process

I tend to explore characters from the margins of what I see presented in literature, attempting to fill in gaps. One of my favourite manuscripts is *The Moon Children* because its depiction of someone with FASD is rare and, I think, necessary if we are to have broad and productive conversations about a spectrum disorder that is preventable but woven in complicated ways into the fabric of our society. At the time I was doing my research, few community resources were available to elicit discussions of this condition outside the traditional medical model. The children I worked with were complex and different from each other, and yet had challenges similar to those faced by other children—challenges related to acceptance and support of their unique profiles—but had the added burden of negative stigma associated with their biological mothers. Literary depictions of characters with FASD seemed much more rare than depictions of characters with autism, a trend I explored in a later study with three graduate students (Barker, Kulyk, Knorr, & Brenna, 2011).

Acceptance and Inclusion

The medical model didn't seem to be affecting either acceptance or inclusion related to further support for students in the teaching context within which I was working, nor did it assist with positive parental engagement, as the stigma for biological mothers of children with FASD was very evident. Also, dishearteningly, over the years that I worked in special education, I didn't see the medical model as a solution related to prevention of FASD. I wondered whether a model based on the arts could help in terms of these positive outcomes. My first conception involved some sort of travelling gallery containing artistic representations of FASD that could visit communities to elicit conversations about various aspects of FASD that weren't in the public consciousness. In addition to assisting with additional support for the population of people with FASD and their families, could such a gallery—Faces of FASD, I thought it could be called—affect prevention? Not an artist myself, this idea, alluring as it was, slowly faded.

What replaced the idea of a travelling gallery was the notion of a children's novel—accessible to adult readers as well as children—featuring FASD and including a non-negative depiction of a biological mother whose son was affected by prenatal alcohol use within a complex family context where a father was encouraging alcohol at the same time as the pregnancy was developing. It took some research, and a lot of time, but when I finished the manuscript that would become my novel *The Moon Children*, I hoped it would be a good story and, in addition, I hoped it might support kids and families now and in the future.

Counterstories and Social Justice

When I first encountered Lindemann Nelson's (1995) conceptualization of a counterstory—a narrative that is created in opposition to the status quo—I was captivated. This seemed to me to be what had driven much of my artistic work for so many years. In *Something to Hang On To* (Brenna, 2009), a collection of a dozen short stories for teens, I had deliberately tried to offer voices to characters I had perceived to be silent in available literature. Thus I included narratives about characters who have Down syndrome, pervasive developmental disorder, and cerebral palsy, in addition to a cameo of the character of Taylor Jane, a teenager with Asperger's syndrome who appears as the protagonist in my trilogy of young adult novels.

One of the decisions I made in the books about Taylor Jane was to concentrate on filling a gap in literature regarding characters who are differently abled, as from my research I had learned that these characters don't often travel beyond their home community. In my trilogy, Taylor spends time at Waskesiu—Saskatchewan's national park—then Cody, Wyoming, and then Lourmarin, France. The latter setting was achieved in part due to financial support from a Canada Council grant that allowed me research funding in order to travel to France during the book's conceptualization.

At the time I was conceptualizing Taylor Jane for *Wild Orchid*, I was also thinking about the need for research into Canadian literature for young people. In particular, I wondered what fiction was available that portrayed characters with disabilities, and what this fiction might offer in terms of patterns and trends. What began as a small-scale search as part of a project I designed for a local school division extended into a doctoral research project at the University of Alberta, where I completed my PhD in 2010. It was here that I first began to envision how fiction could forward social justice ideals into practical settings through critical literacy frameworks. The remaining sections of this chapter, adapted from my graduate research (Brenna, 2010b), further identify underpinnings in my own background that have inspired my writing and my teaching.

The Power of Stories

In her book *The Kindness of Children*, Vivian Paley (1999) narrates a story about Teddy, a child with disabilities with whom she worked in the context of a group of London schoolchildren. In the anecdote, Teddy's classmates welcome him into their imaginary play, despite the reluctance of a teacher to let him participate, and all the children blossom from the opportunity. Paley relates "the Teddy story" for other children, who offer connected tales of impulsive kindness, and then Paley retells Teddy's story in her own personal narrative, connecting its themes to her elderly mother, whose experiences as a frightened immigrant child illuminate the beauty and importance of finding a friend. Paley's narrative inquiry demonstrates how stories can affect personal identity, in the composing, the telling, the retelling, and the listening. I, too, have been affected by stories. I believe that through the framework of stories—as listeners, storytellers, authors, students, and educators—we truly can change each other and the world.

What from my early landscapes caused me to consider issues of disability, identity, and inclusion? How has this consideration been reflective of my evolution as a teacher? What assisted me in translating insights toward the context of book characters? I sift back through early experiences, searching for elements that outline and colour my conceptualization of identity and disability. Many of my first memories focus on stories told by my mother, a prairie girl born in 1916 on a mixed farm near Indian Head, Saskatchewan. Her stories weave around my current thoughts on teaching and writing, clearly providing threads of wisdom that have bound together my two occupations. In the sections that follow, I have presented narratives from my life as a daughter and teacher, inviting introspection into the events that have informed my work, and, in particular, influenced the social constructions of disability that relate to my classroom landscape as well as my published stories on behalf of lived texts.

My Mother's Stories

Many of the stories my mother told me as a child underpin my work as a teacher. These are narratives about the 1920s farming community in which she grew up, her experiences as a child in one-room schoolhouses, and later, stories about her own teaching, about the dilemmas she faced with students and their parents and the new communities she adopted as her own. Within the landscape of my mother's stories about school (Brenna, 2008), I continue to search for foundations to support my own developing landscapes.

When I last spoke with her about what it was like for me as a teacher in schools, my 92-year-old mother shook her head. She told me that she had never encountered children like those I described in "modern" classrooms—kids whose behaviour is at times completely unmanageable by "traditional" school practices. Her classroom landscape of the mid-1930s and early 1940s supported "pale, malnourished depression kids whose lips trembled if the teacher even glanced their way" (personal communication, September, 2008). These children did not ask for control, but for reassurance. A teacher who took the time to think things through would find her way. "Not like how things are today," she said, biting her lip at the challenges I described with classroom management. Her stories, however, are powerful, resonating then and now. Her stories contained more wisdom than perhaps she was aware, and rest here in the upcoming pages as birds with wings.

Johnny and the Pear

This story comes to me from the past, reminding me of a time at home with my mother in our Saskatoon kitchen. I am sitting at the kitchen table waiting for lunch. I am five years old and I have just come home from kindergarten. My mother is mixing milk with the contents of a can of Campbell's mushroom soup and stirring it in a pot on the stove. She is telling me about how things were, when she was a child. "Tell another old one," I say, meaning one of the old-time stories. "Tell 'Johnny and the Pear.'"

> It is 1924 and my mother is a grade five student attending a one-room school in southern Saskatchewan. "Seven-year-old Johnny and his immigrant parents had just moved into the district, and the students were not being very receptive to him. On this particular day in September, a season when cases of peaches, pears, and plums were brought home from town to be preserved in glass jars for winter use, the girls are sitting under the shade of a caragana hedge, eating noon lunch. Mary opens her pail and gives a squeal of disappointment. On top of her sandwiches there is a piece of tissue paper, but the pear her mother had promised is missing. Immediately the students think of Johnny." (Brenna, 2008, p. 255)

As my mother relates the rest of the story, her voice is thick with regret. The students chase Johnny down the road. He runs until he cannot run anymore. Then he falls in the dirt. The students pounce. They assure him that if he admits to taking the pear, they'll let him go. Dutifully, he confesses. Someone runs and tells the teacher. Johnny is herded back into the school, where he receives the strap. It leaves red marks on his hands and wrists. That afternoon the room is uncomfortably quiet, except for Johnny's sobs, coming from the corner where he was asked to stand throughout that long autumn afternoon. The next morning, Mary has a secret. "My mother found the pear, forgotten, on the shelf at home," she says. But nobody told the teacher this news, and nobody spoke about it to Johnny.

I watch my mother carefully as she finishes the story and spoons soup into my bowl. Her nose is red, and her eyes are all watery. I smile. My mother is very predictable. Along with the soup, there is a Prem sandwich and rice pudding for dessert. I am hungry, and I eat. At the time, I am not aware how much this story will mean to me in my future classroom, where I am highly conscious of students like Johnny and Mary, their teacher, and their schoolmates, and where I am willing to do anything to prevent Johnny's situation from repeating. When I was five years old, I inherited this story, but it would take a few years until I inherited the emotions that accompanied it for my mother. When I retell this story now, my eyes automatically fill with tears, mirroring my mother's sentiments during her telling and retellings.

Old Jones

"Tell me another of the old ones," I demand. It's after lunch and my mother's naptime. I am almost six, and too big for naps, although my mother probably wishes I wasn't. I attend Grade 1, but today is a holiday. I want to be loud and play, but my mother is 51 years old and she needs to rest. "It is 1921," she tells me sleepily, taking me back with words to the farm near Indian Head where she and two siblings grew up. It is a work day, not Sunday, and she, not yet school age, is playing on tin-can stilts in the yard, when Old Jones, a "deaf-mute," strides up the road, dust on his clothes and on the hands he uses to gesture greetings and dispense dark chocolate. He'll stay a week and maybe two, helping Grandad with the chores, until the wind pushes him down the road toward the next farm.

"Didn't he have a home?" I ask, as I always do.

"Everyone's home was his home," says my mother. "There was no welfare relief, back then, for people who hadn't the means to live on their own."

I imagine what it would be like if Old Jones came to our door. He'd have to sleep on the couch in the living room, near the heat register, because we don't have a cot in the kitchen near a wood-burning stove.

From an early age, my mother's storytelling of these and other tales has added texture to my life, shading perspectives about diversity and respect for all people. Her story underpins my story, and in the beginning—before my story had amounted to much—her story was my story. My mother drifts off to sleep, and I play with plastic red bricks on the floor beside the bed. I begin to build a house, but it's boring. I creep onto the bed and jump. "Oof," says my mother, my weight on her chest pushing the air out of her lungs. Later, she would tell me that some days she was sure she was never going to be able to get up, that she would be found there by my father— smothered and solidly dead. But she would always be laughing when she said it.

Wild Horses

As I prepare to become a teacher by studying at the university, my mother's stories gain poignancy. She tells me about being 18 years old and attending Normal School in Regina. It is 1935. The $100 fee is an obstacle until her grandmother sends a cheque. Without the extra dollar for paints, my mother sits, flushed and empty-handed, in art class; finally, the instructor pulls her desk alongside a neighbour. "You'll have to share," the instructor snaps. At age 19, my mother graduates from Normal School, and in January of 1936, she heads to her first school, a hamlet near Estevan.

> The train passes brittle fields, gaunt livestock bracing themselves hunch-shouldered against the wind. As the train slows around a bend, she catches sight of a group of hollow-eyed horses pawing the ground for what could only be the most meagre sustenance. But when the train whistles, the animals—transformed—lift their heads and run, manes and tails flowing, sun gleaming on their shining sides. (Brenna, 2008, pp. 254–255)

The image of these animals became the inspiration for my mother's poem "Wild Horses," widely published in Copp-Clark's Grade VI Reader, *All Sails Set*. Her poem, and the context in which it was written, reminds me of the transformative power of fiction. In the words that follow, the skeletal horses have vanished, replaced forever with the vibrant creatures my mother wished them to remain.

Wild Horses

We saw them drink from a quiet stream
    As clear as their own dark eyes,
Their necks were arched in the sunlight's gleam,
    And they were beautiful as a dream
When they drank at dawn from a quiet stream
    As clear as their own dark eyes.

We saw them run on the open plains
    Untouched by the whip and spur,
The wind was soft in their tossing manes,
    The love of freedom was in their veins
As they ran for joy on the open plains,
    Untouched by the whip and spur.

We saw them stand on a hilltop high
    With nostrils wide to the breeze,
Their forms were graceful against the sky,
    And wild and beautiful was their cry
As they stood at eve on a hilltop high
    With nostrils wide to the breeze. (Smith, 1948)

Eddy

After a year of training, my mother is in charge of 20 children in Grades 1 to 8. She has not been given any special teaching strategies for students who might have challenges. There is an older boy at this school, Eddy, who has unique mannerisms and learning needs, a boy who, in a different period of diagnostic medicine, might have qualified for an autism diagnosis. A neighbour woman asks my mother how she is getting along with this student. "He's okay," she replies. "But sometimes he gets on my nerves." On Monday this boy is not at school, nor is he there on Tuesday. My mother telephones. Eddy's tearful parent says, "I heard what you said about my son," and then loudly hangs up the receiver. My mother walks a mile through the snow to the boy's farm. When Eddy's mother opens the door, my mother says, her lips trembling, "I'm very sorry. I did say that. When I'm tired, any of the children get on my nerves. I like your son, and I want him back at school." Difficult words to say, yet they bring the result my mother wishes. Eddy is back in class the next day. My mother's emotion in the telling and retelling of this tale is palpable.

My mother has learned an important lesson, and through her telling and retelling of this story, so have I. In adulthood, I cannot tell any of these stories without feeling the emotion my mother connected to them. And that is one of the legacies my mother has provided: not only do I have these intergenerational family stories, but I have also absorbed her emotional background that accompanies them. This has affected my teaching, in the way I think of my students as all necessary pieces of the classroom puzzle, and it has affected my writing in the choices I make regarding the characterization of people who have not typically been given voices in narrative.

My Teaching Stories

In my years as an elementary classroom teacher, I have countless memories of students who have taught me important lessons, reinforcing the adage that teachers learn as much, or more, than their students. I bring these memories out like polished stones, turn them over in my hands, letting their smooth contours carry me back to a time when I was ready to take the next step in my education. Two students whose stories intertwined powerfully with mine are Brianna and Dan.

Brianna

I was teaching in a primary classroom two afternoons per week. It was October, and I had grown used to the routine of expectations the regular classroom teacher placed upon me, and the expectations I placed on myself, in relation to our ongoing curriculum actualization. There was a child in the classroom, Brianna, who had multiple disabilities, and who had been assigned a teacher associate to assist with the delivery of her alternate program. How this had translated, in the afternoons I spent in the classroom, was that I would teach the rest of the class while "Shirley," a wonderful teacher's assistant in her mid-30s, would work with Brianna. On this particular fall day, I entered the classroom to see three students gathered around Brianna, and no Shirley.

On further investigation, I learned that Shirley was absent from school that afternoon, and no sub was available. I swallowed, panic rising in my throat. I had never actually worked with Brianna. She had always remained at the back of the classroom, with Shirley, and to be honest, I'd had only a minimal idea of what they did there together.

This day proved to be very important in my teaching career. I realized that, as a teacher, I had been acting as if one student in my classroom was not present. Tensions between my lived story and my mother's story cried out for attention. How could I believe in the importance of every learner, and at the same time operate as I had with respect to Brianna?

It was obvious that, in addition to not considering this learner, I had unthinkingly fallen into what was—unfortunately—common classroom practice at that time by allowing a paraprofessional complete jurisdiction in the program of a student with disabilities. And I had done so without paying attention to how such a decision fit with my own value system. I had considered neither my role as Brianna's teacher nor any subject matter with which to engage her in the context of the other students.

From that moment onward, I worked hard to change my position with Brianna and her classmates through the course of that school year, and I now make connections between this and my mother's wisdom with Eddy. My mother's persistence in engaging Eddy's mother toward his return to school demonstrates her belief that all students have the right to be viewed as learners, and that students' differences do not affect their value in the classroom community.

As a result of the tension between my mother's story and my own, I developed multiple methods of engaging Brianna in the school setting. Sometimes, I asked Shirley to work with other students while I worked with Brianna. Sometimes Brianna and I worked with other students. Sometimes Brianna and Shirley and other students worked together. Sometimes Brianna and her friends worked all together, and Shirley and I assisted, as needed. Sometimes Brianna's friends helped her, and sometimes she helped them—not with the concrete aspects of grade-level subject-specific curriculum, as these were not part of Brianna's individualized program plan, but with subtler outcomes related to social skills and communication that were important classroom goals for everyone.

By treating Brianna as null, and being allowed to do so, I had demonstrated how powerful teachers can be in designating to whom, as well as to what, classrooms attend. Difficult as a story like this is for a teacher to admit, for me it inspired tremendous professional growth. Brianna taught me that children have important lessons to offer the adults privileged to work with them. Teachers and learners together can explore regions of learning that have been previously neglected, and reap tremendous rewards. In classrooms, change is always possible.

As I examine Saskatchewan's most recent iteration of subject-specific curriculum, I note that many goals, previously unachievable by particular students, are now absent. In place of these goals are more general outcome statements that all students can move toward—a step forward in creating inclusive classrooms where learning is not only possible, but expected, for everyone.

Dan

When I met Dan, I was a new teacher working with a large and diverse class of middle years students in a rural school division. His inconsistencies from day to day were mystifying. He was bright with a very advanced vocabulary, and seemed to have the basic academic skills intact. Yet, most days he would defy even my simplest instructions. On our first morning of school together, he remained silently sullen at his desk during an independent assignment. When asked why he wasn't doing the work, his response was: "Because it's bullshit."

"He's a monster," I was told by others in the school. The advice of colleagues was to take as many sick days as I could. I quickly enrolled in a behaviour management course at the local university, hoping it wasn't too late for Dan and me. Maybe I could learn enough to salvage the rest of the year. But although the course focus on behaviour modification was somewhat successful with the class in general, with Dan it was of very little help.

The culmination of events that fall was a situation on the playground that propelled Dan into the principal's office, with me as a reluctant witness. He had broken a safety contract designed the previous year and reviewed by the principal earlier that month, and must suffer the consequences, which involved getting the strap. I was made to observe as the principal produced the leather belt and gave him three swift raps across the palm. I saw Dan's colour rise and his facial muscles contract with each blow. Before me wasn't a monster; instead, I saw a little boy. The failure evident to me wasn't his breaking a school rule; the failure wasn't in Dan himself. The failure was ours as an educational system because we were not meeting Dan's needs.

He and I left the office, both powerless for the moment in our respective worlds, both fighting tears. As time went on, I tried to find out more about Dan's background. I learned he lived with a single parent who was away most of the time, even on weekends. Siblings lived in another province. His preference was for gin, but he drank beer. He had a keen interest in geography and a smart sense of humour. When the windows were broken in a local seniors' centre, everyone thought Dan had done it. Maybe he had. He looked thin and pale, as if he never got enough exercise or fresh air. And later, a mother myself, I thought more about Dan's home life. I wondered what he had been eating in those days, mealtimes spent alone. The school counsellor, who began meeting regularly with Dan, assured me that he liked school and he liked me. "Then why is he so difficult?" I asked, and she had no answers. It was a time when no one in schools mentioned mental illness in relation to children, but I have often wondered since if Dan's environment, combined with other factors, had produced childhood depression.

I read to the class for the first part of every afternoon, and I suddenly noticed that Dan was listening hungrily. It became evident that this was the only part of the day when I could count on his respect for me and the other students. After we finished Judy Blume's (1972) *Tales of a Fourth Grade Nothing*, a book I loved, he asked to borrow it. It was the first book he read diligently during silent reading, without any behaviour disruptions. I have often mused about the appeal of this particular book for Dan. Was it the humour? Was it the fact that Fudge, the youngest in the family, as he was, lived in a warm nuclear family the opposite of Dan's?

One day Dan came to school and blurted that it was to be his last day with us. He and his mother were moving out of town. I couldn't believe the suddenness of this transition. Why had his mother not phoned the school to give us time to prepare for his departure? Now, I wonder what Dan's mother thought of the school, where very likely the only contact she had ever had with us had been negative. Meetings with teachers are sometimes tense occasions for many parents, even when things are going reasonably well. I wonder how difficult it had been for Dan's mother to connect. At the time of their departure from our community, many years ago, I tried to communicate with her, but to no avail. She had never taken my calls before; why should this day be any exception? I felt numbly saddened by the imminent loss of this student and wished I could bargain for a little more time with Dan and with his mother.

"See ya," Dan said roughly as he left the classroom, overtly leaving behind the bag we had quickly packed containing his school things. I chased after him and pressed something into his hands. It wasn't the school supplies, as he had likely expected. It was my copy of *Tales of a Fourth Grade Nothing*. The book we had both liked. "This is for you," I said, and the look in his eyes was not one of gratitude. It registered as incredulity. He knew how difficult he had been for me in this class. Yet I had given him something precious to me, something that he knew that I knew he admired. The idea that I liked him must have been completely foreign.

That last image of Dan in my classroom is eclipsed by a future where I visualize him experiencing greater positive relationships at school, just as my mother's picture of the horses running beside the train was transformed in her imagination. I think back to my mother's stories about teaching, and about my beliefs regarding learner, milieu, teacher, and subject matter, and the ways my mother's landscapes intersect with mine. Stories, I believe, are deeply connected to identity. Since that time with Dan, I have often wondered what exactly about Blume's book had touched him so deeply. If I had, in those early years of teaching, known more about critical literacy, about how to engage students in talking about their thoughts in regards to literature, I might have learned more about Dan that would have assisted us in working together. My work with this student occurred over 25 years ago; although I never heard from him again, what I learned from him has remained part of my teaching practice.

Summary

My legacy from my mother's stories is that I approach characterization, and teaching, with a perspective that seeks to discover people's gifts as well as their challenges. This is a unifying point where fiction and non-fiction connect, allowing me a research platform related to children's literature that underpins my current artistic endeavours through writing fiction for young people. Like the other authors spotlighted in this text, I consider that many of our stories have emerged from a consideration of the human condition, and a desire to affect social justice in positive ways. The world is our triggering town (Hugo, 1979), and it is through our individual and naturally limited perceptions of the world that our writing develops. That young people have access to a wide array of literature by many and varied authors becomes much more critical as we consider the different ways each writer might address similar subjects. Similarly, that young people encounter characters with traits similar to their own, as well as perspectives different from their own, are goals that make sense as we consider the importance of critical reading.

Annotated Bibliography of Canadian Young Adult Novels Portraying Characters with Disabilities

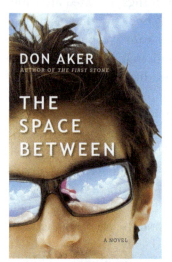

Aker, D. (2007) *The space between.* **Toronto, ON: HarperCollins.**

In Mexico celebrating his 18th birthday, events unfold for Jace—a Grade 12 kid from Halifax—that are completely unexpected. Instead of losing his virginity, as was his plan, he develops a perplexing friendship with a guy whom he later discovers is gay, and then watches the girl of his dreams head back home to her boyfriend. With new insight regarding what it means to be "different," Jace is better equipped to understand his elder brother's suicide and allow himself to grieve over Stefan's death. At the same time, Jace values even more deeply his relationship with his little brother, Luke, a nine-year-old boy with autism. For ages 14 and up.

Description: realistic fiction; themes include loss, self-acceptance, and self-discovery.

Read-ons: Craig Thompson's autobiographical graphic novel *Blankets* contains a similar journey of awakening and discovery for two characters: Craig, the narrator, and Raina, a girlfriend who has two siblings with intellectual disabilities. Francis Chalifour's *After* and Brenda Bellingham's *Drowning in Secrets* are other titles involving the aftermath of suicide in a teen's family. Julie Burtinshaw's *The Perfect Cut* is an even more mature read about surviving the death of a sibling. Julie Roorda's *Wings of a Bee* and Marthe Jocelyn's *Would You* also deal with sibling rivalry and loss of a sibling. Katherine Paterson's *Jacob Have I Loved* is another title that explores sibling rivalry.

Andrews, J. (2013). *The silent summer of Kyle McGinley.* Winnipeg, MB: Great Plains Teen Fiction.

Kyle remembers all too well the abuses in his past and silence, through elective mutism, is how he has decided to respond to the world. His first-person narrative emerges as a stream of consciousness, with the inventive inclusion of two imaginary other voices in addition to Kyle's own thoughts. The first is a character in Kyle's head who offers good advice, and the second provides a barrage of constant negative feedback. The latter, included in bold italicized print, is soon attributed to Kyle's father—a man who abandoned Kyle at an early age, but not before cementing his assaults, both verbal and physical, in the boy's memory. Kyle is a nice guy and an artist who quickly endears himself to Scott and Jill, the couple who provide the latest foster home in the series of homes Kyle has endured. In similar fashion, he endears himself to readers, and from early in the book we share his story and remarkable insight, hoping he will triumph over adversity. And we are not disappointed. Andrews has achieved a masterful relationship between Kyle, his imaginary self, and his recreation of his abuser's voice, a dialogue that well serves the book in that it clearly advances the plot. For its ingenuity and strong characterization, as well as a poignant storyline, this title is highly recommended. For ages 14 and up.

Description: realistic fiction; themes include family relationships and dealing with past trauma.

Read-ons: Another title about a young man abused as a child is Diane Linden's *On Fire*. Bev Brenna's *The Moon Children* has a contrasting portrayal of a young person with selective mutism. Comparisons may also be made with Tim Wynne-Jones' summertime context in *The Uninvited*.

Austin, C. (2011). *All good children.* **Victoria, BC: Orca.**

This is a story for mature readers about mind control—with homophobic dialogue alongside intolerance for intellectual disability—in the context of a small American community rife with prejudice. Compulsory "vaccinations" that turn typical school kids into unusually well-mannered citizens raise the suspicions of 17-year-old graffiti artist Maxwell Connors, who postpones being "treated," along with his friend Dallas, thanks to the ingenuity of his mother. Max's younger sister, however, is not so lucky; because of what appears to be a mild intellectual disability she is sent to a trade school "for throwaways." Max is powerless to avoid his impending fate as a zombie, however, until the conceptualization of a dangerous escape to Canada. This edgy saga offers distant parallels to underground railways in other periods of history. For ages 12 and up.

Description: dystopian fantasy; themes include corporate power, a warning about the use of medication for behaviour control, and a tribute to the power of art as well as individuality.

Read-ons: *Feed*, a novel for older teens by M.T. Anderson, also generates responses regarding corporate power, albeit in a more futuristic time period. Tricia Martineau Wagner's *It Happened on the Underground Railway* could provide fuel for connections to how slaves also sought freedom in Canada. Madeleine L'Engle's *A Wrinkle in Time* has parallels in terms of mind control on the planet Camazotz. Another strong fantasy to compare is Carrie Mac's *The Droughtlanders* (first in a series).

Bell, W. (2006). *The blue helmet.* **Random House of Canada.**

Lee is a high school dropout living with his aunt in New Toronto; a part-time job as a courier introduces him to some interesting people, and one of these—Bruce Cutter, a man with a mental illness—changes his life forever. Their unlikely friendship offers Lee a different perspective on violence, and Lee faces his own aggressive habits with transformative results. Cutter's characterization includes the richness of a man who

exists in light and dark phases, whose uniqueness accompanies but doesn't overshadow his humanness, and whose backstory as a soldier evolves as a framework for the mental health issues that have developed. Cutter's eventual suicide leads Lee further into an attempt to understand the man who has brought Lee peace and establishes that Cutter has at last been the peacekeeper he envisioned himself to be. For ages 14 and up.

Description: realistic fiction; themes include anger management, developing friendships, and father-son relationships.

Read-ons: S.E. Hinton's *The Outsiders* makes a good connection in terms of teen choices regarding anger and violence, as does Faye Harvest's title *Girl Fight*. Michèle Marineau's *The Road to Chlifa* (translated by Susan Ouriou) offers a portrayal of another teen whose past threatens his future. Paul Zindel's *The Pigman's Legacy* offers an additional look at how one human being can affect others. Beth Goobie's *Something Girl* presents another side of anger through the perspective of an abuse victim.

Bobet, L. (2012). *Above.* New York, NY: Arthur A. Levine.

This complex novel explores the characters who live in Safe, an underground community open to those rejected by the city Above. The plot revolves around Matthew, whose claws and scales can be hidden enough to allow him passage, Ariel, a shapeshifter whose character becomes a metaphor for schizophrenia, and Corner—whose gender ambiguity underpins the initial casting out by a society clearly organized around exclusion while at the same time supporting medical experiments that actually create more "misfits." With an uplifting first-person voice, Matthew narrates the fast-paced tale with poise and consistency, his insights speaking to the power of the human spirit and the necessity of stories that remind us of who we are and who we might become. For ages 14 and up.

Description: dystopian fantasy; themes involve a focus on diversity in its many forms, as well as the battle between science and humanity.

Read-ons: M.T. Anderson's remarkable science fiction title *Feed* and Beth Goobie's hard-edged realistic novel *Born Ugly* will both make strong companion reads. C.K. Kelly Martin's dystopian books, beginning with *Yesterday*, is another connection.

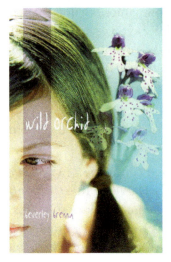

Brenna, B. (2005). *Wild orchid*. Calgary, AB: Red Deer Press.

Taylor Jane Simon is an 18-year-old with Asperger's Syndrome who is reluctantly spending the summer with her mother in Prince Albert National Park. Due to Taylor's ingenuity and perseverance, the summer has its ups as well as its downs. Taylor gets her first job. She sees her first live theatre—*The Birthday Party*—a unique look at social interaction by Nobel Prize–winning playwright Harold Pinter. And she makes headway in reaching a personal goal—acquiring a boyfriend. Readers explore universal themes related to coming of age in this first-person account recorded in Taylor's journal. For ages 12 and up.

Description: realistic fiction; themes include coming of age, teen independence, friendship, and mother-daughter relationships.

Read-ons: *The Catcher in the Rye* by J.D. Salinger is a book Taylor mentions in the story; mature readers are encouraged to explore parallel coming-of-age themes with this title, as well as Mark Haddon's adult crossover novel, *The Curious Incident of the Dog in the Night Time*, and Terry Spencer Hesser's *Kissing Doorknobs*. In Cathy Ytak's *Nothing But Your Skin*, translated from the French by Paula Ayer, a girl narrates the story of a teen with an intellectual disability who becomes sexually active and whose boyfriend is charged with assault. Madeleine L'Engle's *The Joys of Love* involves an idealistic girl's apprenticeship in summer theatre. Steve Kluger's *My Most Excellent Year: A Novel of Love, Mary Poppins, & Fenway Park* is a story with mature themes that contains diary entries, emails, and text messages following the lives of three high-school students, with a focus on elements of exceptionality, including disability and a same-sex crush. Alyxandra Harvey-Fitzhenry's *Broken* and Beth Goobie's *Kicked Out* contain perspectives on first boyfriends that compare to Taylor's relationship with Kody.

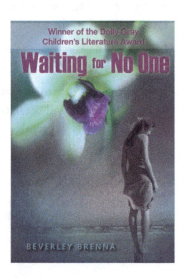

Brenna, B. (2010c). *Waiting for no one*. Markham, ON: Red Deer Press.

In this second book of the Wild Orchid trilogy, 18-year-old Taylor Jane Simon, a young woman with autism, seeks independence through university classes and the world of work. Because of Taylor's unique characteristics, she is a whiz at first-year biology, but struggles with finding employment. For ages 12 and up.

Description: realistic fiction; themes include coming of age, teen independence, friendship, and job hunting.

Read-ons: References in *Waiting for No One* include Harold Pinter's play *The Birthday Party*. Carlo Gebler's book *Caught on a Train* illustrates a different kind of rail adventure. The first chapter in *Waiting for No One* appears in Bev Brenna's collection of short stories about diverse characters, *Something to Hang On To*.

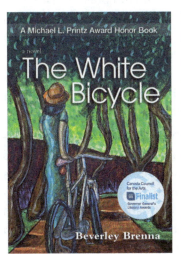

Brenna, B. (2012). ***The white bicycle.*** **Markham, ON: Red Deer Press.**

In this third book of the Wild Orchid trilogy, 19-year-old Taylor Jane Simon, a young woman with autism, achieves increased independence through considering and altering her relationship with her mother. Set in the south of France, this book works to dislodge stereotypes about characters with disabilities and travel. For ages 12 and up.

Description: realistic fiction; themes include coming of age, teen independence, friendship, and travel in the south of France, as well as the power of art. Winner of a Printz Honor and shortlisted for a 2013 Governor General's Award.

Read-ons: References in *The White Bicycle* include Samuel Beckett's play *Waiting for Godot* and Jean-Paul Sartre's *Being and Nothingness*. Cynthia Lord's *Rules* has a character with cerebral palsy that could be compared to Martin Phoenix in *The White Bicycle*. Other books about mother-daughter relationships include *Life on the Refrigerator Door* by Alice Kuipers.

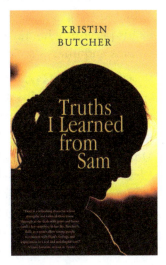

Butcher, K. (2012). ***Truths I learned from Sam.*** **Toronto, ON: Dundurn.**

This is a fast-paced read that combines a character study with light romance, appealing to readers who are looking for a title that is thought-provoking but not troubling, and a main character in Dani who is resilient and positive. When Dani's mom gets married for the sixth time and jets away on honeymoon, 17-year-old Dani must change her summer plans and head to Cariboo Country, where she stays with an uncle she never knew she had. At least she thinks he's her uncle... Told with exaggerated narrative, the story, while certainly not "happy ever after," offers much to smile over and provides a good introduction to this author of over 20 titles. Sam's illness and eventual death aren't strictly disability material; however, this book has been included for its sensitive look at a chronic illness. For ages 12 and up.

Description: realistic fiction; themes include romance and family relationships.

Read-ons: *Broken* by Alyxandra Harvey-Fitzhenry offers a comparable character in Ash Perrault, a modern day Cinderella with a new stepmother and stepsisters as well as a rocky relationship with the school prince. David Poulson's *Old Man* is another title that compares well in terms of a teen connecting with a parent previously distanced.

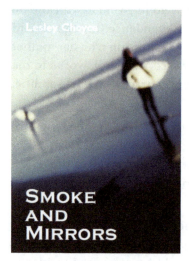

Choyce, L. (2004). *Smoke and mirrors.* Toronto, ON: Dundurn Press.

Sixteen-year-old Simon has always been considered odd; born with prenatal effects from his mother's use of prescription medication, he has always had attention difficulties. Since a skateboarding accident that caused a serious brain injury, he has had short-term memory loss. When a mysterious girl that no one else can see becomes his life-skills coach, readers at first assume that she is simply an effect of his brain differences; the discovery that she is actually a real girl in a coma, somehow having out-of-body experiences, lends fantasy to otherwise realistic elements of the story. Simon's eventual realization of his power as a healer attests to a balance of gifts and challenges overlooked by his parents, who have concentrated on his difficulties to the exclusion of his dreams and interests. For ages 12 and up.

Description: fantasy; themes include self-acceptance and self-discovery, as well as developing friendships and parent-teen relationships. Possible metafictional elements appear in the occasional shift from first-person into third-person narrative.

Read-ons: In the course of this novel, Simon makes references to Shakespeare's *Macbeth*, as well as to writers James Joyce and William James. Beth Goobie's *Kicked Out* is an Orca Sounding's teen read dealing with another difficult parent-teen relationship, as is Don Trembath's *The Tuesday Cafe*. Meg Rosoff's *What I Was* also explores how a mysterious companion named Finn changes the protagonist, who wants to have an effect on Finn in return. The subject of imaginary friends is also included in Deborah Ellis's *Looking for X*. The paranormal is explored further in titles by Margaret Buffie, including her novel *Someone Else's Ghost,* as well as Bruce McBay and James Heneghan's *Waiting for Sarah,* and Sean Stewart and Jordan Weisman's Cathy series, beginning with their title *Cathy's Book.* Another character caught in the spirit world is Adrien in Beth Goobie's mature read *Before Wings.*

Davey, D. (2013). *M in the abstract*. Markham, ON: Red Deer Press.

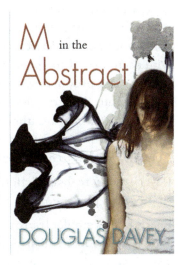

After the disappearance of her father, Mary ("M") and her mother move to a new town. Mary is haunted by hallucinations, voices, and shadows, with many oblique references to mental illness, although no diagnosis or mental health support is provided. She learns to cope, reach for help, and make friends, metaphorically moving from grub to butterfly and emerging as a new person at the end of the book. For ages 14 and up.

Description: realistic fiction; themes include self-help and self-acceptance.

Read-ons: K.L. Denman's *Me Myself and Ike* offers a similar inner perspective of mental confusion.

Denman, K.L. (2008). *Spiral*. Victoria, BC: Orca Books.

Abby is a 15-year-old girl who becomes a paraplegic due to a fall. Anger causes her to lash out at friends and a few key relationships end. A man she meets in rehab introduces her to cocaine and she plummets into darkness until a connection with a horse at Spiral, a residential treatment program, offers hope. Assisted by Taylor, a worker in the program who also uses a wheelchair, Abby begins to learn to live with herself. For ages 12 and up.

Description: hi-lo realistic fiction; themes include facing challenges and accepting support.

Read-ons: Just as Abby's father tries to punish Abby's employer for the accident, the mother of an injured football player attempts to target an opposing teammate in Jeff Rud's intermediate read *Paralyzed.* Abby's dismissal of her boyfriend is similar to another teen break-up in Sandra Richmond's *Wheels for Walking.*

Denman, K.L. (2009). *Me, myself and Ike.* Victoria, BC: Orca.

This fiction title is an edgy read about a young man with schizophrenia. The story, told in 17-year-old Kit's own voice, follows his plan, along with his friend Ike, for a bizarre expedition in which Kit intends to become the next Ice Man, frozen in time for future generations to study. As the story unfolds, however, readers catch hints that make us a little uncomfortable about Ike, and Kit's challenges grow greater with each turn of the page. When we finally realize that Ike is a product of Kit's illness, it offers deep insights into the struggles of this suicidal teen and his family. Denman's Author's Note offers a hope that as we come to a greater understanding of mental illnesses, we are, as a society, in a better position to help. For ages 14 and up.

Description: realistic fiction; themes involve insights into mental illness through first-person projections as well as family challenges.

Read-ons: A similar frank voice from a teen narrator appears in Valerie Sherrard's *Watcher*. Readers will also find connections in Caroline Pignat's *Greener Grass: The Famine Years* where a young woman named Kit must explore seemingly insurmountable challenges related to the Irish famine. Clues from multiple characters also add up in Tim Wynne-Jones's *The Uninvited*.

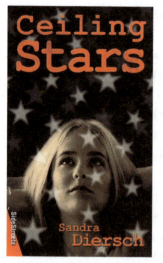

Diersch, S. (2011). *Ceiling stars.* Toronto, ON: James Lorimer.

A first-person story told by Christine about the journey with her best friend Danelle, who is diagnosed with bipolar disorder. Danelle goes from extreme emotional highs to extreme lows and changes the way she dresses, struggling with the emotions both the diagnosis and her behaviour elicit. Chris stresses over what to do to help her friend and her own guilt at being "normal." For ages 12 and up.

Description: realistic fiction; themes include acceptance of mental illness, information about bipolar disorder, and friendship.

Read-ons: Sarah N. Harvey's novel *The Lit Report* also deals with one friend helping the other, this time through a teen pregnancy. Another complex story about friendship and coming of age is *Aristotle and Dante Discover the Secrets of the Universe* by Benjamin Alire Saenz.

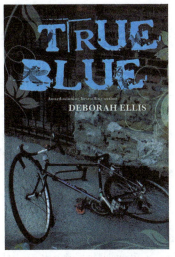

Ellis, D. (2011). *True blue*. Toronto, ON: Pajama Press.

When Casey, a camp counsellor, is wrongly arrested for the murder of a child, Jess, another counsellor, lets jealousy get in the way of loyalty and manages to make things even more difficult for Casey. Whether her actions are due to her mother's mental illness, or being daunted by homophobic remarks, or just simply being self-centred, a reader isn't sure; Jess is an unusual narrator whose warts show clearly through her actions. The town's response to Casey's arrest is extensive, including a scene that shows how the wheelchair ramp has been removed from the local church, while the only character we see using a wheelchair is Casey's father. For ages 12 and up.

Description: mystery; themes include friendship and loyalty.

Read-ons: Other mysteries, such as Valerie Sherrard's Shelby Belgarden novels, could make good connecting titles, as would Eric Walters's *The Money Pit Mystery* and *Rattled: A Mystery* by Lisa Harrington. Another novel where a single event catalyzes change in the life of a teen is Lesley Choyce's *Dumb Luck*.

Fairfield, L. (2009). *Tyranny*. Toronto, ON: Tundra Books.

This graphic novel follows Anna's chronological journey as she succumbs to an eating disorder named as her personal demon, Tyranny, and then recounts her eventual triumph. The author cites a long-term personal struggle with eating disorders as her inspiration for writing this book. For ages 12 and up.

Description: realistic fiction graphic novel; themes include self-acceptance and identity, and information about eating disorders is presented in a straightforward manner.

Read-ons: Another mature graphic novel from an adolescent girl's perspective is Mariko Tamaki and Jillian Tamaki's *Skim*. *Monster* by Walter Dean Myers involves the perspectives of a 16-year-old boy who is being tried for felony murder; readers might wish to compare Steve's self-image and external pressures with the societal pressures that have influenced Anna, as well as the strength of character Steve and Anna share. Francis Chalifour's *Call Me Mimi* and Robin Stevenson's *Big Guy* are additional titles for teens that explore body image. Other novels that deal with eating disorders include *The Hunger* by Marsha Skrypuch, *thinandbeautiful.com* by Liane Shaw, *Ms. Zephyr's Notebook* by K.C. Dyer, and Marnelle Tokio's *More Than You Can Chew*, as well as Diane Tullson's *Zero*.

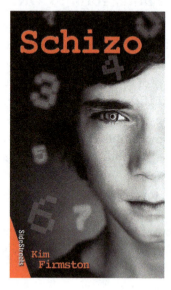

Firmston, K. (2012). *Schizo*. Toronto, ON: James Lorimer.

Daniel and his brother, Dustin, live a challenging life with their single mother, who refuses to take her medication for schizophrenia. How her health spirals out of control, impossible for Dan to manage, is the heart of a book about a teen trying to survive unusual circumstances. For ages 13 and up.

Description: realistic fiction; themes include the complexities of mental illness and its effects.

Read-ons: K.L. Denman's *Me Myself and Ike* also examines schizophrenia; other titles about youth caring for parents who are mentally ill include C. Gingras' *Pieces of Me*.

Fournier, K. M. (2007). *Sandbag shuffle*. Saskatoon, SK: Thistledown Press.

Owen and Andrew are two teens escaping a group home during the Manitoba Red River flood of 1997. What makes this book so original as compared to other books of its genre is that Owen, a boy of rapid-fire wit, has no legs and doesn't refrain from exploiting their absence. The action takes place as the boys travel via the river from Grand Forks to Emerson, Manitoba, then make their way on land to Winnipeg. For ages 12 and up.

Description: realistic fiction: contextually realistic profanity in addition to transgressive politics raise the reading age; themes include life-altering journeys and coming of age.

Read-ons: Progressive attitudes toward disability are also presented in William Bell's title, *Absolutely Invincible!* Sherman Alexie's mature read *The Absolutely True Diary of a Part-time Indian* involves a different kind of journey as 14-year-old Arnold Spirit Jr. tries to escape the reservation, and Barbara Smucker's *Underground to Canada* deals with escape from slavery. Three other quests for escape are found in Wendy A. Lewis' *Freefall*, a realistic title dealing with child abuse and set against the backdrop of skydiving, Meg Rosoff's *What I Was*, the story of a young man during a transformative summer, and Mark Twain's classic text *The Adventures of Huckleberry Finn*. Michael Noel's *Good for Nothing* is another teen novel that deals with the effects of history and culture on coming of age.

Frizzell, C. (2006). *Chill*. Victoria, BC: Orca Books.

Chill is a high school boy with a "bum leg" whose story is told through the eyes of Sean, a friend and classmate. Chill stereotypically "overcomes" his disability by using art to confront an abusive teacher who bullies Chill because of his physical differences. For ages 12 and up.

Description: realistic fiction contrived to suit the grade 3.5 reading level of the Orca Soundings imprint; themes include the triumph of good versus evil, and human cruelty.

Read-ons: David Poulsen's *Numbers* is another story of a high school student who challenges a teacher, in this case for dispersing hate literature. William Bell's *Stones* could also be used to further explore hate crimes. Other links involve the power of art, such as represented by the magic realism of Alyxandra Harvey-Fitzhenry's *Broken*. A look at artists and their self-concepts appears in Peter H. Reynold's picture book, *Ish*.

Froese, D. (2002). *Out of the fire*. Toronto, ON: Sumach Press.

Dayle's desire to be with the "in crowd" explodes when she and another teen are badly burned in an out-of-control bonfire. While dealing with the aftermath of Pete's death, Dayle must also undergo painful physiotherapy, dreams induced by morphine treatment, and a permanently disfigured body. For ages 12 and up.

Description: realistic fiction; themes include dealing with challenges and developing relationships.

Read-ons: Other novels involving racism include Allan Stratton's *Borderline*; further navigations of one's place within peer groups include Adwoa Badoe's *Between Sisters* and Paul Kropp's *Playing Chicken*. More on physical beauty can be found in Erin Bow's fantasy novel *Plain Kate*.

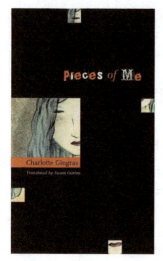

Gingras, C. (2009). *Pieces of me* (S. Ouriou, Trans.). Toronto, ON: Kids Can Press.

This title is Susan Ourious's Governor General's Award–winning English translation of the novella *La Liberté? Connais pas*. The book follows the story of Mira, a Quebec teenager living with a domineering and mentally unstable mother. Catherine, the new girl, is at first drawn to Mira because of the artistic talents they share, but in the end proves not to be the friend Mira thinks she is. With the death of her father, Mira sinks into a depression, recovering with the help of Paule, the school counsellor, who is blind. For ages 14 and up.

Description: realistic fiction; mature themes include sexuality, powerlessness, living with mental illness, and the search for personal identity.

Read-ons: Susan Juby's *Alice, I Think*, is told within a similar context; *Egghead* by Carolyne Pignat is another young adult novel that tackles identity-issues, as well as bullying, through the voices of three first-person narrators, one of whom uses free-verse poetry. An Na's *A Step from Heaven* and Rukhsana Khan's *Dahling If You Luv Me, Would You Please, Please Smile* also involve high-school settings, following protagonists who navigate displacement, immigration, and cultural identity toward self-acceptance. Shem Salvadurai's *Swimming in the Monsoon Sea* engages readers with similar themes of self-acceptance as a young boy identifies his homosexuality. A more esoteric link is to Shaun Tan's *The Arrival*, through which the experiences of immigrants could be compared to any confused encounters with one's own world.

Goobie, B. (2002). *Kicked out*. Victoria, BC: Orca Books.

Dime, a rebellious Winnipeg teen, goes to live with her brother Darren, who has been quadriplegic since an accident three years earlier. In a different context, away from her domineering parents, Dime begins to sort out aspects of her life that need exploration including her dreamy new boyfriend, Gabe, whose looks and motorbike initially trump his abusive nature. For ages 12 and up.

Description: realistic fiction with a grade 3.5 reading level representative of the Orca Soundings label; themes include self-discovery, family dynamics, and coming of age as well as abusive relationships.

Read-ons: Other titles by Beth Goobie that include similar themes are her novel *Mission Impossible*, as well as her title *Something Girl*. *One More Step* by Sheree Fitch depicts a teenage boy with a voice just as angry as Dime's. Bev Brenna's

Wild Orchid and Alyxandra Harvey-Fitzhenry's *Broken* offer perspectives on first boyfriends that compare with Dime's. Eric Walters' *Rebound* offers another look at societal response to disability. Lisa Bird-Wilson's short story collection, *Just Pretending,* focuses on living through transitions through the window of adoption.

Holeman, L. (2002). *Search of the moon king's daughter.* Toronto, ON: Tundra Books.

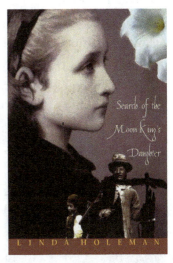

This historical fiction saga involves a young girl's quest to find her brother, sold as a chimney sweep in Victorian England. Emmaline's little brother, Tommy, is born to an alcoholic mother; although not explicitly defined, it is possible his hearing impairment was caused by prenatal alcohol abuse in addition to a fever he had as a baby and brain injuries sustained in a fall. After the death of their father from cholera, their mother suffers a factory-related injury and becomes addicted to laudanum, at which point she sells Tommy to a master sweep. In her desperate search to find him, Emmaline experiences the appalling conditions that workers in the 19th century endured, as well as the strong class distinctions made during that time and place. For ages 12 and up.

Description: historical fiction; themes include hope and the enduring power of love.

Read-ons: Charles Dickens offers a compelling companion read in *The Adventures of Oliver Twist*. Sharon McKay's *Esther* presents a similarly emotionally charged and dramatic rendering of early 18th century France, although with somewhat more mature content. *To Dance at the Palais Royale* by Janet McNaughton is another gripping historical read, as is Alice Walsh's *A Sky Black with Crows*. In the latter, a teen tries to care for her youngest sister, making a nice comparison with Emmaline's situation.

Janz, H. (2004). *Sparrows on wheels.* Edmonton, AB: DocCrip Press.

Originally written as a master's thesis, this semi-autobiographical novel presents the story of Tallia, a young person with cerebral palsy, who, over the course of the story, grows from an anxious Grade 7 student in a special school to the co-editor of the school newspaper and a high school senior considering university courses. It is not Tallia's choice to leave Inglewood School Hospital and attend a regular high school, although one of her peers made that transition, with conflicting results. Much of the omniscient narration includes factual details about the day-to-day life of characters with physical disabilities in the pre-integration era, and while these facts slow the plot, they also add a layer of richness to the story's content. For ages 12 and up.

Description: historical novel adapted from academic writing; themes include self-actualization and coming of age.

Read-ons: Don Trembath's *The Tuesday Cafe* portrays a protagonist with similar dreams of being a writer. *Mabel Riley* by Marthe Jocelyn also explores a young teen's quest to find her voice.

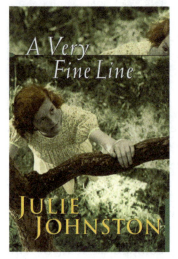

Johnston, J. (2006). *A very fine line*. Toronto, ON: Tundra Books.

Rosalind is a 13-year-old in a family of girls who decides that coming of age isn't for her, and works hard to become the boy she believes her mother has always wanted. Peers in small-town Ontario in 1941 make her gender presentation difficult, but she perseveres as "Ross" until a crush on Adrian, a young man who has been hired to tutor her at home, causes her to think differently about womanhood. One of the complications for Rosalind is that she struggles with second sight, and stories told by her elderly aunts confirm the potential of this gift in a seventh daughter of a seventh daughter, which she actually is, until she "becomes" a son through clothes and gesture. The actuality of her birth order has been hidden until now through the banishment of a sister with intellectual disabilities, sent to live with aunts. Aspects of this sister, Lucy, ring with gothic description and she operates as a metaphor in this novel about difference and belonging. This is a title where many characters are presented as "different," from Rosalind's own giftedness and gender confusion, to Adrian's lameness, to cousin Corny's birth-marked face, in addition to Lucy. Even Rosalind's elder sister, a female medical doctor at a time when women are expected to prioritize marriage and children over careers, is a character worth consideration for her actions as a "rule-breaker." For ages 13 and up.

Description: realistic fiction with shades of magic realism; themes include respect for diversity and coming of age.

Read-ons: Other titles exploring the burdens of second sight include Anne Louise MacDonald's *Seeing Red*, Cora Taylor's *Julie*, and Robin Stevenson's *Impossible Things*, as well as Carol Matas' psychic adventure series beginning with her title *The Freak*. Exceptionality and birth order is further explored in Patricia C. Wrede's *Thirteenth Child*, and Barbara Haworth-Attard's *Irish Chain* also considers the weight of gifts and challenges. Other titles that employ fairy tale imagery include Iain Lawrence's *Gemini Summer* and *Broken* by Alyxandra Harvey-Fitzhenry. Glen Huser's *Stitches* also explores issues related to gender roles. References to Lucy could be compared to Charlotte Brontë's Bertha Mason in *Jane Eyre*. Other references within the text include George Bernard Shaw's play *Saint Joan*, about Joan of Arc, and William Shakespeare's *Macbeth*.

Ketchen, S. (2012). *Grows that way*. Fernie, BC: Oolichan.

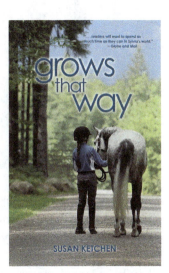

Sylvia has Turner's syndrome. She discovers a Sasquatch while on a trail ride, which leads to her assisting her boyfriend's father with research. In previous titles, Sylvia learns that her lack of growth is due to a genetic condition and that she will need to take growth hormones and estrogen. In this third title, Sylvia chooses to discontinue the growth hormones due to unwanted side effects, and accepts her short stature. For ages 12 and up.

Description: magic realism; this is the third book in Ketchen's series about this character, following *Born That Way* and *Made That Way*. Themes include acceptance of diversity and horse savvy.

Read-ons: For other humorous and quirky voices in teen fiction, look at J.D. Salinger's *The Catcher in the Rye* and Paul Zindel's *The Pigman*, as well as Glen Huser's *The Runaway*. Also see Joe Campbell's collection of essays, *Take Me Out of the Ball Game*.

Kropp, P. (2004). *Against all odds*. Toronto, ON: HIP Books.

Larry thinks of his brother Jeff as "not the brightest crayon in the box" and takes an overbearing stance on how to protect Jeff from everyone's "bullying." When the siblings are caught in a storm cellar with Jeff's friend Tank, Jeff seems to be the one who is most capable, saving his friend who can't swim and never giving up. Larry is forced to reconsider how he views his brother's effectiveness and judgment in light of current achievements. For ages 12 and up.

Description: Hi-lo young adult realistic fiction; themes include not underestimating people with disabilities, perseverance, and not judging a book by its cover.

Read-ons: John Lekich's *The Losers' Club* also allows for multiple perspectives on self and other. Another title by the same name is Natale Ghent's *Against All Odds*, for this reason alone making an interesting connection.

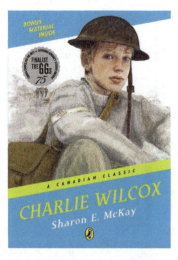

McKay, S. (2000). *Charlie Wilcox*. Toronto, ON: Penguin Books.

Charlie, born into a Newfoundland sealing family, tries to prove his competence in light of the stigma associated with his club foot. After the foot is repaired through surgery, he stows away at age 14 on what he thinks is a fishing vessel, emerging days later bound for France and World War I. For ages 12 and up.

Description: historical fiction introducing ideas about how disability is socially, rather than physically, constructed; themes include the brutality of war and coming of age.

Read-ons: Other war-based accounts for a similar age group are found in Carol Matas's *After the War* and *The Garden*, John Wilson's *And in the Morning*, and David Richards' *The Lady at Batoche*. Janet McNaughton's *Catch Me Once, Catch Me Twice* offers a contrasting picture of Newfoundland. Marguerite de Angeli's Newbery Medal winner *The Door in the Wall* offers another depiction of an adventuresome protagonist with a physical disability. A title intended for younger readers, but whose bravado and clever language make it a possible match for *Charlie Wilcox*, is Sarah Ellis's *The Several Lives of Orphan Jack*. John Lekitch's *The Losers' Club* offers a similar look at physical disability and the taunts of bullies.

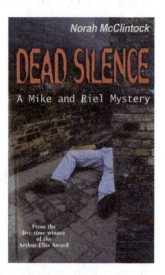

McLintock, N. (2008). *Dead silence*. Toronto, ON: Scholastic.

After Mike skips out on his friend Sal, he discovers that Sal has been stabbed to death near their high school in an inner-city Toronto neighbourhood. Bystanders give mixed messages, so Mike starts asking some deeper questions of his own. Various suspects are considered and cleared, including Alex, a young man with an intellectual disability whose own family expects he's guilty. Eventually the mystery is solved in a way that lets readers retrospectively consider the clues. For ages 12 and up.

Description: mystery; themes involve bullying and societal stereotypes.

Read-ons: Kristin Butcher's mystery *Return to Bone Tree Hill* would make a good companion read as Jessica searches for the killer of a school companion much as Mike is desperate to solve the murder of his friend. Graham McNamee's *Acceleration,* and *Whalesinger* by Welwyn Katz are other novels for similar age groups, told with adventure and energy, each touching in a peripheral way on disability themes. Margaret Thompson's *Eyewitness* is another title involving a murder as well as cultural stereotypes.

McNicoll, S. (2003). *A different kind of beauty.* Markham, ON: Fitzhenry & Whiteside.

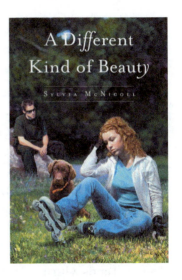

With alternating chapters told in the separate voices of two teenagers, this sequel to *Bringing Up Beauty* cleverly juxtaposes scenes about the training of a guide dog with the story of the young man who is eventually to receive the dog. Elizabeth's difficulty is learning to let go of an animal she has grown to love, as well as a previous boyfriend. Kyle's story is heavier and relates to diabetes-induced blindness and a failed relationship with his old girlfriend. For ages 12 and up.

Description: realistic fiction; themes include dealing with loss, teen relationships, and self-acceptance.

Read-ons: Teen relationships are further explored in *Bone Dance* by Martha Brooks and Stephanie Meyer's Twilight series. Self-acceptance and first-love are two of the themes in Madeleine L'Engle's *A Wrinkle in Time,* as well as *Lean Mean Machines* by Michèle Marineau and translated from the French by Susan Ouriou—a title also written from alternating points of view. Another title about a teen with a vision impairment is Mary Blakeslee's *Hal*.

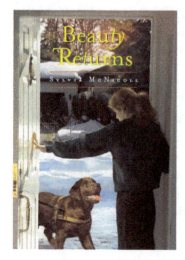

McNicoll, S. (2006). *Beauty returns*. Markham, ON: Fitzhenry & Whiteside.

This realistic novel continues the story introduced in two earlier works, *Bringing Up Beauty* and *A Different Kind of Beauty*, and as in the latter, the chapters are told in the alternating teen voices of Elizabeth and Kyle. Liz is adjusting to life at home with her sister and Teal, her sister's little boy; Kyle is a senior at high school dealing with the prejudices of others regarding his blindness as well as his own resistance to health restrictions. Liz and Kyle's relationship is not an easy one, complicated by concerned parents. Kyle's death corresponds with traditional literary stereotypes about people with disabilities while at the same time contrasting with readers' understandings of the strong and independent character Kyle has become. For ages 12 and up.

Description: realistic fiction; themes include dealing with loss and self-acceptance, with an interesting social commentary on attitudes toward people who are visually impaired.

Read-ons: As above for *A Different Kind of Beauty*.

Nicholson, L.S. (2012). *Vegas tryout*. Toronto, ON: James Lorimer.

Carrie is a synchronized swimmer with big dreams, but anorexia forces her to prioritize her health and the novel ends with a successful period in rehab. This is a believable story that includes details about competitive swimming, as well as rich supporting characters. For ages 12 and up.

Description: realistic fiction; themes include coming of age, overcoming challenges, and parent-teen relationships.

Read-ons: Nicholson's other sports books would make good companion reads.

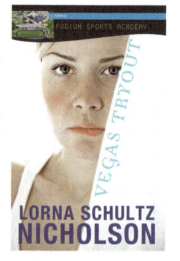

Polak, M. (2011). *Miracleville*. Victoria, BC: Orca.

Sixteen-year-old Ani and her family run a tourist shop in Sainte-Anne-de-Beaupré, catering to the pilgrims who come to the Quebec town seeking a miracle. Ani's younger sister Colette has ADHD and is plunging into a casual sexual relationship that Ani discovers and worries about while their mother recovers from an accident that has left her a paraplegic, although this disability is possibly temporary. Many references in the novel about physical disability demonstrate Ani's changing perspectives as she at first views the many tourists with physical differences, and even a neighbour in a wheelchair, with fear and revulsion. For ages 13 and up.

Description: realistic fiction; themes include teen sexuality, religious faith, and attitudes toward physical disability.

Read-ons: *Tripping* by Heather Waldorf provides a contrasting matter-of-fact attitude toward physical disability; *Between Sisters* by Adwoa Badoe is a different kind of cautionary tale about coming of age and sexuality, and will contrast well with the relationship between the sisters in Polak's book.

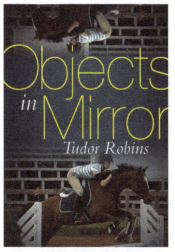

Robins, T. (2013). *Objects in mirror*. Markham, ON: Red Deer Press.

Fifteen-year-old Grace is spending the summer working with horses at a nearby stable. She contributes to the care of spirited and sometimes damaged animals as best she can until an eating disorder almost prevents her from doing the job she loves. The careful weaving of Grace's challenges into complex family dynamics, a new love interest, and aspects of riding that only a seasoned rider could present demonstrate the author's strong storytelling abilities. For ages 12 and up.

Description: realistic fiction; themes include eating disorders and family relationships.

Read-ons: Grace's relationship with her stepmother can be compared to Ella's relationship with her stepmother in *Broken* by Alyxandra Harvey-Fitzhenry. The latter is suggestive of a character with an eating disorder as well. Mother and daughter growth and bonding can also be found in Sarah Ellis's *Outside In*.

Roorda, J. (2007). *Wings of a bee*. Toronto, ON: Sumach Press.

This is the tender story of a young girl whose sister eventually dies from an illness complicated by her cerebral palsy. Bronwyn experiences typical sibling rivalries with Carey, and is sometimes jealous of the attention Carey receives because of her disability, but there are also many happy times that, related in the warm, sure voice of reminiscence, make this title a positive yet realistic depiction of family life. The title refers to Bronwyn's belief that her sister has many hidden depths, including the ability to read complex texts and write plays, even if her school and community don't believe she can, just as the wings of a bee are invisible to the naked eye. Roorda herself grew up alongside a younger brother with cerebral palsy and includes here a compelling description of a time before inclusion was commonly practiced in communities. For ages 12 and up.

Description: realistic fiction; themes include family relationships, living with diversity, loss, and coming of age.

Read-ons: Other titles that involve sibling rivalry and loss include Don Aker's *The Space Between* and Marthe Jocelyn's *Would You*. Books exploring issues regarding school inclusion for students with disabilities include Heidi Janz's *Sparrows on Wheels* as well as Christina Minaki's book for a younger audience, *Zoe's Extraordinary Holiday Adventures*. Jean Little's autobiographical *Little by Little: A Writer's Education* explores another childhood where disability is negotiated alongside dreams of becoming a writer. Other books for young people that involve a protagonist's consideration of faith include Judy Blume's *Are You There God? It's Me, Margaret* and Anita Horrock's *Amost Eden*. Titles mentioned in *Wings of a Bee* include: the Bible; Laura Ingalls Wilder's titles *On the Banks of Plum Creek* and *On the Shores of Silver Lake*; E.B. White's *Charlotte's Web*, and C.S. Lewis's The Chronicles of Narnia series.

Ryan, D. (2012). *Cuts like a knife*. Victoria, BC: Orca.

Told from a first-person perspective, *Cuts Like a Knife* is a story about Daniel and his crush Mac, who starts to act suspiciously after she is humiliated at a school dance. Signs of depression and possibly a potential suicide nudge Daniel to confide his worries to his mother, and Mac is located just in time to save her life. For ages 12 and up.

Description: realistic fiction; themes include depression, loss, friendship, and the importance of confiding difficult secrets.

Read-ons: Other books dealing with the aftermath of suicide include *Karma* by Cathy Ostlere and Don Aker's *The Space Between*.

Scarsbrook, R. (2010). *The monkeyface chronicles*. Saskatoon, SK: Thistledown Press.

Phillip Skylar, born with Van der Woude syndrome, which causes a facial deformity, narrates this fictional journey into his complex family and school dynamics. Compared to his perfect twin brother, Michael, Phillip has always felt handicapped. When Michael receives an almost fatal sports injury, it catalyzes events that irrevocably change Phillip's life. Phillip finds out that his dad, Landon, is not his dad but his brother, that Landon is gay, and that their real father is actually Grandfather. A motorcycle accident destroys his jaw and body, requiring facial reconstruction surgery and physical therapy, and he eventually returns to his hometown physically changed toward "normalcy" while his brother Michael must use a wheelchair. For ages 13 and up.

Description: realistic fiction; themes include self-acceptance, issues related to physical beauty, forgiveness, family relationships, and anger management.

Read-ons: Arthur Slade's series *The Hunchback Assignments* will make a good companion read in terms of perspectives on physical beauty.

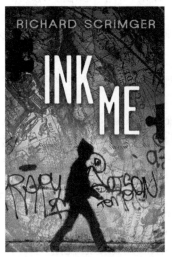

Scrimger, R. (2012). *Ink me.* **Victoria, BC: Orca.**

Told from the first-person perspective of 15-year-old Bernard, better known as "Bunny," this novel relates the story of a young man with an intellectual disability. Bunny's trouble understanding certain situations leads him down a rabbit hole of confusion when his Grampa dies and leaves instructions for Bunny to get a tattoo. Bunny goes to the tattoo parlour, where a mix-up results in him receiving a tattoo intended for a gang member. In a humorous sequence of events, Bunny ends up in trouble with the law when he is caught with the gang doing a gun-drug deal. Bunny ends up going to jail because he won't identify his gang member friends. For ages 12 and up.

Description: realistic comic fiction; themes include developing friendships and coming of age.

Read-ons: Other titles where authors have used spelling or other structural signs to represent intellectual disability include Gina McMurchy-Barber's *Free as a Bird*. The other seven books in Orca's Seven The Series collection, detailing the adventures of each of the other grandkids when Grampa dies, are written by other Canadian young adult authors.

Shaw, L. (2009). *thinandbeautiful.com*. Toronto, ON: Second Story Press.

This fictional account of a high school girl's struggle with an eating disorder is told in diary format. Flashbacks in different font allow a richer perspective on Maddie's past as well as her present. Maddie will not admit she is sick, and it isn't until she spends time in a rehabilitation clinic that she begins to acknowledge reality and start the process of healing. One of the threads in the story occurs through emails between Maddie and her online friends via a pro-anorexia website. This site supports Maddie's illness through conversations with people who normalize her behaviour; however, the eventual death of a friend from this site becomes an important catalyst for change. For ages 12 and up.

Description: realistic fiction that is issues-based; themes include self-acceptance and self-discovery as well as friendships.

Read-ons: Cecily von Ziegesar's Gossip Girl series could be a stepping stone into this more realistic title. A book narrated with a similar issues-based slant is Terry Spencer Hesser's *Kissing Doorknobs*, a fictional, first person account of growing up with Obsessive Compulsive Disorder. Marsha Skrypuch's *The Hunger*, Diane Tullson's *Zero*, Lesley Fairfield's *Tyranny*, Marnelle Tokio's *More Than You Can Chew*, and K.C. Dyer's *Ms. Zephyr's Notebook* are other titles that include characters with eating disorders. Teresa Toten's *The Game* also explores the story of a teen who surfaces for help in a residential psychiatric treatment centre.

Shaw, L. (2011). *Fostergirls*. Toronto, ON: Second Story Press.

Sadie is a foster girl who is moving into a group home. She has a reading disability and has a tough time fitting in with new people. She doesn't like school until the support of her counsellor offers a new perspective on her challenges as well as methods for coping. For ages 14 and up.

Description: realistic fiction; themes include developing friendships, negotiating life transitions, and dealing with challenges.

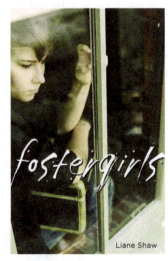

Read-ons: Katherine Patterson's *The Great Gilly Hopkins* has a similar female protagonist who has learned various self-protection strategies. Lisa Bird-Wilson's collection of short stories *Just Pretending* contains many tales about identity related to unstable home environments and adoption.

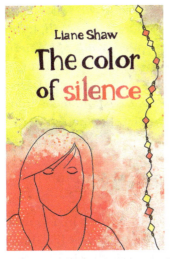

Shaw, L. (2013). *The color of silence*. Toronto, ON: Second Story Press.

Seventeen-year-old Alex, involved in a car accident that killed her best friend, withdraws into selective mutism, using her voice for only the most necessary exchanges. A court order mandating community service is initially just another situation in which she feels powerless. Yet coming to know Joanie, a teenager whose genetic condition has left her with minimal control of her body and no speech, is revelatory for Alex. She begins to see outside her own life and into Joanie's reality, and both characters learn and grow through their relationship. The developing bond between the two girls is narrated through their alternating first-person voices. In addition, flashbacks take readers through what really happened to Cali, Alex's friend, in the accident that killed her. This read is psychologically complex, character driven, and told with flair. For ages 12 and up.

Description: realistic fiction; themes include recovery from trauma and developing friendships.

Read-ons: S.J. Laidlaw's *An Infidel in Paradise* also explores themes of loss and friendship, as does Alice Kuipers' novel *The Worst Thing She Ever Did*. Gilles Abier's short novel *The Pool Was Empty* also deals with a teen involved with the law.

Skrypuch, M. (1999). *The hunger*. Toronto, ON: Boardwalk Books.

Paula is a contemporary 15-year-old girl who is struggling with an eating disorder. As her body becomes ravaged, she metamorphoses into Marta, an orphaned teen living during the 1915 Armenian genocide. The equating of Paula's rejection of food with Marta's enforced starvation gives Paula the strength to battle her illness at Homewood, a treatment program. As Paula tries to research the events in her "dream," her grandmother admits her own Armenian roots. For ages 12 and up.

Description: historical fiction told through the lens of fantasy and contemporary realism; themes include human cruelty and the struggle to survive, as well as issues related to perfectionism and self-acceptance.

Read-ons: Other novels that explore genocide include *Nobody's Child*—Marsha Skrypuch's sequel to *The Hunger*—and Eric Walters' *Shattered*. Books that deal with eating disorders include Liane Shaw's *thinandbeautiful.com*, Diane Tullson's *Zero*, Lesley Fairfield's *Tyranny*, *Ms. Zephyr's Notebook* by K.C. Dyer, and Marnelle Tokio's *More Than You Can Chew*. Books where protagonists time slip and become historical characters include K.C. Dyer's Eagle Glen series beginning with the title *Seeds of Time*, Lynne Kositsky's *A Question of Will*, Judith Silverthorne's *The Secret of the Stone House*, Lois Donovan's *Winds of L'Acadie*, and Lynne Fairbridge's *Tangled in Time*, as well as Nicholas Maes' combination of futuristic science fiction and time travel in *Laughing Wolf*. Characters in Darren Krill's *The Uncle Duncle Chronicles: Escape from Treasure Island* move into a fictional past. One other connecting fantasy is Barbara Nickel's *Hannah Waters and the Daughter of Johann Sebastian Bach*.

Sobat, G.S. (2008). *Gravity journal*. Winnipeg, MB: Great Plains Publications.

Anise's story unfolds here in first-person perspective as written in a journal, relating her struggle with anorexia and self-mutilation. Anise has very little home support and for most of the story resides in a facility to assist her in managing the eating disorder. A developing friendship with Boyd, another resident of the facility who is dealing with bipolar disorder, offers a love interest. The end of the story shows Anise in a group home where she finally seems to be on the road to recovery. For ages 12 and up.

Description: realistic fiction; themes include coming of age, family relationships and dynamics, and self-acceptance.

Read-ons: Another title about self-acceptance is Denise Jaden's *Never Enough*. Caroline Pignat's *Egghead* also embeds poetry in a journal-like narrative.

Spring, D. (2010). *The kayak*. Saskatoon, SK: Thistledown Press.

Teresa must now use a wheelchair after a tragic accident in her teenage years. In this novel, she and her family take a camping trip, while Teresa finds herself in a summer love triangle. For ages 14 and up.

Description: realistic fiction novel expanded from Spring's short story *The Kayak*; themes include coming of age and developing relationships.

Read-ons: Teresa could be compared to Rainy in Heather Waldorf's *Tripping*. Another love story may be found in Paul Zindel's *The Pigman*. Debbie Spring's short story *The Kayak* is available in Thistledown's anthology *Takes*, edited by R.P. MacIntyre.

Stevenson, R. (2008). *Big guy*. Victoria, BC: Orca Books.

This coming of age story is told in the first-person voice of 17-year-old Ethan, chatting online to Derek, a newfound love interest, but afraid to reveal his true, overweight self. Ethan, a high school dropout, worries about a lot of things, including his single father's reaction to a gay son. A job as a physical care assistant offers Ethan a chance at mutual friendship with Aaliyah, a woman who has been a paraplegic since she experienced a brain aneurism. The two have more in common than they at first realize, and eventually push each other toward seizing the day and following their dreams. For ages 13 and up.

Description: realistic fiction with a grade 3.5 reading level consistent with the Orca Soundings label; themes include self-acceptance and prejudice.

Read-ons: Kristyn Dunnion's *Mosh Pit* is an even edgier read that explores the journey of a lesbian teen involved in the punk scene. *Skim*, a graphic novel by Mariko Tamaki and illustrated by Jillian Tamaki, explores the life of a "not-slim" wannabe wiccan goth high school student who falls for a female teacher. One other title about sexual orientation is Benjamin Alire Saenz's *Aristotle and Dante Discover the Secrets of the Universe*. Lesley Fairfield's *Tyranny* and Francis Chalifour's *Call Me Mimi* also deal with issues of weight and self-acceptance.

Stinson, K. (2012). *What happened to Ivy*. Toronto, ON: Second Story Press.

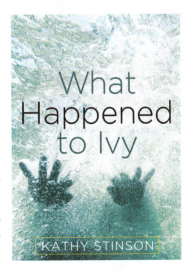

David wants to be a regular teenager, but he has to take a lot of responsibility for his sister, Ivy, who has cerebral palsy. David regrets his complaints when Ivy drowns at the family lake, and his father seemingly lets her slip away. This first-person mature look at the topic of mercy killing is brave and sensitive, offering fuel for classroom discussions of this highly controversial topic. One point to deliberate involves society's view of Ivy and people like her, as people's reactions to Ivy in the story are not all sympathetic. For ages 14 and up.

Description: realistic fiction; themes include mercy killing and sibling relationships, as well as family dynamics related to a person with a disability and grief and loss.

Read-ons: Comparisons to Robert Latimer's murder of his daughter Tracy, called a "compassionate homicide" by Justice Ted Noble, are worthy; information online from various websites, including the following, may be connected to Stinson's novel: www.robertlatimer.net; www.ccdonline.ca/en/humanrights/endoflife/latimer/2000/06b

Tokio, M. (2003). *More than you can chew.* Toronto, ON: Tundra Books.

Marty has survived an alcoholic mother, an absent father, and a break with a boyfriend she thinks she loves, but the death of a younger friend named Lily, who has been with her at the treatment centre, sends her reeling into an attempted suicide. For ages 14 and up.

Description: semi-autobiographical realistic fiction; this is an issues book whose themes include family dynamics, power and control, and teen sexuality.

Read-ons: Other books about characters reclaiming power over their lives include Beth Goobie's *The Good, the Bad and the Suicidal* and Brian Doyle's *Boy O'Boy*.

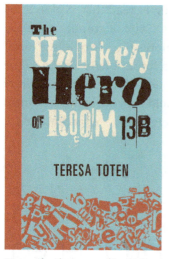

Toten, T. (2013). *The unlikely hero of room 13B.* Toronto, ON: Doubleday.

Adam, a 15-year-old with Obsessive Compulsive Disorder (OCD), joins a group where participants with various forms of OCD discuss their challenges and adopt superheroes as alter egos. Adam falls head over heels with Robyn, another group member, and must juggle his rituals, love life, and off-the-rails family responsibilities in this comic yet sensitive view of mental illness. Winner of the 2013 Governor General's Literary Award for Children's Literature (text). For ages 13 and up.

Description: realistic fiction; themes include individuality, self-acceptance, and mental health.

Read-ons: The character of Adam will make an interesting comparison to the character of Matti in Dianne Linden's *On Fire*. A similar combination of humour and pathos can be found in Paul Zindel's *The Pigman*.

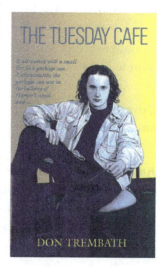

Trembath, D. (1996). *The Tuesday cafe.* Victoria, BC: Orca Books.

Harper Winslow is a high school kid who's trying to get attention from his emotionally distant parents; when he's caught and charged for lighting fires at school, the judge orders him to write an essay on how he's going to turn his life around. The problem is, he doesn't know … until The Tuesday Cafe—a writing class in which his mother's enrolled him—becomes an unexpected source of support. His classmates turn out to be adults with special needs, and Harper learns some new and valuable perspectives here. For ages 12 and up.

Description: realistic fiction; themes include family relationships, self-discovery, and personal writing development.

Read-ons: Similar family dynamics are presented in Lesley Choyce's young adult title *Smoke and Mirrors. Shattered*, by Eric Walters, is another story of a teen learning about himself and others through experiencing a local community, in this case, a soup kitchen. Heidi Janz's *Sparrows on Wheels* narrates the story of another teen intent on becoming a writer.

Trembath, D. (2005). *Rooster*. Victoria, BC: Orca Books

Rooster is failing Grade 12, so the school principal and counsellor decide he needs to make up his work by volunteering with a group of mentally challenged adults who bowl. Rooster goes from resenting this group of people to championing their human rights. For ages 14 and up.

Description: realistic fiction; themes include personal growth and identity as well as social justice.

Read-ons: John Lekich's *Loser's Club* and Don Trembath's other books, including *The Tuesday Cafe*, make good companion reads. Another young adult novel with the same unusual title, *Rooster,* is by T.D. Thompson, and a comparison of how characters deal with tragic events as well as a search for identity can be made between these two titles.

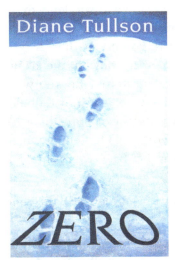

Tullson, D. (2006). *Zero*. Markham, ON: Fitzhenry & Whiteside.

Kas is attending a school for the arts, hoping to perfect her painting ability. When she begins to suffer from anorexia and bulimia, she tells no one, and since no one recognizes the signs, she becomes very ill until at last her secret is out. Even her new boyfriend, Jason, isn't strong enough to help her, and Kas is filled with self-loathing when her parents take her back home for treatment. For ages 12 and up.

Description: realistic fiction; themes include self-acceptance and issues related to eating disorders.

Read-ons: Kas's critical internal voice can be contrasted with the self-perception Anubis has learned from her social context in Deborah Ellis's *Jackal in the Garden*.

Hope's War by Marsha Skrypuch relates a different dilemma for a gifted teen attending a school for the arts. Other books about eating disorders include Marsha Skrypuch's *The Hunger*, Lesley Fairfield's *Tyranny*, K.C. Dyer's *Ms. Zephyr's Notebook*, Liane Shaw's *thinandbeautiful.com*, and Marnelle Tokio's *More Than You Can Chew*.

Tullson, D. (2009). *Riley Park*. Victoria, BC: Orca.

Recovering from a brain injury in an attack that killed his friend Darius, Corbin navigates unfamiliar territory as he comes to terms with both physical restrictions and the law, as well as his unreturned admiration for an abused girl named Rubee. For ages 13 and up.

Description: hi-lo realistic fiction; themes include grief and loss, and responsible use of alcohol.

Read-ons: Rubee's story may be expanded by reading other titles involving spousal abuse, including Monique Polak's *So Much It Hurts*. Various connections will also be found to short stories in Linda Holeman's collection *Toxic Love*.

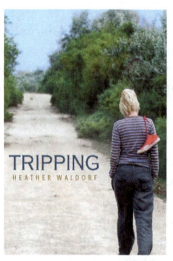

Waldorf, H. (2008). *Tripping*. Calgary, AB: Red Deer Press.

A group of six teenagers signs on for a cross-Canada summer field trip, each attempting to exorcise personal demons. Rainey—who turns 17 en route—is concerned about her future and about her past as well; the mother she never knew is suddenly available for contact, and during this trip Rainey must decide whether or not to go and see her. A relationship with Alain, one of the boys in the group, suddenly turns serious, and Rainey doesn't want it to be a temporary fling. One aspect of Rainey's characterization involves the use of a prosthetic leg due to the "amniotic band syndrome" she was born with. It is her employment of the "Flexileg" in a variety of situations that confirms her true zest for life. For ages 14 and up.

Description: realistic fiction; themes include coming of age, teen sexuality, and mother/daughter relationships.

Read-ons: Other titles that explore coming of age and teen sexuality include Beth Goobie's *Hello Groin* and Susan Juby's *Miss Smithers* as well as Don Aker's *The Space Between*. Julie Johnston's *In Spite of Killer Bees* further examines a daughter's reunion with a long absent mother.

Read-on Bibliography

Abier, G. (2009). *The pool was empty.* Ontario: Firefly Books.
Aker, D. (2007). *The space between.* Toronto, Ontario: HarperCollins.
Alexie, S. (2007). *The absolutely true diary of a part-time Indian.* New York, NY: Little, Brown.
Alire Saenz, B. (2012). *Aristotle and Dante discover the secrets of the universe.* Toronto, ON: Simon & Schuster Books for Young Readers.
Anderson, M.T. (2002). *Feed.* Cambridge, MA: Candlewick Press.
Badoe, A. (2010). *Between sisters.* Toronto, ON: Groundwood Books/House of Anansi Press.
Beckett, S. (1994). *Waiting for Godot.* New York, NY: Grove.
Bell, W. (1991). *Absolutely invincible!* Toronto, ON: Stoddart Kids.
Bell, W. (2001). *Stones.* Toronto, ON: Doubleday.
Bellingham, B. (1998). *Drowning in secrets.* Toronto, ON: Scholastic Canada.
Bird-Wilson, L. (2013). *Just pretending.* Regina, SK: Coteau Books.
Blakeslee, M. (1991). *Hal.* Toronto, ON: Stoddart.
Blume, J. (1970). *Are you there God? It's me, Margaret.* New York, NY: Yearling.
Bobet, L. (2012). *Above.* New York, NY: Arthur A. Levine Books.
Bow, E. (2010). *Plain Kate.* New York, NY: Arthur A. Levine Books.
Brenna, B. (2007). *The moon children.* Calgary, AB: Red Deer Press.
Brenna, B. (2009). *Something to hang on to.* Saskatoon, SK: Thistledown Press.
Brontë, C. (2008). *Jane Eyre.* Radford, VA: Wilder Productions. (Original work published 1847).
Brooks, M. (1997). *Bone dance.* Toronto, ON: Douglas & McIntyre.
Buffie, M. (1992). *Someone else's ghost.* New York, NY: Scholastic.
Burtinshaw, J. (2008). *The perfect cut.* Vancouver, BC: Raincoast Books.
Butcher, K. (2009). *Return to Bone Tree Hill.* Saskatoon, SK: Thistledown Press.
Campbell, J. (2005). *Take me out of the ball game.* Saskatoon, SK: Thistledown Press.
Chalifour, F. (2005). *After.* Toronto, ON: Tundra Books.
Chalifour, F. (2005). *Call me Mimi.* Toronto, ON: Tundra Books.
Choyce, L. (2004). *Smoke and mirrors.* Toronto, ON: Boardwalk Books.
Choyce, L. (2011). *Dumb luck.* Markham, ON: Red Deer Press.
De Angeli, M. (1949). *The door in the wall.* New York, NY: Doubleday.
Denman, K.L. (2009). *Me, myself and Ike.* Victoria, BC: Orca Book Publishers.
Dickens, C. (1838). *The adventures of Oliver Twist.* New York, NY: Quality Paperback.
Donovan, L. (2007). *Winds of L'Acadie.* Vancouver, BC: Ronsdale Press.
Doyle, B. (2003). *Boy O'Boy.* Toronto, ON: Douglas & McIntyre.
Dunnion, K. (2005). *Mosh pit.* Red Deer, AB: Red Deer Press.
Dyer, K.C. (2002). *Seeds of time.* Toronto, ON: Dundurn.
Dyer, K.C. (2007). *Ms. Zephyr's notebook.* Toronto, ON: Boardwalk.
Ellis, D. (1999). *Looking for X.* Toronto, ON: Douglas & McIntyre.
Ellis, D. (2006). *Jackal in the garden.* New York, NY: Watson-Guptill Publications.

Ellis, S. (2003). *The several lives of Orphan Jack.* Toronto, ON: Groundwood Books/Douglas & McIntyre.
Ellis, S. (2014). *Outside in.* Toronto, ON: Groundwood Books/House of Anansi Press.
Fairbridge, L. (1999). *Tangled in time.* Vancouver, BC: Ronsdale Press.
Fairfield, L. (2009). *Tyranny.* Toronto, ON: Tundra Books.
Fitch, S. (2002). *One more step.* Victoria, BC: Orca Book Publishers.
Gebler, C. (2001). *Caught on a train.* Lawrence, KA: Mammoth Publications.
Ghent, N. (2011). *Against all odds.* Toronto, ON: HarperCollins.
Gingras, C. (2009). *Pieces of me.* Toronto, ON: Kids Can Press.
Goobie, B. (1994). *Mission impossible.* Red Deer, AB: Red Deer College Press.
Goobie, B. (1997). *The good, the bad and the suicidal.* Montreal, QC: Roussan.
Goobie, B. (2000). *Before wings.* Victoria, BC: Orca Book Publishers.
Goobie, B. (2002). *Kicked out.* Scarborough, ON: Prentice Hall Canada.
Goobie, B. (2005). *Something girl.* Victoria, BC: Orca Book Publishers.
Goobie, B. (2006). *Hello groin.* Victoria, BC: Orca Book Publishers.
Goobie, B. (2011). *Born ugly.* Markham, ON: Red Deer Press.
Haddon, M. (2003). *The curious incident of the dog in the night-time.* Toronto, ON: Anchor Canada.
Harrington, L. (2010). *Rattled: A mystery.* Halifax, NS: Nimbus Publishing.
Harvest, F. (2011). *Girl fight.* Toronto, ON: J. Lorimer.
Harvey, S.N. (2008). *The lit report.* Victoria, BC: Orca Book Publishers.
Harvey-Fitzhenry, A. (2008). *Broken.* Vancouver, BC: Tradewind.
Haworth-Attard, B. (2002). *Irish chain.* Toronto, ON: HarperTrophy Canada.
Hinton, S.E. (1967). *The outsiders.* New York, NY: Viking Press.
Holeman, L. (2003). *Toxic love.* Toronto, ON: Tundra Books.
Horrock, A. (2006). *Almost Eden.* Toronto, ON: Tundra Books.
Huser, G. (2003). *Stitches.* Toronto, ON: Groundwood Books.
Huser, G. (2011). *The runaway.* Vancouver, BC: Tradewind Books.
Ingalls Wilder, L. (1937). *On the banks of Plum Creek.* New York, NY: HarperTrophy.
Ingalls Wilder, L. (1939). *On the shores of Silver Lake.* Los Angeles, CA: LR Publishing.
Jaden, D. (2012). *Never enough.* New York, NY: Simon Pulse.
Janz, H.L. (2004). *Sparrows on wheels.* Edmonton, AB: Doc Crip Press.
Jocelyn, M. (2004). *Mabel Riley: A reliable record of humdrum, peril, and romance.* Toronto, ON: Tundra Books.
Jocelyn, M. (2008). *Would you.* Toronto, ON: Tundra Books.
Johnston, J. (2001). *In spite of killer bees.* Toronto, ON: Tundra Books.
Juby, S. (2000). *Alice, I think.* Saskatoon, SK: Thistledown Press.
Juby, S. (2004). *Miss Smithers.* New York, NY: HarperTempest.
Katz, W.W. (1990). *Whalesinger.* Toronto, ON: Douglas & McIntyre.
Kelly Martin, C.K. (2013). *Yesterday.* Toronto, ON: Doubleday Canada.
Khan, R. (1999). *Dahling if you luv me, would you please, please smile.* Toronto, ON: Stoddart Kids.

Kluger, S. (2008). *My most excellent year: A novel of love, Mary Poppins, & Fenway Park.* New York, NY: Dial Books.
Kositsky, L. (2000). *A question of Will.* Montreal, QU: Roussan Pub.
Krill, D. (2006). *The Uncle Duncle chronicles: Escape from Treasure Island.* Montreal, QC: Lobster Press.
Kropp, P. (1986/2003). *Playing chicken.* Toronto, ON: HIP Books.
Kuipers, A. (2007). *Life on the refrigerator door.* Toronto, ON: HarperCollins.
Kuipers, A. (2010). *The worst thing she ever did.* Toronto, ON: HarperTrophyCanada.
Laidlaw, S.J. (2013). *An infidel in paradise.* Toronto, ON: Tundra Books.
Lawrence, I. (2006/2008). *Gemini summer.* New York, NY: Yearling.
Lekich, J. (2002). *The losers' club.* Toronto, ON: Annick Press.
L'Engle, M. (2008). *The joys of love.* New York, NY: Farrar Straus Giroux.
L'Engle, M. (2011). *A wrinkle in time.* New York, NY: Square Fish.
Lewis, C.S. (1950). *The lion, the witch and the wardrobe.* New York, NY: HarperTrophy.
Lewis, W.A. (2008). *Freefall.* Toronto, ON: Key Porter Books.
Linden, D. (2013). *On fire.* Saskatoon, SK: Thistledown Press.
Little, J. (1987). *Little by little: A writer's education.* Markham, ON: Viking Kestrel.
Lord, C. (2006). *Rules.* New York, NY: Scholastic Press.
Mac, C. (2006). *The Droughtlanders.* Toronto, ON: Puffin Canada.
MacDonald, A.L. (2009). *Seeing red.* Toronto, ON: KidsCan Press.
MacIntyre, R.P. (Ed.) (1997). *Takes.* Saskatoon, SK: Thistledown Press.
Maes, N. (2009). *Laughing wolf.* Toronto, ON: Dundurn Press.
Marineau, M. (1995). *The road to Chlifa.* Red Deer, AB: Red Deer College Press.
Marineau, M. (2000). *Lean mean machines.* Calgary, AB: Red Deer Press.
Martineau Wagner, T. (2007). *It happened on the underground railway.* Guilford, CT: Globe Pequot Press.
Matas, C. (1996). *After the war.* New York, NY: Simon & Schuster Books for Young Readers.
Matas, C. (1997). *The freak.* Toronto, ON: Key Porter Books.
Matas, C. (1997). *The garden.* New York, NY: Simon & Schuster Books for Young Readers.
McBay, B., & Heneghan, J. (2003). *Waiting for Sarah.* Victoria, BC: Orca Books.
McKay, S. (2004) *Esther.* Toronto, ON: Penguin Canada.
McMurchy-Barber, G. (2010). *Free as a bird.* Toronto, ON: Dundurn Press.
McNamee, G. (2003). *Acceleration.* New York, NY: Wendy Lamb Books.
McNaughton, J. (1994). *Catch me once, catch me twice.* Toronto, ON: Stoddart.
McNaughton, J. (1996). *To dance at the Palais Royale.* St. John's, NL: Tuckamore Books.
Meyer, S. (2005). *Twilight.* New York, NY: Little, Brown and Co.
Minaki, C. (2007). *Zoe's extraordinary holiday adventures.* Toronto, ON: Second Story Press.
Myers, W.D. (1999). *Monster.* New York, NY: HarperCollins Publishers.
Na, A. (2001/2002). *A step from heaven.* New York, NY: Speak.

Nickel, B. (2005). *Hannah Waters and the daughter of Johann Sebastian Bach.* Toronto, ON: Penguin Canada.

Noël, M. (2004). *Good for nothing.* Toronto, ON: Groundwood Books.

Ostlere, C. (2011/2012). *Karma.* Toronto, ON: Penguin Group (Canada).

Patterson, K. (1978). *The great Gilly Hopkins.* New York, NY: Crowell.

Paterson, K. (1980). *Jacob have I loved.* New York, NY: Crowell.

Pignat, C. (2008). *Egghead.* Calgary, AB: Red Deer Press.

Pignat, C. (2008). *Greener grass: The famine years.* Calgary, AB: Red Deer Press.

Pinter, H. (2006). The birthday party. In *The essential Pinter.* New York, NY: Grove.

Polak, M. (2013). *So much it hurts.* Victoria, BC: Orca Book Publishers.

Poulsen, D. (2008). *Numbers.* Toronto, ON: Key Porter Books.

Poulsen, D. (2013). *Old man.* Toronto, ON: Dundurn Press.

Reynold, P.H. (2004). *Ish.* Cambridge, MS: Candlewick Press.

Richards, D. (1999). *The lady at Batoche.* Saskatoon, SK: Thistledown Press.

Richmond, S. (1983/2009). *Wheels for walking.* Vancouver, BC: Douglas & McIntyre.

Roorda, J. (2007). *Wings of a bee.* Toronto, ON: Sumach Press.

Rosoff, M. (2007/2009). *What I was.* Toronto, ON: Doubleday Canada.

Rud, J. (2008). *Paralyzed.* Victoria, BC: Orca Book Publishers.

Salinger, J.D. (1945). *The catcher in the rye.* New York, NY: Little, Brown.

Salvadurai, S. (2005). *Swimming in the Monsoon Sea.* Toronto, ON: McClelland & Stewart.

Sartre, J.P. (1956/1992). *Being and nothingness.* New York, NY: Washington Square Press.

Shakespeare, W. (2008). Macbeth. In N. Brooke (Ed.), *The Oxford Shakespeare: Macbeth.* Oxford, UK: Oxford University Press.

Shaw, G.B. (1924). *Saint Joan: A chronicle play in 6 scenes and an epilogue.* London, UK: Constable & Co.

Shaw, L. (2009). *thinandbeautiful.com.* Toronto, ON: Second Story Press.

Sherrard, V. (2009). *Watcher.* Toronto, ON: Dundurn Press.

Silverthorne, J. (2005). *The secret of the stone house.* Regina, SK: Coteau Books.

Skrypuch, M. (1999). *The hunger.* Toronto, ON: Boardwalk Books.

Skrypuch, M. (2001). *Hope's war.* Toronto, ON: Boardwalk Books.

Skrypuch, M. (2003). *Nobody's child.* Toronto, ON: Dundurn Press.

Slade, A. (2009). *The hunchback assignments.* Toronto, ON: HarperCollins.

Smucker, B. (1977). *Underground to Canada.* Toronto, ON: Clarke, Irwin.

Spencer Hesser, T. (1998). *Kissing doorknobs.* New York, NY: Delacorte Press.

Stevenson, R. (2008). *Big guy.* Victoria, BC: Orca Books.

Stevenson, R. (2008). *Impossible things.* Victoria, BC: Orca Book Publishers.

Stewart, S., & Weisman, J. (2008). *Cathy's book.* Philadelphia, PA: Running Press.

Stratton, A. (2010). *Borderline.* Toronto, ON: HarperTrophy Canada.

Tamaki, M., & Tamaki, J. (2008). *Skim.* Toronto, ON: Groundwood Books.

Tan, S. (2007). *The arrival.* New York, NY: Arthur A. Levine Books.

Taylor, C. (1985). *Julie.* Saskatoon, SK: Western Producer Prairie Books.

Thompson, C. (2003). *Blankets.* Marietta, GA: Top Shelf Productions.
Thompson, M. (2000). *Eyewitness.* Vancouver, BC: Ronsdale Press.
Thompson, T.D. (2011). *Rooster.* Winnipeg, MB: Pemmican Publications.
Tokio, M. (2003). *More than you can chew.* Toronto, ON: Tundra Books.
Toten, T. (2001). *The game.* Calgary, AB: Red Deer Press.
Trembath, D. (1996). *The Tuesday café.* Victoria, BC: Orca Books.
Tullson, D. (2006). *Zero.* Markham, ON: Fitzenry & Whiteside.
Twain, M. (1884). *The adventures of Huckleberry Finn.* New York, NY: Tom Doherty Associates.
Waldorf, H. (2008). *Tripping.* Calgary, AB: Red Deer Press.
Walsh, A. (2006). *A sky black with crows.* Calgary, AB: Red Deer Press.
Walters, E. (1999). *The money pit mystery.* Toronto, ON: HarperCollins.
Walters, E. (2000). *Rebound.* Toronto, ON: Stoddart Kids.
Walters, E. (2006). *Shattered.* Toronto, ON: Penguin.
White, E.B. (1939). *Charlotte's web.* New York, NY: Harper & Row.
Wilson, J. (2003). *And in the morning.* Toronto, ON: Kids Can Press.
Wrede, P.C. (2009). *Thirteenth child.* New York, NY: Scholastic Press.
Wynne-Jones, T. (2009). *The uninvited.* Somerville, MA: Candlewick Press.
Ytak, C. (2009). *Nothing but your skin.* Richmond Hill, ON: Firefly Books.
Ziegesar, C. (2002). *Gossip girl.* Boston, MA: Little, Brown and Co.
Zindel, P. (1968). *The pigman.* New York, NY: Harper & Row.
Zindel, P. (1980). *The pigman's legacy.* New York, NY: Harper & Row.

Three Essential Questions for This Chapter

1. Explore a bookstore or a public library; where are books for older teens located? What seems to differentiate these books from adult books? What seems to separate them from books for younger readers?
2. Consider the lack of books that include other types of difference alongside disability in characterizations. Why do you think this might be so? What message does it send to readers?
3. Select a young adult novel that is new to you from the annotated bibliography. After you read it, list at least four age-appropriate response activities, in the following categories, that students could do that are related to the book: drama; art; creative writing; and music.

CHAPTER 7

Contemporary Canadian Books on an International Landscape

Book Selection Ideas

It is clear that children's and young adult literature related to portrayals of characters with disabilities is available, but not easily located in terms of bookstore browsing or even online searches. Once titles are located, professionally published reviews such as those found online in CM Magazine (http://www.umanitoba.ca/cm/) can be helpful; however, it is locating titles related to particular disabilities that may pose a challenge. Hopefully the volume at hand will support readers in locating titles of interest, and connecting these titles to other books in the field.

The Promise of Radical Change

Books Past and Present

Books portraying characters with disabilities have evolved through a number of stages to the current state of the field. From didactic 19th-century titles where characters with disabilities were predominantly killed or cured (Keith, 2001), across texts where literary characters who are disabled remain "on the margins ... as uncomplicated figures or exotic aliens" and rarely appear as main characters (Thomson, 1997), and through a new wave of books in the 1960s and '70s where writers were not able to create characters who were not weighed down with feelings of inadequacy and self-hatred (Keith, 2001), there have been changes to how disability is perceived and interpreted. In her provocative book *Take Up Thy Bed and Walk*, Lois Keith describes lists of books about characters with disabilities, such as the ones prepared by Baskin and Harris (1977), as promoting social rather than literary outcomes.

When Dresang (1999) discusses Radical Change that pushes the field of children's literature into new territory, including changing forms and formats, changing boundaries, and changing perspectives, she offers that new depictions of characters with mental and physical disabilities began appearing in the late

1990s, and categorizes the evolution of disability in characterizations in terms of particular stages. At that time, exclusively positive portrayals dominated, possibly as a mechanism to counteract previous negative stigma in books. Such a book is Elizabeth Helfman's (1993) *On Being Sarah*, an uncomplicated story about a 12-year-old girl with cerebral palsy, described in reviews of the time as a "medical drama" book. Novels that focused on identity crises or blandly positive portrayals did not offer the deepest characterizations possible. Over time, however, portrayals have become richer and more diversified.

At the other end of the spectrum of complexity, as far as disability is concerned, is Leah Bobet's (2012) *Above*, a striking example of how radical changes have moved books that incorporate themes of diversity into interdisciplinary territory. In this dystopian fantasy, a corrupt medical system creates, in a city not unlike contemporary Toronto, "abnormal" people who either die or find secret refuge in Safe. Gritty stuff for mature young adult readers who will explore a variety of controversial topics in Bobet's novel within the safe framework fantasy provides.

A Growing Field

More books are being written for young people than ever before. Good literature inspires good literature. As titles about characters with disabilities appear on awards lists, readers and writers become attuned to the potentiality of difference. Books such as Mark Haddon's (2003) international bestseller *The Curious Incident of the Dog in the Night-Time* and its various iterations on stage and screen have championed other voices previously unheard. My own title, *Waiting for No One* (2010c), second in a trilogy about a young woman with autism, was the first Canadian winner of a Dolly Gray Award in 2012. Various titles that portray characters with disabilities have appeared on Governor General's Literary Award lists and shortlists. According to research conducted for this volume, in Canada we have at least 21 picture books, 10 junior novels, 50 intermediate novels, and 53 young adult novels presenting characterizations that include disability. The word is out: taking risks to create characters unique in children's literature is valued.

Complex characterizations that include two or more aspects of diversity are appearing, albeit infrequently, on the world's bookshelves. Jamaican-born California writer Nalo Hopkinson's (2012) young adult novel *The Chaos* presents a 16-year-old girl whose best male friend, Ben, is gay and uses a wheelchair. In addition to demonstrating combinations of diverse traits related to characterizations, Hopkinson's book also demonstrates how themes related to disability can operate in speculative fiction, assisting in changing the dominant status of realistic fiction as far as diverse characterizations are concerned. Another title that pushes boundaries is Belfast author Sarah Wray's (2007) fantasy *The Forbidden Room*, where Jenny, an orphan who uses a wheelchair, discovers a horrifying secret in her new bedroom, and from there the novel spirals into a hard-edged thriller.

Influences of Non-Fiction

Increasing numbers of non-fiction titles, such as David Wright's (2011) highly regarded text *Downs: The History of a Disability*, offer information to support writers of fiction. Kim Edwards' popular adult novel *The Memory Keeper's Daughter* (2006) may have drawn on research or contemporary news stories to support the very able characterization of Phoebe, a character with Down syndrome. Malone's (2011) adult text *Big Town: A novel of Africville* most certainly has roots in historical research, to the extent of how three characters—one of whom may have acquired prenatal health effects along with an intellectual disability due to an assault on his mother by his father—are placed in time and space.

Other non-fiction titles, such as Karin Melberg Schwier's (2013) *Flourish*, provide inspiration toward the consideration of unique life stories. One stereotype that is overturned in Schwier's book involves the idea that people with disabilities will automatically have dull and uninteresting lives. In contrast, readers meet Allison Cameron Gray, an accomplished actor, playwright, and stand-up comic who has cerebral palsy; Jenny Unrein, an artist with William's Syndrome; and Daniel Desjardins, an Alberta radio broadcaster with Down syndrome. Another biography of a person with Down syndrome appears in the documentary film *Educating Peter* (Goodwin & Wurzburg, 1992), with a sequel in *Graduating Peter* (Wurzburg & Watts, 2001). Stereotypes are also dislodged in various non-fiction titles for younger children, including Sarah E. Turner's (2012) striking picture book *Ribbon's Way*, about a monkey born with malformed feet and no hands.

Influences of Writers with Disabilities

Pat Thomson (1992) surmises that "we are unlikely to be fully satisfied" with books about characters who have disabilities "until disabled writers start to come through in greater numbers" (p. 24). This statement parallels Charlotte Brontë and Virginia Woolf's philosophies regarding perspectives on women, namely that "if women were to achieve equality in society, they first had to make the voices of their own imaginations heard through literature" (Meyer, 2007, p. 70). Kent (1988) suggests that though "a number of disabled women have written autobiographies, few, if any, have ventured to translate their experiences into fiction and drama. As the struggles of women with disabilities draw increasing attention through scholarly studies and autobiographical accounts, perhaps women with impairments will feel more free to express themselves in literary forms accessible to the general public" (p. 110). It is also possible that a past lack of access to literacy in marginalized populations may have limited the "registering of the experience of oppression, or the claiming of a political voice" (Swindells, 1995, p. 7).

New research regarding autobiography and biography implies that change in characterizations may be motivated through "disability life writing," counteracting "marginalizing representations of disability in contemporary culture" (Couser, 2006, p. 401). Daniel Tammet's (2007) memoir of Asperger's and an extraordinary mind, *Born on a Blue Day*, offers remarkable insights into individual experience. Fiction by people whose connections to disability are firsthand, such as Alexei Maxim Russell's young adult novel *Trueman Bradley—Aspie Detective* (2011), and Will Roger's junior fiction title *The Stonking Steps* (2004) may also move further understandings about disability into the field. In the case of these titles, both authors are autism advocates.

Graphic Novels: A Form to Watch

Current research on graphic novels and characters with disabilities is limited, but a study examining 30 high-quality American graphic novels published in 2008 indicates that portrayals of these characters, explored in 12 of the 30 texts, most often fit a negative stereotype, where the disability was a primary trait and either connected to a pitiable state, in the case of female characters, or representative of evil, related to male characters (Irwin & Moeller, 2010). These results indicate that the creators of graphic novels have not yet provided realistic representations of people with disabilities in even the best of their work. The graphic novel form is one to watch as Radical Change moves children's literature into even more authentic territory in terms of characterizations.

Predicted Patterns

As we consider the increasing numbers of novels portraying characters with disabilities, particularly for intermediate and young adult age groups, as well as the current dearth of titles for readers in junior ages eight and up, we can only imagine the patterns soon to appear on the landscape of available material. Rather than fitting a niche of "issues books," where these titles contain didactic information about either the disability or its host, it is clear that characters with disabilities have already broken previous stereotypes related to how disabled literary characters have appeared on the margins of fiction as uncomplicated figures or exotic aliens (Thomson, 1997).

From the marginalization of people with special needs as less than status quo, toward full acceptance of people with differences, the evolution as well as the definition of disability is ongoing. Human rights laws provide important guiding principles regarding the acceptance of all people, but in many aspects of community life—the workplace, living environments, schools—people with disabilities continue to advocate for equal access and respect. Yet, disability as a fundamental human experience is beginning to find a place in critical consciousness. Stories, and the context in which these stories are presented, can provide an important medium for change, drawing disability to the fore alongside other aspects of human diversity.

Is Different Wrong?

"Is different wrong?" a young glider shakily asks his sister in Kenneth Oppel's (2007) intermediate fantasy *Dusk*. This character is aware of his physical difference from the clan that is raising him, and he is afraid. In the context of the story, the sister's response reflects wider and contemporary stereotypes about difference, and the answer, for Dusk, and for us all, is heartbreaking.

I dream of a time when the answer to this question, in real terms, is reflective of a diversity that is more ordinary than society has cared in the past to acknowledge. I dream of a time when children will take their place in schools that reflect their individual strengths and challenges through diverse resources. I dream of a time when the unequivocal answer to the question "Is different wrong?" will be an answer we all may celebrate.

Concluding Thoughts

In addition to representing the world, I believe that stories can also change the world. In this moment of stopped time, I consider my classroom experiences with Dan and Brianna, and retrace my steps into a school curriculum that did not, at that time, support either of these students. The discovery of our shared appreciation for a particular novel might have been the beginning of a new path for Dan and me, had he remained in my room. Reflections on Brianna, as well as the people from my mother's stories—Johnny, Old Jones, and Eddy—cause me to think about how powerful narratives are in terms of offering transformational experiences. I ponder the value of stories, of storytelling. Who says we—teachers, parents, storytellers, writers—cannot change the world? Together, I believe we can.

Stories build understanding of self and other, critical to positive renderings of identity and community. As an educator, I think that the stories we offer to children in our homes and classrooms matter. As a researcher, I think there is important work yet to be done in cataloguing the messages young people receive from contemporary texts, as well as noticing voices yet unheard on the textual landscape. As a writer, I know that my stories have changed me—have changed how I think about the navigation of disabilities from a personal standpoint as I attempt to create characters from the inside out. I predict that as more people are supported in telling their own stories, and as these authentic narratives follow biographies into supporting fictive works, we can heighten the possibility of the appearance of authentic mirrors and informative windows in children's reading—helping our leaders of tomorrow see, understand, and actualize the world in a more complete and just way.

Three Essential Questions for This Chapter

1. Locate a new title representing a character with a disability that could be added to this volume. Summarize it, and suggest questions for students that might extend critical literacy related to the book's content.
2. Write a letter to an imaginary author, asking her or him to write about a particular character whose voice you think is missing on the landscape of available books for young people.
3. Discuss a title (fiction or non-fiction) that had some sort of transformational effect on you or someone you know. How might a title support transformation in a group of students?

REFERENCES

Alcott, L.M. (1958). *Little women*. London, UK: Puffin Books. (Original work published 1868).

Anderson, M.T. (2002). *Feed*. Cambridge, MA: Candlewick.

Asch, A., & Fine, M. (1988). Introduction: Beyond pedestals. In M. Fine & A. Asch (Eds.), *Women with disabilities: Essays in psychology, culture, and politics* (pp. 1–37). Philadelphia, PA: Temple University Press.

Baker, B. (2014). *Camp Outlook*. Toronto, ON: Second Story Press.

Banks, J.A. (2014). *An introduction to multicultural education* (5th ed.). Toronto, ON: Pearson.

Barker, C., Kulyk, J., Knorr, L., & Brenna, B. (2011). Open inclusion or shameful secret: A comparison of characters with Fetal Alcohol Spectrum Disorders (FASD) and characters with Autism Spectrum Disorders (ASD) in a North American sample of books for children and young adults. *International Journal of Special Education, 26*(3), 171–180.

Baskin, B.H., & Harris, K.H. (1977). *Notes from a different drummer: A guide to juvenile fiction portraying the handicapped*. New York, NY: R.R. Bowker.

Bateson, M.C. (1994). *Peripheral visions: Learning along the way*. New York, NY: Harper Collins.

Baynton, D. (2006). A silent exile on this earth: The metaphorical construction of deafness in the nineteenth century. In L.J. Davis (Ed.), *The Disability Studies Reader* (2nd ed., pp. 33–48). New York, NY: Routledge.

Bell, L.A. (1997). Theoretical foundations for social justice education. In M. Adams, L.A. Bell, & P. Griffin (Eds.), *Teaching for diversity and social justice: A sourcebook* (pp. 3–15). New York, NY: Routledge.

Biklen, D., & Bogdan, R. (1977). Media portrayals of disabled people: A study in stereotypes. *Interracial Books for Children Bulletin, 8*(6–7), 4–9.

Blakeslee, M. (1991). *Hal*. Toronto, ON: Stoddart.

Bloom, S.P. (2006). Review of the book *Gemini summer* by I. Lawrence. *The Horn Book Magazine, 82*(6), 717–718.

Blume, J. (1972). *Tales of a fourth grade nothing*. New York, NY: Dutton.

Bobet, L. (2012). *Above*. New York, NY: Arthur A. Levine.

Brenna, B. (2005). *Wild orchid*. Calgary, AB: Red Deer Press.

Brenna, B. (2007). *The moon children*. Calgary, AB: Red Deer Press.

Brenna, B. (2008). Stories in the wind. *Journal of the Association for Research on Mothering, 10*(2), 254–256.

Brenna, B. (2009). *Something to hang on to.* Saskatoon, SK: Thistledown Press.

Brenna, B. (2010a). Assisting young readers in the interpretation of a character with disabilities in Iain Lawrence's juvenile fiction novel "Gemini Summer". *English Quarterly, 41*(1–2), 54–61.

Brenna, B. (2010b). *Characters with disabilities in contemporary children's novels: Portraits of three authors in a frame of Canadian texts.* Unpublished PhD dissertation, University of Alberta.

Brenna, B. (2010c). *Waiting for no one.* Markham, ON: Red Deer Press.

Brenna, B. (2011). *Falling for Henry.* Markham, ON: Red Deer Press.

Brenna, B. (2012a). One literate life: A case study of a ninety-four-year-old reader. *The Reading Professor, 34*(1), 33–37.

Brenna, B. (2012b). *The white bicycle.* Markham, ON: Red Deer Press.

Brenna, B., & Bell, A. (2014, in press). Never too late to learn: The unique literacy profile of a teen with multiple disabilities. *The Reading Professor.*

Brueggemann, B.J., & Lupo, M.E. (2008). *Disability and/in prose.* New York, NY: Routledge.

Bryan, G. (2006). Review of the book *Gemini summer* by I. Lawrence. *CM Magazine, 13*(8). Retrieved from www.umanitoba.ca/cm/vol13/no8/gemini-summer.html

Burke, K.J. (2010). *Ducks on the moon: A parent meets autism.* Regina, SK: Hagios Press.

Bush, E. (2006). Review of the book *Gemini summer* by I. Lawrence. *Bulletin of the Center for Children's Books, 60*(4), 176.

Carle, E. (1969). *The very hungry caterpillar.* New York, NY: Philomel Books.

Carter, A.L. (2001). *In the clear.* Victoria, BC: Orca Books.

Coles, R. (1989). *The call of stories: Teaching and the moral imagination.* Boston: Houghton Mifflin.

Couser, G.T. (2006). Disability, life narrative and representation. In L.J. Davis (Ed.), *The disability studies reader* (2nd ed., pp. 399–401). New York, NY: Routledge.

Crossley, N. (2005). *Key concepts in critical social theory.* Thousand Oaks, CA: Sage.

Crotty, M. (1998). *The foundations of social research: Meaning and perspective in the research process.* Thousand Oaks, CA: Sage.

Damico, J., & Apol, L. (2008). Using testimonial response to frame the challenges and possibilities of risky historical texts. *Children's Literature in Education, 39,* 141–58.

Davidson, M. (2006). Universal design: The work of disability in an age of globalization. In L.J. Davis (Ed.), *The disability studies reader* (2nd ed., pp. 117–128). New York, NY: Routledge.

Davis, L.J. (2006). Constructing normalcy: The bell curve, the novel, and the invention of the disabled body in the nineteenth century. In L.J. Davis (Ed.), *The disability studies reader* (2nd ed., pp. 3–16). New York, NY: Routledge.

Denman, K.L. (2009). *Me, myself and Ike.* Victoria, BC: Orca Book Publishers.

Denman, K.L. (2011). *Stuff we all get.* Victoria, BC: Orca.

Derman-Sparks, L., & the ABC Task Force. (1989). *Anti-bias curriculum: Tools for empowering young children.* Washington, DC: National Association for the Education of Young Children.

de Vries, M. (2011). *Somebody's girl.* Victoria, BC: Orca.

Dolmage, J. (2008). Between the valley and the field. In B.J. Brueggemann, & M.E. Lupo (Eds.), *Disability and/in prose* (pp. 98–109). New York, NY: Routledge.

Dresang, E.T. (1999). *Radical change: Books for youth in a digital age.* New York, NY: H.W. Wilson.

Dresang, E.T., & Kotrla, B. (2009). Radical change theory and synergistic reading for digital age youth. *Journal of Aesthetic Education,* 43(2), 92–107.

Dyches, T.T., & Prater, M.A. (2000). *Developmental disability in children's literature: Issues and annotated bibliography.* Reston, VA: Council for Exceptional Children, Division on Mental Retardation and Developmental Disabilities.

Dyches, T.T., Prater, M.A., & Cramer, S.F. (2001). Characterization of mental retardation and autism in children's books. *Education and Training in Mental Retardation and Developmental Disabilities,* 36(3), 230–243.

Dyches, T.T., & Prater, M.A. (2005). Characterization of developmental disability in children's fiction. *Education and Training on Developmental Disabilities,* 40(3), 202–216.

Dyer, K.C. (2002). *Seeds of time.* Toronto, ON: Dundurn Press.

Dyer, K.C. (2003). *Secret of light.* Toronto, ON: Dundurn Press.

Edwards, K. (2006). *The memory keeper's daughter.* Toronto, ON: Penguin Books Canada.

Edwards, G., & Saltman, J. (2010). *Picturing Canada: A history of Canadian children's illustrated books and publishing.* Toronto, ON: University of Toronto Press.

Eisner, E. (2002). *The educational imagination: On the design and evaluation of school programs* (3rd ed.). Upper Saddle River, NJ: Merrill/Prentice Hall.

Ellis, D. (2011). *No ordinary day.* Toronto, ON: Groundwood Books.

Emmerson, J., Fu, Q., & Brenna, B. (2013, May). Portrayals of characters with disabilities in contemporary North American children's picture books. Canadian Society for the Study of Education (CSSE), Victoria, BC.

Emmerson, J., Fu, Q., Lendsay, A., & Brenna, B. (2014). Picture book characters with disabilities: Patterns and trends in a context of Radical Change. *Bookbird,* 52(4), 12–22.

Fairfield, L. (2009). *Tyranny*. Toronto, ON: Tundra Books.

Filax, G., & Taylor, D. (2014). *Disabled mothers: Stories and scholarship by and about mothers with disabilities*. Toronto, ON: Demeter Press.

Finazzo, D.A. (1997). *All for the children: Multicultural essentials of literature*. New York, NY: Delmar Publishers.

Findlay, J. (2011). *The summer of permanent wants*. Toronto, ON: Doubleday Canada.

Fitch, S., & Flook, H. (Illustrator). (2004). *Pocket rocks*. Victoria, BC: Orca Book Publishers.

Freire, P. (1983). *Pedagogy of the oppressed* (M.B. Ramos, Trans.). New York, NY: Continuum. (Original work published in 1970).

Freire, P. (1991). The importance of the act of reading. In B. Power, & R. Hubbard (Eds.), *Literacy in process* (pp. 21–26). Portsmouth, NH: Heinemann.

Freire, P. (1998). *Teachers as cultural workers: Letters to those who dare teach* (D. Macedo, D. Koike, & A. Oliveira, Trans.). Cambridge, MA: Westview Press.

Galda, L. (1998). Mirrors and windows: Reading as transformation. In T.E. Raphael, & K.H. Au (Eds.), *Literature-based instruction: Reshaping the curriculum* (pp. 1–11). Norwood, MA: Christopher Gordon Publishers.

Gilbert, P. (1997). Discourses on gender and literacy: Changing the stories. In S. Muspratt, A. Luke, & P. Freebody (Eds.), *Constructing critical literacies: Teaching and learning textual practice* (pp. 59–76). Cresskill, NJ: Hampton Press.

Gilbert, P. (2001). (Sub)versions: Using sexist language practices to explore critical literacy. In H. Fehring, & P. Green (Eds.), *Critical literacy: A collection of articles from the Australian Literacy Education Association* (pp. 75–83). Newark, DE: International Reading Association.

Gilmore, R. (1995). *A friend Like Zilla*. Toronto, ON: Second Story Press.

Gilmore, R. (1999). *A screaming kind of day*. Markham, ON: Fitzhenry & Whiteside.

Gilmore, R. (2000). *Mina's spring of colors*. Markham, ON: Fitzhenry & Whiteside.

Giroux, H.A. (2005). *Border crossings* (2nd ed.). New York, NY: Routledge.

Goobie, B. (2012). *Jason's why*. Markham, ON: Red Deer Press.

Goodwin, T.C., & Wurzburg, G. (Producers), & Wurzburg, G. (Director). (1992). *Educating Peter*. (Motion picture). United States: Direct Cinema Limited. Retrieved from www.cloudy.ec/v/be02376fc9d7b

Grandin, T. (2012). *Different—not less: Inspiring stories of achievement and successful employment from adults with autism, Asperger's, and ADHD*. Arlington, TX: Future Horizons.

Greenwell, B. (2004). The curious incident of novels about Asperger's syndrome. *Children's Literature in Education, 35*(3), 271–284.

Gregory, N., & Lightburn, R. (Illustrator). (1997). *How Smudge came*. Markham, ON: Red Deer Press.

Haddon, M. (2003). *The curious incident of the dog in the night-time*. Toronto, ON: Anchor Canada.

Haworth-Attard, B. (2002). *Irish chain*. Toronto, ON: HarperTrophy Canada.

Hays, P.L. (1971). *The limping hero: Grotesques in literature*. New York, NY: New York University Press.

Heffernan, L. (2004). *Critical literacy and writers' workshop: Bringing purpose and passion to student writing*. Newark, DE: International Reading Association.

Helfman, E. (1993). *On being Sarah*. Morton Grove, IL: Albert Whitman.

Hesse, K. (1997). *Out of the dust*. New York, NY: Scholastic.

Higashida, N. (2013). *The reason I jump: The inner voice of a thirteen-year-old boy with autism*. Toronto, ON: Knopf Canada.

Hopkinson, N. (2012). *The chaos*. Toronto, ON: Margaret K. McElderry Books.

Hugo, R. (1979). *The triggering town*. New York, NY: Norton.

Huntley, K. (2006). Review of the book *Gemini summer* by I. Lawrence. *The Booklist, 103*(8), 49.

Huser, G. (2003). *Stitches*. Toronto, ON: Groundwood.

Irwin, M., & Moeller, R. (2010). Seeing different: Portrayals of disability in young adult graphic novels. *School Library Research, 13*. Retrieved from www.ala.org/aasl/sites/ala.org.aasl/files/content/aaslpubsandjournals/slr/vol13/SLR_SeeingDifferent.pdf.

Jackson, L. (2002). *Freaks, geeks and Asperger syndrome: A user guide to adolescence*. London, UK: Jessica Kingsley.

Jaeger, P.T., & Bowman, C.A. (2005). *Understanding disability: Inclusion, access, diversity and civil rights*. Westport, CT: Praeger.

Janz, H. (2004). *Sparrows on wheels*. Edmonton, AB: Doc Crip Press.

Kalke-Klita, T. (2005). Moving forward: The inclusion of characters with Down syndrome in children's picture books. *Language and Literacy, 7*(2).

Kamara, M., with McClelland, S. (2008). *The bite of the mango*. Toronto, ON: Annick Press.

Keith, L. (2001). *Take up thy bed & walk: Death, disability and cure in classic fiction for girls*. New York, NY: Routledge.

Kelly, D. (2010). Media representation and the case for critical media education. In M.C. Courtland, & T. Gambell (Eds.), *Literature, Media & Multiliteracies in Adolescent Language Arts* (pp. 277–304). Vancouver, BC: Pacific Educational Press.

Kent, D. (1987). Disabled women: Portraits in fiction and drama. In A. Gartner, & T. Joe (Eds.), *Images of the disabled, disabling images* (pp. 47–63). New York, NY: Praeger.

Kent, D. (1988). In search of a heroine: Images of women with disabilities in fiction and drama. In M. Fine, & A. Asch (Eds.), *Women with disabilities: Essays in psychology, culture, and politics* (pp. 90–113). Philadelphia, PA: Temple University Press.

Ketchen, S. (2012). *Grows that way*. Fernie, BC: Oolichan.

Klages, M. (1999). *Woeful afflictions: Disability and sentimentality in Victorian America*. Philadelphia, PA: University of Pennsylvania Press.

Klein, B. S. (2006). *Shameless: The ART of disability*. (Motion picture). Montreal, QC: National Film Board.

Kliewer, C. (1998). *Schooling children with Down syndrome: Toward an understanding of possibility*. New York, NY: Teachers College Press.

Kropp, P. (2004). *Against all odds*. Toronto, ON: HIP Books.

Kropp, P. (2014). Paul Kropp's high interest novels. Retrieved from http://www.paulkropp.com/highint.html

Landrum, J. (2001). Selecting intermediate novels that feature characters with disabilities: Characters with disabilities can create opportunities for learning about and accepting differences. *The Reading Teacher, 55*(3), 252–258.

Lawrence, I. (2006). *Gemini summer*. New York, NY: Delacorte Press.

Le Guin, U. (2004). *The wave in the mind: Talks and essays on the writer, the reader, and the imagination*. Boston, MA: Shambhala.

L'Engle, M. (2011). *A wrinkle in time*. New York, NY: Square Fish. (Original work published in 1962).

Lewison, M., Flint, A.S., & Van Sluys, K. (2002). Taking on critical literacy: The journey of newcomers and novices. *Language Arts, 79*(5), 382–392.

Lindemann Nelson, H. (1995). Resistance and insubordination. *Hypatia, 10*(2), 23–40.

Linton, S. (2006). Reassigning meaning. In L.J. Davis (Ed.), *The disability studies reader* (2nd ed., pp. 161–172). New York, NY: Routledge.

Little, J. (2012). *From Anna*. Toronto, ON: Scholastic Canada. (Original work published in 1972).

Little, J. (1987). *Little by Little: A writer's education*. Markham, ON: Viking.

Little, J. (1990). *Stars come out within*. Markham, ON: Penguin Books.

Little, J. (2000). *Willow and Twig*. Toronto, ON: Penguin Canada.

Longmore, P.K. (1987). Screening stereotypes: Images of disabled people in television and motion pictures. In A. Gardner, & T. Joe (Eds.), *Images of the disabled, disabling images*. (pp. 65–78). New York, NY: Praeger.

Luce-Kapler, R. (2004). *Writing with, through, and beyond the text: An ecology of language*. Mahwah, NJ: Lawrence Erlbaum.

Lugones, M. (1987). Playfulness, "world"-travelling, and loving perception. *Hypatia, 2*(2), 3–19.

Luke, A., & Freebody, P. (1997). Shaping the social practices of reading. In S. Muspratt, A. Luke, & P. Freebody (Eds.), *Constructing critical literacies: Teaching and learning textual practice* (pp. 185–225). Cresskill, NJ: Hampton Press.

Maclear, K., & Arsenault, I. (Illustrator). (2012). *Virginia Wolf*. Toronto, ON: Groundwood Books.

Malone, S.G. (2011). *Big town: A novel of Africville*. Halifax, NS: Vagrant Press.

Marlowe, P. (2010). *Knights of the sea*. Sackville, NB: Sybertooth.

Marshall, C.S. (1998). Using children's storybooks to encourage discussions among diverse populations. *Childhood Education, 74,* 194–199.

Matthew, N., & Clow, S. (2007). Putting disabled children in the picture: Promoting inclusive children's books and media. *International Journal of Early Childhood, 39* (21), 65.

May, V.M., & Ferri, B.A. (2008). Fixated on ability. In B.J. Brueggemann & M.E. Lupo (Eds.), *Disability and/in prose* (pp. 110–130). New York, NY: Routledge.

McBay, B., & Heneghan, J. (2003). *Waiting for Sarah*. Victoria, BC: Orca Books.

McDaniel, C.A. (2006). *Critical literacy: A way of thinking, a way of life*. New York, NY: Peter Lang.

McKay, S. (2009). *War brothers*. Toronto, ON: Annick Press.

McKay, S., & Lafrance, D. (2013). *War brothers: The graphic novel*. Toronto, ON: Annick Press.

McMurchy-Barber, G. (2010). *Free as a bird*. Toronto, ON: Dundurn Press.

McNicoll, S. (1994). *Bringing up beauty*. Toronto, ON: Stoddart Kids.

McNicoll, S. (2013). *Dying to go viral*. Markham, ON: Fitzhenry & Whiteside.

Mercer, A. (2011). *Rebound*. Toronto, ON: James Lorimer.

Meyer, B. (2007). *Heroes*. Toronto, ON: HarperCollins.

Mills, C. (2002). The portrayal of mental disability in children's literature: An ethical appraisal. *The Horn Book Magazine, 78*(5), 531–542.

Minaki, C. (2009). Great responsibility: Rethinking disability portrayal in fiction for the real world. *Canadian Children's Book News, 32*(3), 12–14.

Minaki, C. (2011). *Great responsibility: Rethinking disability portrayal in popular fiction & calling for a multi-cultural change* (Unpublished master's thesis). Ontario Institute for Studies in Education, Toronto, ON.

Mitchell, D.T., & Snyder, S.L. (2000). *Narrative prosthesis: Disability and the dependencies of discourse*. Ann Arbor, MI: The University of Michigan Press.

Moll, L.C. (2014). *L.S. Vygotsky and education*. New York, NY: Routledge.

Montgomery, L.M. (1908). *Anne of Green Gables*. Boston, MA: L.C. Page.

Mouttet, J. (2007). Review of the book *Gemini summer* by I. Lawrence. *Library Media Connection, 25*(5), 77.

Muller, R.D. (2009). *The solstice cup.* Victoria, BC: Orca.

Oppel, K. (2007). *Darkwing.* Toronto, ON: HarperCollins.

Orkwis, R., & McLane, K. (1998). *A curriculum every student can use: Design principles for student access.* (ERIC OSEP Topical Brief, 1–20).

Pajka-West, S. (2007). Perceptions of deaf characters in adolescent literature. *ALAN Review, 34*(3), 39–45.

Paley, V.G. (1979). *White teacher.* Cambridge, MA: Harvard University Press.

Paley, V.G. (1992). *You can't say you can't play.* Cambridge, MA: Harvard University Press.

Paley, V.G. (1999). *The kindness of children.* London, UK: Harvard University Press.

Phillips, W. (2010). *Fishtailing.* Regina, SK: Coteau Books.

Pinker, S. (2002). *The blank slate: The modern denial of human nature.* New York, NY: Viking.

Pohl-Weary, E. (2013). *Not your ordinary wolf girl.* Toronto, ON: Penguin.

Polak, M. (in press). *Hate mail.* Vancouver, BC: Orca.

Polak, M. (2007). *Scarred.* Toronto, ON: Lorimer.

Porter, P. (2004). *Sky.* Toronto, ON: Groundwood Books.

Porter, P. (2005). *The crazy man.* Toronto, ON: Groundwood Books.

Porter, P. (2006). *Stones call out.* Regina, SK: Coteau Books.

Porter, P. (2008a). *The intelligence of animals.* Omaha, NE: The Backwaters Press.

Porter, P. (2008b). *Yellow moon, apple moon.* Toronto, ON: Groundwood Books.

Porter, P. (2010). *Cathedral.* Vancouver, BC: Ronsdale Press.

Porter, P. (2011). *I'll be watching.* Toronto, ON: Groundwood Books.

Porter, P. (2012). *No ordinary place.* Vancouver, BC: Ronsdale Press.

Prater, M.A., & Dyches, T.T. (2008a). Books that portray characters with disabilities: A top 25 list for children and young adults. *Council for Exceptional Children, 40*(4), 32–38.

Prater, M.A., & Dyches, T.T. (2008b). *Teaching about disabilities through children's literature.* Westport, CT: Libraries Unlimited.

Priestly, M. (2001). Introduction: The global context of disability. In M. Priestly (Ed.), *Disability and the life course* (pp. 3–5). Cambridge, UK: Cambridge University Press.

Rainfield, C. (2010). *Scars.* Lodi, NJ: Westside Books.

Rayner, R. (2010). *Scab.* Toronto, ON: Lorimer.

Richmond, S. (2009). *Wheels for walking.* Toronto, ON: Groundwood Books. (Original work published in 1983).

Riley, C.A., II. (2005). *Disability and the media: Prescriptions for change.* Lebanon, NH: University Press of New England.

Roger, W. (2004). *The stonking steps.* Bloomington, IN: Trafford Publishing.

Rose, M.L. (2006). Deaf and dumb in ancient Greece. In L.J. David (Ed.), *The disability studies reader* (pp. 17–31). New York, NY: Routledge.

Rosenblatt, L. (1978). *The reader, the text, the poem: The transactional theory of the literary work.* Carbondale, IL: Southern Illinois University Press.

Rosenblatt, L. (2005). *Making meaning with texts: Selected essays.* Portsmouth, NH: Heinemann.

Rubin, J.Z. (1988). Foreword. In M. Fine, & A. Asch (Eds.), *Women with disabilities: Essays in psychology, culture, and politics* (pp. ix–x). Philadelphia, PA: Temple University Press.

Rud, J. (2008*). Paralyzed.* Victoria, BC: Orca Books.

Rudman, M.K. (1995). *Children's literature: An issues approach* (3rd ed.). White Plains, NY: Longman.

Rueda, R. (1998). Addressing the needs of a diverse society. In T.E. Raphael, & K.H. Au (Eds.), *Literature-based instruction: Reshaping the curriculum.* Norwood, MA: Christopher-Gordon Publishers.

Russell, A.M. (2011). *Trueman Bradley—Aspie detective.* London: Jessica Kingsley.

Said, E.W. (2005). The politics of knowledge. In C. McCarthy, W. Crichlow, G. Dimitriadis, & N. Dolby (Eds.), *Race, identity, and representation in education* (2nd ed., pp. 453–460). New York, NY: Routledge.

Saskatchewan Preventions Institute (2009). *FASD "Realities and Possibilities": The Myles Himmelreich Story.* Saskatoon, Saskatchewan.

Scarsbrook, R. (2010). *The monkeyface chronicles.* Saskatoon, SK: Thistledown Press.

Schwab, J.J. (1978). *Science, curriculum, and liberal education: Selected essays.* London, UK: University of Chicago Press.

Schwier, K.M. (2013). *Flourish: People with disabilities living life with passion.* Saskatoon, SK: Copestone.

Shaw, L. (2013). *The color of silence.* Toronto, ON: Second Story Press.

Sherry, M. (2008). Reading me/Reading disability. In B.J. Brueggemann & M.E. Lupo (Eds.), *Disability and/in prose* (pp.153–165). New York, NY: Routledge.

Sidney, M. (1880). *Five little peppers and how they grew.* New York, NY: Lothrop, Lee & Shepard.

Simon, R., & Armitage Simon, W. (1995). Teaching risky stories: Remembering mass destruction through children's literature. *English Quarterly, 28*(1), 27–31.

Smith, M. (1948). Wild horses. In R. McIntosh (Ed.), *All sails set* (p. 97). Toronto, ON: Copp Clark.

Smith, T.E.C., Polloway, E.A., Patton, J.R., Dowdy, C.A., & Heath, N.L. (2001). *Teaching students with special needs in inclusive settings* (Canadian ed.). Toronto, ON: Pearson.

Smith, M., & Wilhelm, J.D. (2002). *Reading don't fix no Chevys: Literacy in the lives of young men.* Portsmouth, NH: Heinemann.

Smith-D'Arezzo, W. (2003). Disability in children's literature: Not just a black and white issue. *Children's Literature in Education, 34*(1), 75–94.

Snyder, M. (2007). Review of the book *Gemini summer* by I. Lawrence. *Resource Links, 12*(4), 14–16.

Snyder, S.L., Brueggemann, B.J., & Garland-Thomson, R. (2002). *Disability studies: Enabling the humanities.* New York, NY: The Modern Language Association of America.

Spring, D. (2008). *Breathing soccer.* Saskatoon, SK: Thistledown Press.

Spufford, F. (2002). *The child that books built.* London: Faber and Faber.

Swindells, J. (Ed.). (1995). *The uses of autobiography.* London: Taylor & Francis.

Tamaki, M., & Tamaki, J. (2008). *Skim.* Toronto, ON: Groundwood Books.

Tammet, D. (2007). *Born on a blue day: Inside the extraordinary mind of an autistic savant.* Toronto, ON: Simon & Schuster Canada.

Thomson, P. (1992). Disability in modern children's fiction. *Books for Keeps, 75*, 24–26.

Thomson, R.G. (1997). *Extraordinary bodies: Figuring physical disability in American culture and literature.* New York, NY: Columbia University Press.

Tomlinson, C.A. (2008). *The differentiated school: Making revolutionary changes in teaching and learning.* Alexandria, VA: Association for Supervision and Curriculum Development.

Tullson, D. (2004). *Blue highway.* Ontario: Fitzhenry and Whiteside.

Turner, S.E. (2012). *Ribbon's way.* Winlaw, BC: Sono Nis Press.

Waldman, D. (2011). *Addy's race.* Victoria, BC: Orca Book Publishers.

Waldorf, H. (2008). *Tripping.* Calgary, AB: Red Deer Press.

Wallace, D.F. (1996). *Infinite jest: A novel.* Boston: Little, Brown and Company.

Walters, E. (2000). *Rebound.* Toronto, ON: Stoddart Kids.

Ward, D. (2011). *Between two ends.* New York, NY: Amulet.

Watson, J. (2013). *Prove it, Josh.* Winlaw, BC: Sono Nis Press.

White, E.B. (1939). *Charlotte's web.* New York, NY: Harper & Row.

Wilhelm, J. (1998). Reading and writing workshop: Focus on drama. *Instructor, 109*(4), 43–48.

Will, E.M. (2013). *Look straight ahead: A graphic novel.* Canada: Cuckoo's Nest Press.

Willis, A.I., Montavon, M., Hall, H., Hunter, C., Burke, L., & Herrera, A. (2008). *Critically conscious research: Approaches to language and literacy research.* New York, NY: Teachers College Press.

Wood, R. (1979). An introduction to the American horror film. In A. Britton, R. Lippe, T. Williams, & R. Wood (Eds.), *American nightmare: Essays on the horror film.* Toronto, ON: Festival of Festivals.

Wormeli, R. (2006). *Fair isn't always equal: Assessing and grading in the differentiated classroom.* Portland, Maine: Stenhouse.

Wray, S. (2007). *The forbidden room.* Dublin, IRL: Children's Books.

Wurzburg, G. (Producer), & Wurzburg, G, & Watts, G. (Directors). (2001). *Graduating Peter.* (Motion picture). United States: HBO.

Wright, D. (2011). *Downs: The history of a disability.* Oxford: Oxford University Press.

Yee, P., & Chan, H. (Illustrator). (1996). *Ghost train.* Toronto, ON: Groundwood Books.

York, S.K. (2012). *The anatomy of Edouard Beaupre.* Regina, SK: Coteau Books.

Young, C. (2011). *Ten birds.* Toronto, ON: Kids Can Press.

Zindel. P. (1971). *The pigman.* Toronto, ON: Fitzhenry & Whiteside. (Original work published in 1968).

COPYRIGHT ACKNOWLEDGEMENTS

Cover from *Aaron's Awful Allergies* written by Troon Harrison and illustrated by Eugenie Fernandes is used by permission of Kids Can Press Ltd., Toronto. Text © 1996 Troon Harrison. Illustrations © 1996 Eugenie Fernandes.

Cover from *All Good Children* by Catherine Austen © 2011. Reproduced with permission of Orca Book Publishers.

Cover from *A Bear in War* by Stephanie Innes and Harry Endrulat © 2008. Cover illustration by Brian Deines. Reproduced with permission of Pajama Press.

Cover from *Beauty Returns* by Sylvia McNicoll © 2006. Reproduced with permission of Fitzhenry & Whiteside, Markham, Ontario.

Cover from *The Black Book of Colors* by Menena Cottin © 2008. Cover illustration by Rosana Faria. Reproduced with permission of Groundwood Books Limited, www.groundwoodbooks.com.

Cover from *The Blue Helmet* by William Bell © 2009. Reproduced with permission of Random House.

Cover from *Camp Outlook* by Brenda Baker © 2013. Reproduced with permission of Second Story Press.

Cover from *Ceiling Stars* by Sandra Diersch © 2011. Reproduced with permission of Lorimer.

Cover from *Charlie Wilcox* by Sharon McKay © 2000. Reproduced with permission of Stoddart Kids.

Cover from *The Color of Silence* by Liane Shaw © 2013. Reproduced with permission of Second Story Press.

Cover taken from *The Crazy Man* by Pamela Porter © 2005. Cover illustration by Karine Daisay, cover design by Michael Solomon. Reproduced with permission of Groundwood Books Limited, www.groundwoodbooks.com.

Cover from *Darkwing* by Kenneth Oppel © 2007. Reproduced with permission of HarperCollins.

Cover from *Dead Silence* by Norah McClintock © 2006. Reproduced with permission of Scholastic Canada.

Cover from *A Different Kind of Beauty* by Sylvia McNicoll © 2004. Reproduced with permission of Fitzhenry & Whiteside, Markham, Ontario.

Cover taken from *Eddie Longpants* by Mireille Levert © 2005. Reproduced with permission of Groundwood Books Limited, www.groundwoodbooks.com.

Cover from *Edward the "Crazy Man"* by Marie Day © 2002. Reproduced with permission of Annick Press.

Cover from *Emily Included* by Kathleen McDonnell © 2011. Reproduced with permission of Second Story Press.

Cover from *Forward, Shakespeare!* by Jean Little © 2005. Cover illustration by Hanne Lore Koehler. Reproduced with permission of Orca Book Publishers.

Cover from *Fostergirls* by Liane Shaw © 2011. Reproduced with permission of Second Story Press.

Cover from *Free as a Bird* by Gina McMurchy-Barber © 2010. Reproduced with permission of Dundurn Press.

Cover from *A Friend Like Zilla* by Rachna Gilmore © 1993. Reproduced with permission of Second Story Press.

Cover from *Ghost Train* by Paul Yee © 2013. Cover illustration by Harvey Chan. Reproduced with permission of Groundwood Books Limited, www.groundwoodbooks.com.

Cover from *Grows That Way* by Susan Ketchen © 2012. Reproduced with permission of Oolichan Press.

Cover from *Heck Superhero* by Martine Leavitt © 2004. Reproduced with permission of Red Deer Press, Markham, Ontario.

Cover from *How Smudge Came* by Nan Gregory © 1995. Cover illustration by Ron Lightburn. Reproduced with permission of Red Deer Press, Markham, Ontario.

Cover from *How to be a Friend* by Nancy Richards © 2011. Reproduced with permission of Scholastic Canada.

Cover from *In the Clear* by Ann Laurel Carter © 2001. Reproduced with permission of Orca Book Publishers.

Cover from *Ink Me* by Richard Scrimger © 2012. Reproduced with permission of Orca Book Publishers.

Cover from *Irish Chain* by Barbara Haworth-Attard © 2002. Reproduced with permission of HarperCollins.

Cover from *The Island of Doom* by Arthur Slade © 2013. Reproduced with permission of HarperCollins.

Cover from *Jason's Why* by Beth Goobie © 2013. Reproduced with permission of Red Deer Press, Markham, Ontario.

Cover from *Jeannie and the Gentle Giants* by Luanne Armstrong © 2002. Reproduced with permission of Ronsdale Press.

Cover from *King of the Skies* by Rukhsana Khan © 2001. Cover illustration by Laura Fernandez and Rick Jacobson. Reproduced with permission of Scholastic Canada.

Cover from *Lily and the Mixed-Up Letters* by Deborah Hodge © 2007. Cover illustration by France Brassard. Reproduced with permission of Tundra Books.

Cover from *The Little Yellow Bottle* by Angèle Delaunois © 2012. Cover illustration by Christine Delezenne. Reproduced with permission of Second Story Press.

Cover taken from *Looking for X* by Deborah Ellis © 1999. Cover illustration by Julia Bell. Reproduced with permission of Groundwood Books Limited, www.groundwoodbooks.com.

Cover from *The Losers Club* by John Lekich © 2004. Reproduced with permission of Annick Press.

Cover from *M in the Abstract* by Douglas Davey © 2013. Reproduced with permission of Red Deer Press, Markham, Ontario.

Cover from *Me, Myself and Ike* by K. L. Denman © 2009. Reproduced with permission of Orca Book Publishers.

Cover from *Meeting Miss 405* by Lois Peterson © 2008. Reproduced with permission of Orca Book Publishers.

Cover from *The Moon Children* by Beverley Brenna © 2007. Reproduced with permission of Red Deer Press, Markham, Ontario.

Cover taken from *Ms. Zephyr's Notebook* by K.C. Dyer © 2007. Reproduced with permission of Dundurn.

Cover taken from *No Ordinary Day* by Deborah Ellis copyright © 2011. Cover photo by Gil Chamberland / Photolibrary, cover design by Michael Solomon. Reproduced with permission of Groundwood Books Limited, www.groundwoodbooks.com.

Cover from *Objects in Mirror* by Tudor Robins © 2013. Reproduced with permission of Red Deer Press, Markham, Ontario.

Cover from *Out of Sight* by Robert Rayner © 2011. Reproduced with permission of Lorimer.

Cover from *Patrick's Wish* by Karen Mitchell and Rebecca Upjohn © 2010. Reproduced with permission of Second Story Press.

Cover from *Pieces of Me* written by Charlotte Gingras is used by permission of Kids Can Press Ltd., Toronto. Text © 2005 Les éditions de la courte échelle inc. English Translation © 2009 Susan Ouriou. Cover illustration © 2005 Stéphane Jorisch. First published by Les editions, Montreal, Quebec, Canada.

Cover from *Pocket Rocks* by Sheree Fitch © 2004. Cover illustration by Helen Flook. Reproduced with permission of Orca Book Publishers.

Cover from *Prove it, Josh* by Jenny Watson © 2013. Reproduced with permission of Sono Nis Press.

Cover from *Pump* by Sharon Jennings © 2006. Reproduced with permission of HIP Books.

Cover from *Rebound* by Eric Walters © 2011. Reproduced with permission of Fitzhenry & Whiteside, Markham, Ontario.

Cover from *The Reluctant Journal of Henry K. Larsen* by Susin Nielsen © 2012. Reproduced with permission of Tundra Books.

Cover from *Run* by Eric Walters © 2003. Reproduced with permission of Penguin.

Cover from *Schizo* by Kim Firmston © 2012. Reproduced with permission of Lorimer.

Cover from *A Screaming Kind of Day* by Rachna Gilmore © 1999. Cover illustration by Gordon Sauve. Reproduced with permission of Fitzhenry & Whiteside, Markham, Ontario.

Cover from *Search of the Moon King's Daughter* by Linda Holeman © 2003. Reproduced with permission of Tundra Books.

Cover from *Secret of Light* by K. C. Dyer © 2003. Reproduced with permission of Dundurn.

Cover from *Seeds of Time* by K. C. Dyer © 2002. Reproduced with permission of Dundurn.

Cover from *Seeing Orange* by Sara Cassidy © 2012. Cover illustration by Amy Meissner. Reproduced with permission of Orca Book Publishers.

Cover from *Seeing Red* written by Anne Louise MacDonald is used by permission of Kids Can Press Ltd., Toronto. Text © 2009 Anne Louise MacDonald.

Cover from *Shades of Red* by K. C. Dyer © 2005. Reproduced with permission of Dundurn.

Cover from *Siena Summer* by Ann Chandler © 2008. Reproduced with permission of Tradewind Books.

Cover from *The Silent Summer of Kyle McGinley* by Jan Andrews © 2013. Reproduced with permission of Great Plains Publications.

Cover from *Smoke and Mirrors* by Lesley Choyce © 2004. Reproduced with permission of Dundurn.

Cover from *The Space Between* by Don Aker © 2010. Reproduced with permission of HarperCollins.

Cover from *Splish, Splat!* by Alexis Domney © 2011. Cover illustration by Alice Crawford. Reproduced with permission of Second Story Press.

Cover taken from *Stitches* by Glen Huser © 2003. Cover illustration by Betsy Everitt, cover design by Michael Solomon. Reproduced with permission of Groundwood Books Limited, www.groundwoodbooks.com.

Cover from *The Summer of Permanent Wants* by Jamieson Findlay © 2011. Reproduced with permission of Doubleday Canada.

Cover from *Ten Birds* written and illustrated by Cybèle Young is used by permission of Kids Can Press Ltd., Toronto. Text and illustrations © 2011 Cybèle Young.

Cover from *Thin and Beautiful.com* by Liane Shaw © 2009. Reproduced with permission of Second Story Press.

Cover from *To Stand on My Own* by Barbara Haworth-Attard © 2010. Reproduced with permission of Scholastic Canada.

Cover from *Tori by Design* by Colleen Nelson © 2011. Reproduced with permission of Great Plains Publications.

Cover from *Triple Threat* by Jacqueline Guest © 2011. Reproduced with permission of Lorimer.

Cover from *Tripping* by Heather Waldorf © 2009. Reproduced with permission of Red Deer Press, Markham, Ontario.

Cover from *True Blue* by Deborah Ellis © 2011. Reproduced with permission of Pajama Press.

Cover from *Truths I Learned from Sam* by Kristin Butcher © 2013. Reproduced with permission of Dundurn.

Cover from *The Tuesday Cafe* by Don Trembath © 1996. Reproduced with permission of Orca Book Publishers.

Cover from *The Unlikely Hero of Room 13B,* © 2013 by Teresa Toten. Reproduced with permission of Doubleday Canada.

Cover from *Vegas Tryout* by Lorna Schultz Nicholson © 2012. Reproduced with permission of Lorimer.

Cover from *A Very Fine Line* by Julie Johnston © 2008. Reproduced with permission of Tundra Books.

Cover from *Virginia Wolf* written by Kyo Maclear and illustrated by Isabelle Arsenault is used by permission of Kids Can Press Ltd., Toronto. Text © 2012 Kyo Maclear. Illustrations © 2012 Isabelle Arsenault.

Cover from *Waiting for No One* by Beverley Brenna © 2010. Reproduced with permission of Red Deer Press, Markham, Ontario.

Cover from *The Weber Street Wonder Work Crew* by Maxwell Newhouse © 2010. Reproduced with permission of Tundra Books.

Cover from *What Happened to Ivy* by Kathy Stinson © 2012. Reproduced with permission of Second Story Press.

Cover from *The White Bicycle* by Beverley Brenna © 2012. Reproduced with permission of Red Deer Press, Markham, Ontario.

Cover from *Wild Orchid* by Beverley Brenna © 2006. Reproduced with permission of Red Deer Press, Markham, Ontario.

Cover from *Zero* by Diane Tullson © 2007. Reproduced with permission of Fitzhenry & Whiteside, Markham, Ontario.

Cover from *Zoe's Extraordinary Holiday Adventures* by Christina Minaki © 2007. Reproduced with permission of Second Story Press.

Cover from *Zoom* by Robert Munsch © 2003. Cover illustration by Michael Martchenko. Reproduced with permission of Scholastic Canada.

INDEX

A

Aaron's Awful Allergies (Harrison and Fernandes), 47
Abier, Gilles, 141
ableist language, 28
ableist metaphors, 13
ableist thinking, 68
abnormal, concept of, 13
Aboriginal characters, 33, 45, 81
Above (Bobet), 105, 121, 154
Absolutely Invincible! (Bell), 128
The Absolutely True Diary of a Part-time Indian (Alexie), 128
Acceleration (McNamee), 135
acceptance, 54–55, 71–73, 108–109
Across the Steel River (Stenhouse), 89
Adam and Eve and Pinch-Me (Johnston), 88
addictions, 38
Addison Addley series (McMillan), 57
Addy's Race (Waldman), 68, 96
adoption, 65, 76
The Adventures of Huckleberry Finn (Twain), 129
The Adventures of Oliver Twist (Dickens), 131
After (Chalifour), 119
After the Fire (Citra), 57, 88
After the War (Matas), 134
Against All Odds (Ghent), 134
Against All Odds (Kropp), 106, 133–134
age-appropriate reading, 51–52
Aker, Don, 118–119, 138, 146
Aksomitis, Linda, 77
Alberta, 28
Alcott, Louisa May, 24, 53
Alexie, Sherman, 128
Alice, I Think (Juby), 130
All Good Children (Austin), 120
allergies, 47, 61, 80
Alma (Bell), 93
Almost Eden (Horrocks), 83–84, 138
Amado, E., 45
American Library Association, 40
American Psychological Association, 66
amputation, 19, 97
An Infidel in Paradise (Laidlaw), 141
The Anatomy of Edouard Beaupré (York), 19
And in the Morning (Wilson), 134
Anderson, M.T., 105, 120, 121
Andrews, J., 119
Anne of Green Gables (Montgomery), 24, 83

annotated bibliographies
  books not included in, 38
  generally, 8
  intermediate novels, 75–98
  junior novels, 57–62
  picture books, 44–50
  young adult novels, 118–146
anorexia. *See* eating disorders
Are You There God? It's Me, Margaret (Blume), 138
Aristotle and Dante Discover the Secrets of the Universe (Saenz), 127, 143
Armstrong, L., 75
The Arrival (Tan), 130
Arsenault, Isabelle, 41, 44
Asperger's syndrome, 28, 42, 109, 122–123, 155–156
  see also autism
asthma, 82, 96
asylum tourism, 66
Atlantis Time (Gilmore), 54
attention deficit hyperactivity disorder (ADHD), 15, 137
Austin, C., 120
autism, 6, 7, 18–19, 80, 85, 88–89, 94, 107, 114, 118, 122–123, 154, 156
  see also Asperger's syndrome
autobiography, 18–19, 138, 155
Avi, 60
Awake and Dreaming (Pearson), 77, 89
awards, 25, 40–41

B

Babbitt, Natalie, 80
The Bad Beginning (Snicket), 92
Badoe, Adwoa, 129, 137
Baker, Brenda, 67, 75–76
Banks, James A., 32
basketball, 59, 90, 96
Bates, Sonya Spreen, 75
Bateson, Catherine, 56
Bat Summer (Winthrow), 93
A Bear in War (Innes, Endrulat, and Deines), 48
Beauty Returns (McNicoll), 136
Beckett, Samuel, 123
Becoming Holmes (Peacock), 96
Before Wings (Goobie), 125
behavioural challenges, 58–59, 66
Being and Nothingness (Sartre), 123
Belgue, Nancy, 94

Bell, William, 93, 120–121, 128, 129
Bellingham, Brenda, 119
The Belonging Place (Little), 83
Berg, Elizabeth, 84
Better than Weird (Goobie), 59
Between Sisters (Badoe), 129, 137
Between Two Ends (Ward), 36
Big Guy (Stevenson), 127, 143
Big Town (Malone), 155
biography, 18–19
bipolar disorder, 126–127, 142
Bird-Wilson, Lisa, 131, 141
The Birthday Party (Pinter), 123
The Bite of the Mango (Kamara), 19
Black Beauty (Sewell), 77
The Black Book of Colors (Cotting and Faria), 45
Blakeslee, Mary, 4, 135
Blankets (Thompson), 118–119
blended families, 65
blended genres, 65
blindness. *See* visual impairments
Blink & Caution (Wynne-Jones), 96
Blood Upon Our Land (Trottier), 77
The Blue Helmet (Bell), 120–121
Blue Highway (Tullson), 38
Blume, Judy, 57, 117, 138
The Boat (Ward), 98
Bobet, L., 105, 121, 154
Bone Dance (Brooks), 135
bone disease, 84
book awards, 25, 40–41
Bookbird, 3
"Books That Portray Characters with Disabilities" (Prater and Dyches), 13
Boot Camp (Walters, Williams, and Williams III), 90
Borderline (Stratton), 129
Born on a Blue Day (Tammet), 19, 155–156
Born Ugly (Goobie), 121
Bow, Erin, 82, 129
Boy O'Boy (Doyle), 144
Brain Camp (Kim and Klavan), 75
brain injury, 146
Brassard, F., 47
Breathing Soccer (Spring), 67–68, 96
Brenna, Beverley, 2, 19, 28, 37, 57, 61, 76, 82, 93, 98, 107–118, 119, 122–123, 123, 130–131, 154
    acceptance and inclusion, 108–109
    Brianna, 114–116
    counterstories and social justice, 109
    Dan, 116–117
    Eddy, 113–114
    "Johnny and the Pear," 111–112
    mother's stories, 110–114
    "Old Jones," 112
    power of stories, 110
    teaching stories, 114–117
    "Wild Horses" (Smith), 112–113
    writing process, 108

Bridge to Terabithia (Patterson), 57, 84, 86, 97
Brignall, Richard, 94
Bringing Up Beauty (McNicoll), 31, 76
Broken (Harvey-Fitzhenry), 86, 122, 124, 129, 131, 133, 137
Brontë, Charlotte, 133, 155
Brooks, Martha, 135
Buffie, Margaret, 125
bulimia. *See* eating disorders
bullying, 7, 33, 67, 68, 84
Burke, Kelley Jo, 18–19
Burnett, Frances Hodgson, 8, 77
Burtinshaw, Julie, 119
Butcher, Kristin, 93, 123–124, 135
Byars, Betsy, 58, 59, 62, 76

C

Caldecott winners, 40
Call Me Mimi (Chalifour), 127, 143
Cameron, Ann, 76
Campbell, Joe, 133
Campbell, Nicola, 60
Camp Outlook (Baker), 67, 75–76
Camp Wild (Withers), 75
Canadian Journal of Disability Studies, 3
Canadian materials, focus on, 6
Canadian settings, 28
cancer, 46
Carle, Eric, 23
Carter, Anne Laurel, 28, 67, 76–77, 83
Carver, Peter, 94
Cassidy, Sara, 57
Catch Me Once, Catch Me Twice (McNaughton), 134
The Catcher in the Rye (Salinger), 122, 133
categories of exceptionality, 14–15, 66
Cathedral (Porter), 69
Cathy's Book (Stewart and Weisman), 125
Caught on a Train (Gebler), 123
Ceiling Stars (Diersch), 126–127
cerebral palsy, 20, 60, 87, 123, 131–132, 137–138, 143, 154, 155
Chalifour, Francis, 119, 127, 143
Chambers, J.M., 45
Chan, H., 41, 44
Chandler, A., 77
changing boundaries, 28
changing forms and formats, 28
changing perspectives, 28
The Chaos (Hopkinson), 154
characters with disabilities
    contemporary trends, 17–21
    current research findings, 18–19
    current state of the field, 2–3
    diversity within characterization, 29, 31, 154
    early discoveries, 2
    early questions, 1–2
    evolution of disability in characterizations, 154

evolution of the reflection of, 20–21
future predictions, 21
historical patterns and trends, 15–17
history of, in children's texts, 11–21
"kill or cure" mentality, 28
multiple disabilities, 41
past limitations, 17–18
pervasive ideologies in the classics, 16–17
primary characters, 1, 66
rubric, 34–35
secondary characters, 1, 66
testimonial response activities, 36–37
writing books about, 6–7
see also diverse characters
Characters with Disabilities in Contemporary Children's Novels (Brenna), 2
Charlie Wilcox (McKay), 134
Charlotte's Web (White), 24, 138
Chartrand, J., 45
child abuse, 119
childhood depression. *See* depression
children's literature
book awards, 25
characters with disabilities. *See* characters with disabilities
curricular intent, 7–8
diverse perspectives, value of, 7–8
evaluation of, 24–25
history of characters with disabilities, 11–21
reviews, 25
selection of texts, 37
value of stories, 19–20
Children's Literature (Rudman), 3
child soldiers, 37
The Child That Books Built (Spufford), 9
Chill (Frizzell), 86, 129
China Clipper (Brignall), 94
Choice of Colours (Danakas), 94
Choyce, Lesley, 80, 89, 97, 124–125, 127, 145
The Chronicles of Narnia series (Lewis), 138
Chrisholm, M., 46
Christmas at Wapos Bay (Wheller and Jackson), 61
Christopher, Matt, 97
chronic illness, 125
Citra, Becky, 57, 59, 75, 88
Cleary, Beverly, 60, 61
club foot, 85, 134
CM Magazine, 153
collectivist orientation, 36
The Color of Silence (Shaw), 67, 141
combined disability traits. *See* multiple disabilities
A Complicated Kindness (Toews), 83–84
constructed oppression, 14
contemporary trends, 17–21
content integration, 33
Cottin, M., 45
counterstories, 55–56, 73–74, 109

Crawford, Alice, 46
Crazy About Basketball (Lesynski), 59, 90
The Crazy Man (Porter), 2, 11, 29, 31, 67, 69–74, 76, 93
Creech, Sharon, 93
crime novels. *See* mystery
critical literacy, 25–27
applied, 27–35
changing the world through, 9
classroom resources, 29
disrupting the commonplace, 29–30
educational frameworks, 29
intermediate novels, 67–68
meaning of, 26
multiple viewpoints, integration of, 30–31
sociopolitical issues, 31–32
supports for, 3–4
taking action and promoting social justice, 32–35
Crohn's Disease, 79–80
Crow Medicine (Haynes), 97
cultural construction, 15
culture, 32–33
The Curious Incident of the Dog in the Night-Time (Haddon), 7, 122, 154
Curtis, Christopher Paul, 84
Cuts Like a Knife (Ryan), 138
cutting, 38, 142

D
Dahl, Roald, 92
Dahling If You Luv Me, Would You Please, Please Smile (Khan), 130
Dalen & Gole (Deas), 60
Danakas, John, 94
Dancing Through the Snow (Little), 80, 88
Danger in Dead Man's Mine (Glaze), 83
Dann, Sarah, 96
The Dark Deeps (Slade), 95
Darkwing (Oppel), 15, 92–93
dashes, 51
Davey, D., 125
Day, Marie, 45
de Angeli, Marguerite, 134
de Vries, Maggie, 65, 75
Dead in the Water (Stevenson), 98
Dead Silence (McLintock), 134–135
deafness. *See* hearing impairments
Dear Canada series, 83
Dear George Clooney: Please Marry My Mom (Nielsen), 92
Deas, Mike, 60, 96
Debon, Nicolas, 93
Deines, B., 48
Delaunois, A., 46
Delezenne, C., 46
Delisle, A., 50
dementia, 50
Denman, K.L., 7, 15, 125, 126, 128

depression, 41, 44, 116, 138
developmental disabilities, 18, 54, 58, 85
    see also intellectual disabilities; physical disabilities
diabetes, 97
DiCamillo, Kate, 58, 76
Dickens, Charles, 131
Diersch, Sandra, 126–127
Different Dragons (Little), 89
differently abled, 15
A Different Kind of Beauty (McNicoll), 135
Different—Not Less (Grandin), 19
disability
    categories of exceptionality, 14–15, 66
    disability, definition of, 14–15
    disability vs. *handicap*, 5, 12
    evolution of disability, 11–14, 154
    historical responses to, 17
    metaphors of disability, 13
    multiple disabilities, 41
    as a social construction, 12–14
    societal assumptions about, 17
    writers with disabilities, 155–156
    see also characters with disabilities; people with disabilities
disability life writing, 155
disability studies, 13
Disabled Mothers (Filax and Taylor), 21
disfigurement, 129, 138–139
disrupting the commonplace, 29–30
diverse characters
    ethnicity, 7, 31, 33, 107
    LGBT characterizations, 7–8, 31, 105, 107, 130
    see also characters with disabilities
diverse perspectives, 7–8
diversity
    within characterization, 29, 31, 154
    in intermediate novels, 65
    multicultural diversity, 42
Dolly Gray Award, 3, 18, 41, 108, 154
Domney, Alexis, 46
Donovan, Lois, 78, 142
The Door in the Wall (de Angeli), 134
Dorsey, Angela, 77
Down syndrome, 7, 18, 37, 42, 47, 75, 89–90, 91, 155
Downs (Wright), 155
Doyle, Brian, 144
Draper, Penny, 83
Dresang, Eliza, 7
    see also Radical Change theory
The Droughtlanders (Mac), 120
Drowning in Secrets (Bellingham), 119
The Druid's Tune (Melling), 90
Ducks on the Moon (Burke), 18–19
Dumb Luck (Choyce), 127
Dunnion, Kristyn, 143
Dusk (Oppel), 156–157
Dyches, Tina Taylor, 2, 13

Dyer, K.C., 65, 67, 78–79, 79–80, 128, 140, 142, 146
Dying to Go Viral (McNicoll), 38
dyslexia, 47, 67, 98
dystopian fantasy. *See* fantasy

E
eating disorders, 7, 79, 107, 127–128, 136, 137, 140–142, 145–146
Eddie Longpants (Levert), 48
edginess, 37, 105
Edmonton Public Library, 28
Educating Peter (Goodwin and Wurzburg), 155
Edward the "Crazy Man" (Day), 45
Edwards, Gail, 39
Edwards, Kim, 155
Egghead (Pignat), 130, 142
The 18th Emergency (Byars), 62, 76
Elijah of Buxton (Curtis), 84
Elixir (Walters), 97
Ellis, Deborah, 67, 80, 81, 86, 97, 125, 127, 145
Ellis, Sarah, 80, 86, 90, 134, 137
Emily Included (McDonnell), 60
emotional investment, 36
Empire of Ruins (Slade), 95
The Encyclopedia of Me (Rivers), 94
Endrulat, H., 48
epilepsy, 62
Epp, M., 46
equity pedagogy, 33–34
Esther (McKay), 131
ethnicity, 7, 31, 33, 107
evil, trope for, 32, 35–36, 65, 66
exceptionality, 15, 21
Eyewitness (Thompson), 135

F
Fairbridge, Lynne, 78, 142
Fairfield, L., 7, 127–128, 140, 142, 143, 146
fairy tales, 16, 32, 66, 85, 86
Falling for Henry (Brenna), 108
The False Prince (Nielsen), 85
fantasy, 28
    dystopian fantasy, 105, 120, 121, 154
    intermediate novels, 65, 78–79, 82, 85, 89, 90–91, 92–93
    young adult novels, 105, 106, 120, 121, 124–125
Faria, R., 45
FASD "Realities and Possibilities" (Saskatchewan Preventions Institute), 19
Feed (Anderson), 105, 120, 121
Fernandes, E., 47
Fernandez, Laura, 48
Fetal Alcohol Spectrum Disorder, 6, 19, 76, 108–109
Fetal Alcohol Syndrome, 28
Fight for Justice (Saigeon), 84
Findlay, Jamieson, 68, 81–82
fire images, 88

Firmston, K., 128
Fishtailing (Phillips), 7, 38
Fitch, Sheree, 42, 46, 57, 130
Five Little Peppers and How They Grew (Sidney), 24
Floodland (Sedgwick), 82
Flook, Helen, 42, 46, 57
Flourish (Schwier), 155
Floyd the Flamingo and his Flock of Friends (Stone), 60
Flying Geese (Haworth-Attard), 82, 83
A Fly Named Alfred (Trembath), 87
folktales, 8, 16, 35
Following My Own Footsteps (Hahn), 87
Food Fight (O'Donnell), 60
football, 67, 94
The Forbidden Room (Wray), 154
Forward, Shakespeare! (Little), 59–60
foster care, 59, 75, 88, 119, 140–141
Fostergirls (Shaw), 140–141
Fournier, K.M., 128–129
Francesca and the Magic Bike (Nugent), 86, 92
The Freak (Matas), 89, 133
Freaks, Geeks and Asperger Syndrome (Jackson), 19
Freckle Juice (Blume), 57
Free as a Bird (McMurchy-Barber), 7, 37, 60, 89–90, 139
Freefall (Lewis), 129
Freire, Paulo, 9, 25–26, 27, 29
A Friend Like Zilla (Gilmore), 30–31, 52, 53, 54–55, 58
Frizzell, Colin, 86, 129
Froese, D., 129
Frog Face and the Three Boys (Trembath), 96
From Anna (Little), 4, 88, 94
From the Top of a Grain Elevator (Nickel), 93
Funk, Cornelia, 92

G
The Game (Toten), 140
Gantos, Jack, 57, 76
The Garden (Matas), 134
Gathering Blue (Lowry), 92
Gebler, Carlo, 123
Gemini Summer (Lawrence), 32, 35–36, 65, 66, 85–86, 133
gender, 33, 42
gender ambiguity, 121, 132
genres. *See specific genres*
Ghent, Natale, 134
Ghost Boy (Lawrence), 80
Ghost Train (Yee and Chan), 41, 44
ghosts, 89
Giff, Patricia Reilly, 58
Gilmore, Rachna, 2, 25, 30–31, 41, 44, 52–56, 58, 70
    acceptance and inclusion, 54–55
    counterstories and social justice, 55–56
    writing process, 53–55

Gingras, C., 128, 130
Girl Fight (Harvest), 121
Glaze, Dave, 83
Goertzen, Glenda, 60
Goobie, Beth, 15, 58–59, 96, 121, 122, 124, 125, 130–131, 144, 146
The Good, the Bad and the Suicidal (Goobie), 144
The Good Dog (Avi), 60
Good for Nothing (Noel), 129
Gorrell, Gena K., 60
Gossip Girl series (von Ziegesar), 140
Goto, H., 82
Governor General's Literary Awards for Children's Literature: Children's Illustration, 25, 41
Governor General's Literary Awards for Children's Literature: Children's Text, 2, 7, 25, 41, 44, 52, 69, 80, 84, 88, 91, 93
Graduating Peter (Wurzburg and Watts), 155
The Gramma War (Butcher), 93
Grandin, Temple, 19
graphic novels, 25, 37, 43, 51, 60, 75, 85, 86, 96, 105, 118, 127–128, 143, 156
Gravity Journal (Sobat), 142
The Great Gilly Hopkins (Paterson), 80, 141
Greener Grass (Pignat), 126
Gregory, Nan, 42, 47
group homes, 42, 47, 58–59, 128
Grows That Way (Ketchen), 106, 107, 133
The Guardian of Isis (Hughes), 92
Guest, Jacqueline, 59
guide dogs, 135

H
Haddix, Margaret Peterson, 85
Haddon, Mark, 7, 122, 154
Hahn, Mary Downing, 87
Hal (Blakeslee), 4, 135
Hancock, Pat, 89
A Handful of Time (Pearson), 57
handicap, 5, 12
Hannah Waters and the Daughter of Johann Sebastian Bach (Nickel), 78, 142
Hansen's Disease. *See* leprosy
Harrington, Lisa, 127
Harrison, T., 47
Harry Flammable (O'Keefe), 88
Harvest, Faye, 121
Harvey, Sarah N., 126
Harvey-Fitzhenry, Alyxandra, 86, 122, 124, 129, 131, 133, 137
Hate Mail (Polak), 6
Haunted Canada (Hancock), 89
Haworth-Attard, Barbara, 67, 82–83, 83, 133
hearing impairments, 2, 12, 16, 41, 44, 46, 52, 54, 66, 88, 96, 131
Heck, Superhero (Leavitt), 84, 86
Heidi (Spyri), 8, 77

Helfman, Elizabeth, 32, 61, 154
Hello Groin (Goobie), 146
hemophilia, 49
Heneghan, James, 67, 89, 125
Hero of Lesser Causes (Johnston), 77
Hesse, Karen, 93
Hesser, Terry Spencer, 122, 140
Higashida, Naoki, 19
The Higher Power of Lucky (Patron), 86, 92
hi-lo (high interest-low vocabulary) books, 51, 85, 90, 106, 125, 134, 146
Hinton, S.E., 121
historical engagement, 36
historical fiction, 28
    intermediate novels, 77, 82–84, 85, 93, 97
    junior novels, 60, 65
    young adult novels, 106, 131–132, 134, 141
historical patterns and trends, 15–17
history of characters with disabilities, 11–21
Hodge, D., 47
Holeman, Linda, 88, 131, 146
Holman, Felice, 86
Home Free (Jennings), 77
Hoop Magic (Howling), 59
Hope and the Dragon (Epp and Chrisholm), 46
Hope's War (Skrypuch), 146
Hopkinson, Deborah, 82
Hopkinson, Nalo, 154
Horrocks, A., 83–84, 138
A Horse Called Freedom (Dorsey), 77
horse stories, 77, 88–89, 137
How Raven Freed the Moon (Cameron), 76
How Smudge Came (Gregory and Lightburn), 42, 47
How To Be a Friend (Richards), 62
Howling, Eric, 59
Hughes, Monica, 92
Hugo, Richard, 74, 118
human rights laws, 9, 156
The Hunchback Assignments (Slade), 95, 139
The Hunger (Skrypuch), 78, 97, 128, 140, 141–142, 146
Hunter, Bernice Thurman, 77
Hunter, Mollie, 90
Huser, Glen, 67, 84, 91, 93, 133

I
I Am Algonquin (Revelle), 81
I Want to Be In the Show (Nolan and Chambers), 45
IBBY Canada, 3
IBBY Collection for Young People with Disabilities, 3
IBBY Outstanding Books for Young People with Disabilities, 3
ideal, concept of, 13
I'll Be Watching (Porter), 69
illustrated books. *See* graphic novels; picture books

Impossible Things (Stevenson), 89, 133
inclusion, 54–55, 71–73, 108–109
inclusive education, 20
In Spite of Killer Bees (Johnston), 146
In the Clear (Carter), 28, 67, 76–77, 83
In the Same Boat series, 82
individual differences, 24
Infinite Jest (Wallace), 14
Initiation (Schwartz), 93
Inkheart (Funk), 92
Ink Me (Scrimger), 90, 139
Innes, S., 48
intellectual disabilities, 6, 30–31, 52, 54, 106, 120, 132–133, 133–134, 139, 145, 155
    see also developmental disabilities; Down syndrome
The Intelligence of Animals (Porter), 69
intermediate novels
    annotated bibliography, 75–98
    critical literacy suggestions, 67–68
    patterns and trends, 65–66
    read-on bibliography, 98–102
International Conference on Education, 2
international landscape, 153–157
An Introduction to Multicultural Education (Banks), 32–33
Invention of Hugo Cabret (Selznik), 86
Irish Chain (Haworth-Attard), 67, 82–83, 133
Ish (Reynold), 129
The Island of Doom (Slade), 95–96
It Happened on the Underground Railway (Wagner), 120

J
Jackal in the Garden (Ellis), 145
"Jack and the Beanstalk," 8
Jackson, Dennis, 61
Jackson, Luke, 19
Jacob Have I Loved (Paterson), 119
Jacob's Little Giant (Smucker), 60
Jacobson, Rick, 48
Jaden, Denise, 142
Jane Eyre (Brontë), 133
Janz, Heidi, 20, 131–132, 138, 145
Jason's Why (Goobie), 15, 58–59
Jeannie and the Gentle Giants (Armstrong), 75
Jennings, Sharon, 77, 84–85
Jocelyn, Marthe, 119, 132, 138
Joey Pigza series (Gantos), 57
Joey Pigza Swallowed the Key (Gantos), 76
Johansen, K.V., 85
Johnston, Julie, 77, 88, 89, 132–133, 146
Jolted (Slade), 92
Joy School (Berg), 84
The Joys of Love (L'Engle), 122
Juby, Susan, 130, 146
Julie (Taylor), 89, 93, 133
Junie B. Jones series (Park), 62

junior novels
  age-appropriate reading, issues related to, 51–52
  annotated bibliography, 57–62
  patterns and trends, 52
  read-on bibliography, 62–63
junior readers, 28
Just Ella (Haddix), 85
Just Pretending (Bird-Wilson), 131, 141
juvenile arthritis, 90

K
Kamara, Mariatu, 19
Karma (Ostlere), 138
Katz, Welwyn, 135
The Kayak (Spring), 142
The Keeper of the Trees (Brenna), 82
Keith, Lois, 153
Kent, Deborah, 18
Kent, Trilby, 76
Kerz, Anna, 59, 77
Ketchen, S., 106, 107, 133
Khan, Rukhsana, 48, 130
Kicked Out (Goobie), 96, 122, 124, 130–131
Kim, Susan, 75
The Kindness of Children (Paley), 110
King of the Skies (Khan, Fernandez, and Jacobson), 48
Kissing Doorknobs (Hesser), 122, 140
Klaven, Laurence, 75
Klein, Bonnie Sherr, 19
Kluger, Steve, 122
Knights of the Sea (Marlowe), 14
knowledge construction process, 33
Korman, Gordan, 87
Kositsky, Lynne, 78, 142
Krill, Darren, 78, 142
Kropp, Paul, 106, 129, 133–134
Kuipers, Alice, 123, 141

L
The Lady at Batoche (Richards), 134
Lafrance, Daniel, 37
Laidlaw, S.J., 141
Last Chance Summer (Wieler), 96
Latimer, Robert, 143
Laughing Wolf (Maes), 78, 142
Lawrence, Iain, 32, 35–36, 65, 66, 77, 80, 85–86, 133
Lean Mean Machines (Marineau), 135
learning disabilities, 46, 47, 57, 67, 82–83, 98, 140–141
Leaving Fletchville (Schmidt), 89, 98
Leavitt, Martine, 80, 84, 86
Leber's Disease, 94
Lekich, John, 87, 134, 145
L'Engle, Madeleine, 24, 120, 122, 135
leprosy, 67, 81
Lesynski, Loris, 59, 90

Letters from a Nut (Nancy), 87
Levert, Mireille, 48
Levy, Myrna Neuringer, 58
Lewis, C.S., 138
Lewis, Wendy A., 129
LGBT (lesbian, gay, bisexual, and transgender) characterizations, 7–8, 31, 105, 107, 130
Life on the Refrigerator Door (Kuipers), 123
Lightburn, Ron, 42, 47
Lilly's Crossing (Giff), 58
Lily and the Mixed-Up Letters (Hodge and Brassard), 47
Linden, Dianne, 86, 87–88, 119, 144
The Lit Report (Harvey), 126
Little, Jean, 4, 13–14, 18, 59–60, 60, 61, 66, 80, 83, 88, 89, 94, 138
Little by Little (Little), 138
Little Women (Alcott), 24, 53
The Little Yellow Bottle (Delaunois and Delezenne), 46
Lohans, Alison, 80
Look Straight Ahead (Will), 37
Looking for X (Ellis), 80, 86, 97, 125
Lord, Cynthia, 80, 123
Losers' Club (Lekich), 87, 134, 145
Love That Dog (Creech), 93
Lowry, Lois, 92
Lunn, Janet, 82

M
Mabel Riley (Jocelyn), 132
Mac, Carrie, 120
Macbeth (Shakespeare), 124, 133
MacDonald, Anne Louise, 88–89, 133
MacIntyre, R.P., 142
Maclear, Kyo, 41, 44
Maes, Nicholas, 78, 142
The Magic Beads (Nielsen), 57
magic realism, 65, 81–82, 85, 92, 106, 132–133, 133
Maguire, Gregory, 88
Malone, Stephens Gerrard, 155
Manson, Ainslie, 59
Manuel, Lynn, 98
Marineau, Michèle, 121, 135
Markoti, Nicole, 2
Marlowe, Paul, 14
Martchenko, Michael, 49
Martin, C.K. Kelly, 121
Martineau, Tricia, 120
Matas, Carol, 86, 89, 133, 134
Mazer, Norma Fox, 91
McBay, Bruce, 67, 89, 125
McDonnell, Kathleen, 60
McKay, Sharon, 37, 131, 154
McLintock, N., 134–135
McMillan, Melody DeFields, 57
McMurchy-Barber, Gina, 7, 37, 60, 89–90, 139
McNamee, Graham, 135

McNaughton, Janet, 131, 134
McNicoll, S., 31, 38, 76, 135, 136
Me, Myself and Ike (Denman), 7, 125, 126, 128
The Mealworm Diaries (Kerz), 59, 77
medical model, 13, 108
Medina Hill (Kent), 76
Meeting Miss 405 (Peterson), 61
Melling, O.R., 90
The Memory Keeper's Daughter (Edwards), 155
mental illness, 2, 11, 29, 31, 37
    in intermediate novels, 66, 69, 75, 83–84, 86, 87–88, 90, 91, 93
    in junior novels, 52
    in picture books, 45, 50
    in young adult novels, 105, 107, 120–121, 125, 126–127, 128, 130, 137, 142, 144
    see also specific mental illnesses
Mercer, A., 90
Meyers, Stephanie, 135
Minaki, Christina, 20, 60, 61, 138
Mina's Spring of Colors (Gilmore), 53, 61
Mine for Keeps (Little), 60, 61
M in the Abstract (Davey), 125
Miracleville (Polak), 136–137
Missing (Citra), 75
Missing Sisters (Maguire), 88
missing voices, 42–43
Mission Impossible (Goobie), 130
Miss Smithers (Juby), 146
Mitchell, Karen, 49
Modo (Slade and Steininger), 96
The Money Pit Mystery (Walters), 127
The Monkeyface Chronicles (Scarsbrook), 107, 138–139
Monster (Myers), 127
Montgomery, L.M., 24, 52, 83
The Moon Children (Brenna), 28, 57, 76, 93, 98, 108, 109, 119
More Than You Can Chew (Tokio), 128, 140, 142, 144, 146
Mormor Moves In (Nielsen), 61
Mosh Pit (Dunnion), 143
mothers with mental illness, 52, 66, 75, 83–84, 86, 90, 91, 130
Mouse Mountain, 24
Ms. Zephyr's Notebook (Dyer), 79–80, 128, 140, 142, 146
Mulder, M., 90
Muller, Rachel Dunstan, 66, 68, 90–91
multicultural diversity, 42, 61
multicultural education, 32–33
multiple disabilities, 41, 66, 106, 114
multiple viewpoints, 30–31
Munsch, Robert, 49
My Most Excellent Year (Kluger), 122
My Mother is Weird (Gilmore), 53
Myers, Walter Dean, 127
mystery, 28, 96, 127, 135

N

Na, An, 130
Nancy, Ted L., 87
Narsimhan, Mahtab, 88
National Film Board, 19
negative stereotypes, 16
Nelson, C., 91
Never Enough (Jaden), 142
Newhouse, Maxwell, 49
Nicholson, Lorna Schultz, 136
Nickel, Barbara, 78, 93, 142
Nielsen, Jennifer A., 85
Nielsen, Susin, 57, 61, 80, 91–92, 92, 94
No Ordinary Day (Ellis), 67, 81
No Ordinary Place (Porter), 69
No Place for Kids (Lohans), 80
Nobody's Child (Skrypuch), 142
Nodelman, Perry, 86
Noel, Michael, 129
Nolan, D., 45
non-fiction, 19, 155
normal, concept of, 13
North York Central Library, 3
Northwest Territories, 28
The Nose from Jupiter (Scrimger), 97
Nothing But Your Skin (Ytak), 122
Not Your Ordinary Wolf Girl (Pohl-Weary), 38
Nugent, Cynthia, 86, 92
null curriculum, 8
Numbers (Poulsen), 129
Nunavut, 28

O

Objects in Mirror (Robins), 137
Obsessive Compulsive Disorder (OCD), 144
Odd Man Out (Ellis), 86, 90
O'Donnell, Liam, 60, 85, 96
O'Keefe, Frank, 88
Old Man (Poulson), 124
On Being Sarah (Helfman), 32, 61, 154
One More Step (Fitch), 130
On Fire (Linden), 87–88, 119, 144
On the Banks of Plum Creek (Wilder), 138
On the Shores of Silver Lake (Wilder), 138
Ontario, 28
Opening Tricks (Carver), 94
Oppel, Kenneth, 15, 92–93, 156–157
Ostlere, Cathy, 138
Ouriou, Susan, 121, 128, 130, 135
Out of Sight (Rayner), 94
Out of the Box (Mulder), 90
Out of the Dust (Hesse), 93
Out of the Fire (Froese), 129
Outside In (Ellis), 137
The Outsiders (Hinton), 121

P

Paley, Vivian, 110
Paralyzed (Rud), 66, 67, 94, 125

paraplegic, 125, 137, 143
Park, Barbara, 62
Parkinson, Curtis, 98
Paterson, Katherine, 57, 80, 84, 86, 97, 119, 141
Patrick's Wish (Mitchell and Upjohn), 49
Patron, Susan, 86, 92
patterns and trends
    historical patterns and trends, 15–17
    intermediate novels, 65–66
    junior novels, 52
    predicted patterns, 156
    young adult novels, 106–107
Peacock, Shane, 96
Pearson, Kit, 57, 77, 89
pedagogy of love, 29
people with disabilities
    "cultural burdens," 9
    marginalization, 9
    older readers with disabilities, 40
    segregation, 9
    see also characters with disabilities; disability
The Perfect Cut (Burtinshaw), 119
Peripheral Visions (Bateson), 56
Peterson, Lois, 61
Phillip, Wendy, 7, 38
physical differences, 32, 35–36, 41, 48, 66, 92–93, 95–96, 133, 138–139
physical disabilities, 2, 6, 8, 16, 19, 29–30, 37
    in intermediate novels, 66, 77, 78–79, 85, 87, 89, 90–91, 93, 97
    in junior novels, 59, 60, 61
    in picture books, 41, 44, 46, 48
    in young adult novels, 107, 125, 128–129, 130–132, 134, 137–138, 142–143, 146
    see also specific physical disabilities
Pick-Up Sticks (Ellis), 80, 90
picture books
    for adult audiences, 40
    adult facilitators, 42
    age-related boundaries, blurring of, 39
    annotated bibliography, 44–50
    current explorations and comparisons, 41–42
    intergenerational picture books, 40
    introduction, 39–40
    missing voices, 42–43
    for older readers, 42
    previous studies, 40–41
    reader response, 42
Picturing Canada (Edwards and Saltman), 39
Pieces of Me (Gingras), 128, 130
The Pigman (Zindel), 24, 80, 133, 142, 144
The Pigman's Legacy (Zindel), 121
Pignat, Caroline, 126, 130, 142
The Pinballs (Byars), 59, 76
Pinter, Harold, 123
A Place for Margaret (Hunter), 77
Plain Kate (Bow), 82, 129
Playing Chicken (Kropp), 129

Play Like a Pro (Dann), 96
Pocket Rocks (Fitch and Flook), 42, 46, 57
Pohl-Weary, Emily, 38
Polak, Monique, 6, 38, 136–137, 146
polio, 16, 28, 48, 66, 76, 83
The Pool Was Empty (Abier), 141
Porter, Pamela, 2, 11, 29, 31, 67, 69–74, 76, 93
    acceptance and inclusion, 71–73
    counterstories and social justice, 73–74
    writing process, 70
post-traumatic stress, 57, 67
Poulsen, David, 124, 129
power of stories, 110
The Prairie Dogs (Goertzen), 60
Prater, Mary Anne, 2, 13
predicted patterns, 156
prejudice reduction, 33
prenatal effects, 124
Printz Honour Award, 108
The Proof That Ghosts Exist (Matas and Nodelman), 86
prosthetics, 19, 29, 37, 78–79, 107, 146
Prove It, Josh (Watson), 67, 98
Pump (Jennings), 84–85

Q

quadriplegic, 130
Queen of the Toilet Bowl (Wishinsky), 86
A Question of Will (Kositsky), 78, 142

R

Radical Change (Dresang), 7
Radical Change theory, 3, 5, 20, 21, 28, 33, 36, 37, 52, 56, 65
    books past and present, 153–154
    graphic novels, 156
    a growing field, 154
    intermediate novels, 68–69
    is different wrong?, 156–157
    non-fiction, influences of, 155
    picture books, 40
    predicted patterns, 156
    promise of, 153–157
    writers with disabilities, influences of, 155–156
    young adult novels, 105, 106
Rainfield, Cheryl, 7, 38
Ramona the Pest (Cleary), 61
Ramp Rats (O'Donnell), 85
Rattled (Harrington), 127
Rayner, Robert, 38, 94
Razzell, Mary, 81
reader response, 42
Reading Don't Fix No Chevys (Smith and Wilhelm), 37
read-on bibliographies
    intermediate novels, 98–102
    junior novels, 62–63
    young adult novels, 147–151

read-ons, 4
    see also read-on bibliographies; annotated bibliographies
realistic fiction, 28
    intermediate novels, 65, 75–76, 77, 79–81, 84–85, 86–89, 89–90, 91–92, 94, 96, 98
    junior novels, 57–60, 61–62
    young adult novels, 106, 118–119, 120–121, 122–124, 125–127, 127–131, 132–133, 135–141, 142–146
Really and Truly (Rivard and Delisle), 50
The Reason I Jump (Higashida), 19
Rebound (Mercer), 90
Rebound (Walters), 28, 96, 131
religious diversity, 31
The Reluctant Journal of Henry K. Larsen (Nielsen), 91–92
Replay (Sandor), 94
Rescue Pup (Little), 60
residential schools, 60
Return to Bone Tree Hill (Butcher), 135
Revelle, Rick, 81
reviews, 25
Reynold, Peter H., 129
Ribbon's Way (Turner), 155
Ribsy (Cleary), 60
Richards, David, 134
Richards, N.W., 62
Richmond, Sandra, 4, 19, 125
Riley Park (Tullson), 146
risky texts, 36–38
Rivard, E., 50
Rivers, K., 94
The Road to Chlifa (Marineau), 121
Robins, T., 137
Roger, Will, 156
Roll On (Manson), 59
Roorda, Julie, 119, 137–138
Rooster (Trembath), 145
The Root Cellar (Lunn), 82
Rosoff, Meg, 124, 129
rubric, 34–35
Rud, Jeff, 66, 67, 94, 125
Rules (Lord), 80, 123
Run (Aksomitis), 77
Run (Walters), 96, 97
Run, Billy, Run (Christopher), 97
The Runaway (Huser), 133
Russell, Maxim, 156
Ryan, D., 138

S
Saenz, Benjamin Alire, 127, 143
Saigeon, Lori, 84
Saint Joan (Shaw), 133
Salinger, J.D., 122, 133
Saltman, Judith, 39
Salvadurai, Shem, 130
Sandbag Shuffle (Fournier), 128–129

Sandor, Steven, 94
Sartre, Jean-Paul, 123
Sauve, Gordon, 2, 44
Scab (Rayner), 38
Scarred (Polak), 38
Scars (Rainfield), 7, 38
Scarsbrook, R., 107, 138–139
Schizo (Firmston), 128
schizophrenia, 7, 45, 121, 126, 128
Schmidt, René, 89, 98
Schneider Family Book Award, 3, 40
Schwartz, Virginia Frances, 93
Schwier, Karin Melberg, 155
A Screaming Kind of Day (Gilmore and Sauve), 2, 25, 41, 44, 52, 53, 54, 55
Scrimger, Richard, 90, 97, 139
Sea Chase (Parkinson), 98
Search of the Moon King's Daughter (Holeman), 88, 131
The Secret Garden (Burnett), 8, 77
Secret of Light (Dyer), 67, 78–79
The Secret of Sentinel Rock (Silverthorne), 82
The Secret of the Stone House (Silverthorne), 78, 142
Sedgwick, Marcus, 82
Seeds of Time (Dyer), 65, 78, 142
seeing-eye dogs, 59–60
Seeing Orange (Cassidy), 57
Seeing Red (MacDonald), 88–89, 133
selective mutism. See speech loss
self-harm, 38
self-mutilation. See cutting
Selznik, Brian, 86
A Semester in the Life of a Garbage Bag (Korman), 87
The Several Lives of Orphan Jack (Ellis), 134
Sewell, Anna, 77
The Sewing Basket (White), 84
sexual abuse, 7
sexual orientation, 33
    see also LGBT (lesbian, gay, bisexual, and transgender) characterizations
Shades of Red (Dyer), 79
Shakespeare, William, 124, 133
Shameless (Klein), 19
shared reading, 23–24
Shattered (Walters), 142, 145
Shaw, George Bernard, 133
Shaw, Liane, 67, 128, 140–141, 141, 142, 146
Shelby Belgarden series (Sherrard), 127
Sherrard, Valerie, 98, 126, 127
Shimmerdogs (Linden), 86
Shin-chi's Canoe (Campbell), 60
Sidney, M., 24
Siena Summer (Chandler), 77
The Silent Summer of Kyle McGinley (Andrews), 119
Silverthorne, Judith, 78, 82, 142
single fathers, 31–32

Skim (Tamaki and Tamaki), 25, 127, 143
skin disease, 61
Skinnybones and the Wrinkle Queen (Huser), 93
Skrypuch, Marsha, 78, 97, 128, 140, 141–142, 142, 146
Sky (Porter), 69
A Sky Black with Crows (Walsh), 83, 131
Slade, Arthur, 92, 95–96, 139
Slake's Limbo (Holman), 86
Smith, Michael W., 37
Smoke and Mirrors (Choyce), 80, 89, 97, 124–125, 145
Smucker, Barbara, 60, 128
Smuggler's Moon (Razzell), 81
Snicket, Lemony, 92
Sobat, G.S., 142
soccer, 67–68, 94, 96
Soccer Sabotage (O'Donnell and Deas), 96
social action, 27
social construction, 5, 11, 12–14
social disability, 16
social justice, 4–5, 55–56, 73–74, 109
    see also taking action and promoting social justice
societal values and definitions, 5
sociopolitical issues, 31–32
The Solstice Cup (Muller), 66, 68, 90–91
Somebody's Girl (de Vries), 65, 75
Someone Else's Ghost (Buffie), 125
Something Girl (Goobie), 121, 130
Something to Hang On To (Brenna), 109, 123
So Much It Hurts (Polak), 146
Sower of Tales (Gilmore), 53–54
The Space Between (Aker), 118–119, 138, 146
Sparrows on Wheels (Janz), 20, 131–132, 138, 145
Special Edward (Walters), 98
special needs, 145
speech loss, 68, 81–82, 119, 141
Speechless (Sherrard), 98
Spider Summer (Brenna), 61
Spinelli, Jerry, 97
Spiral (Denman), 125
Splish, Splat! (Domney and Crawford), 46
sports stories, 45, 59, 67–68, 90, 94, 96, 136
Spring, D., 67–68, 96, 142
Spyri, Johanna, 8, 77
steampunk, 65, 93, 95–96
Steininger, Christopher, 96
Stenhouse, Ted, 89
A Step from Heaven (Na), 130
Stephen Fair (Wynne-Jones), 86
stereotypes, 8, 67
stereotypical language, 68
Stevenson, Robin, 89, 98, 127, 133, 143
Stewart, Sean, 125
Stinson, K., 143
Stitches (Huser), 67, 84, 91, 133
Stone, Tiffany, 60
Stones (Bell), 129
Stones Call Out (Porter), 69
The Stonking Steps (Roger), 156
Storm-Blast (Parkinson), 98
Straight Ahead (Will), 105
A Stranger Came Ashore (Hunter), 90
Stratton, Allan, 129
Stuff We All Get (Denman), 15
suicide, 79, 91, 118, 138, 144
The Summer Kid (Levy), 58
The Summer of Permanent Wants (Findlay), 68, 81–82
The Summer of the Marco Polo (Manuel), 98
Summer of the Swans (Byars), 58
Summer on the Run (Belgue), 94
Sweet Clara and the Freedom Quilt (Hopkinson), 82
Swimming in the Monsoon Sea (Salvadurai), 130
Sydor, Colleen, 93

T

Take Me Out of the Ball Game (Campbell), 133
Takes (MacIntyre, ed.), 142
Take Up Thy Bed and Walk (Keith), 153
taking action and promoting social justice, 26–27, 32–35
Tales of a Fourth Grade Nothing (Blume), 117
Tamaki, Jillian, 25, 127, 143
Tamaki, Mariko, 25, 127, 143
Tammet, Daniel, 19, 155–156
Tan, Shaun, 130
Tangled in Time (Fairbridge), 78, 142
Taylor, Cora, 89, 93, 133
Teaching About Disabilities through Children's Literature (Prater and Dyches), 13
Ten Birds (Young), 41, 45
Ten Ways to Make My Sister Disappear (Mazer), 91
Terror at Turtle Mountain (Draper), 83
testimonial response activities, 36–37
thinandbeautiful.com (Shaw), 128, 140, 142, 146
The Third Eye (Narsimhan), 88
Thirteenth Child (Wrede), 93, 133
Thompson, Craig, 118–119
Thompson, Margaret, 135
"Three Billy Goats Gruff," 8, 35
Three on Three (Walters), 90
Thunder Creek Ranch (Bates), 75
The Tiger Rising (DiCamillo), 58, 76
Timmerman Was Here (Sydor and Debon), 93
To Dance at the Palais Royale (McNaughton), 131
Toews, Miriam, 83–84
Tokio, Marnelle, 128, 140, 142, 144, 146
Tom Finder (Leavitt), 80
Tori by Design (Nelson), 91
Toronto, 28
Torrie & the Snake-Prince (Johansen), 85
To Stand on My Own (Haworth-Attard), 83
Toten, Teresa, 140, 144

Tourette Syndrome, 87–88
Toxic Love (Holeman), 146
transgender character, 105
Trembath, Don, 87, 96, 124, 132, 144–145, 145
The Triggering Town (Hugo), 74, 118
Triple Threat (Guest), 59
Tripping (Waldorf), 29–30, 37, 107, 137, 142, 146
Trottier, Maxine, 77
True Blue (Ellis), 127
Trueman Bradley—Aspie Detective (Russell), 156
Truths I Learned From Sam (Butcher), 123–124
Tuck Everlasting (Babbitt), 80
The Tuesday Cafe (Trembath), 124, 132, 144–145
Tullson, Diane, 38, 128, 140, 142, 145–146, 146
Turner, Sarah E., 155
Turner's syndrome, 107, 133
Twain, Mark, 129
Twilight (Meyers), 135
The Twits (Dahl), 92
Tyranny (Fairfield), 7, 127–128, 140, 142, 143, 146

U
The Uncle Duncle Chronicles (Krill), 78, 142
Underground to Canada (Smucker), 128
The Uninvited (Wynne-Jones), 119, 126
The Unlikely Hero of Room 13B (Toten), 144
Upjohn, Rebecca, 49

V
value of stories, 19–20
Van der Woude syndrome, 107, 138–139
Vegas Tryout (Nicholson), 136
A Very Fine Line (Johnston), 89, 132–133
The Very Hungry Caterpillar (Carle), 23
Virginia Wolf (Maclear and Arsenault), 41, 44
visual impairments, 12, 13–14, 16, 28, 31, 45, 59–60, 66, 77, 88, 92, 94, 135, 136
von Ziegesar, Cecily, 140
Vygotsky, Lev, 12

W
Waiting for Godot (Beckett), 123
Waiting for No One (Brenna), 108, 122–123, 154
Waiting for Sarah (McBay and Heneghan), 67, 89, 125
Waldman, D., 68, 96
Waldorf, Heather, 29–30, 37, 107, 137, 142, 146
Wallace, David Foster, 14
Walsh, Alice, 83, 131
Walter (Wersba), 62
Walters, Eric, 28, 90, 96, 97, 98, 127, 131, 142, 145
War Brothers (McKay), 37
Ward, David, 36
Ward, Helen, 98
Watcher (Sherrard), 126
The Water of Possibility (Goto), 82
Watson, J., 67, 98
The Way Home (Citra), 59

The Weber Street Wonder Work Crew (Newhouse), 49
Weisman, Jordan, 125
Wersba, Barbara, 62
Weyburn Mental Hospital, 71–72
Whalesinger (Katz), 135
What Happened to Ivy (Stinson), 143
What I Was (Rosoff), 124, 129
Wheelchair Challenge, 59
wheelchairs, 14, 28, 49, 59, 61, 77, 85, 96, 107, 125, 127, 137, 142, 154
Wheeler, Jordan, 61
Wheels for Walking (Richmond), 4, 19, 125
White, E.B., 24, 138
White, Susan, 84
The White Bicycle (Brenna), 108, 123
Wieler, Diana, 96
Wild Orchid (Brenna), 2, 19, 28, 37, 109, 122, 130–131
Wilder, Laura Ingalls, 138
Wilhelm, Jeffrey D., 37
Will, Elaine M., 37, 105
Williams, Jerome, 90
Williams, Johnnie III, 90
William's Syndrome, 155
Willow and Twig (Little), 66, 88
Wilson, John, 134
Winds of L'Acadie (Donovan), 78, 142
Wings of a Bee (Roorda), 119, 137–138
The Winter Pony (Lawrence), 77
Winthrow, Sara, 93
Wishinsky, Frieda, 86
Withers, Pam, 75
Woolf, Virginia, 155
Word Nerd (Nielsen), 80, 92, 94
Working Like a Dog (Gorrell), 60
The Worst Thing She Ever Did (Kuipers), 141
Would You (Jocelyn), 119, 138
Wray, Sarah, 154
Wrede, Patricia C., 93, 133
Wright, David, 155
Wringer (Spinelli), 97
A Wrinkle in Time (L'Engle), 24, 120, 135
writers with disabilities, 155–156
Wynne-Jones, Tim, 86, 96, 119, 126

Y
Yee, P., 41, 44
Yellow Moon, Apple Moon (Porter), 69
Yesterday (Martin), 121
York, Sarah, 19
Young, C., 41, 45
Young Adult Library Services Association's Great Graphic Novels for Teens 2008, 43
young adult novels
    annotated bibliography, 118–146
    patterns and trends, 106–107
    Radical Change in action, 105
    read-on bibliography, 147–151

Ytak, Cathy, 122
Yukon, 28

Z
Zero (Tullson), 128, 140, 142, 145–146
Zindel, Paul, 24, 80, 121, 133, 142, 144
Zoe's Extraordinary Holiday Adventures
 (Minaki), 60, 61, 138
Zoom (Munsch and Martchenko), 49